DALEY

Power and Presidential Politics

F. RICHARD CICCONE

CONTEMPORARY BOOKS
A TRIBUNE COMPANY

Library of Congress Cataloging-in-Publication Data

Ciccone, F. Richard.
    Daley : power and presidential politics / F. Richard Ciccone.
      p.   cm.
    Includes index.
    ISBN 0-8092-3151-4
    1. Daley, Richard J., 1902–1976.   2. Mayors—Illinois—
Chicago—Biography.   3. Chicago (Ill.)—Politics and
government—1951–   I. Title.
F548.54.D34C53   1996
997.3'1104'092—dc20
[B]   96-20514
                                                  CIP

For Joan

Interior design by Terry Stone

Copyright © 1996 by The Chicago Tribune Company
All rights reserved
Published by Contemporary Books
An imprint of NTC/Contemporary Publishing Company
Two Prudential Plaza, Chicago, Illinois 60601-6790
Manufactured in the United States of America
International Standard Book Number: 0-8092-3151-4
10   9   8   7   6   5   4   3   2   1

Contents

Preface

NO ONE IN AMERICAN CITY POLITICS EVER ROSE AS HIGH IN
national prominence or recognition as Richard J. Daley. In
the twenty years he served as mayor of Chicago, he was the
gatekeeper of presidential nominations, the confidant of the
Oval Office, and the national symbol for the vanishing era of
a system that had been remarkably successful—as well as
occasionally immoral—for more than a century. This book
is an attempt to place Daley's life in that context. It is important to place Daley against the backdrop of his times: the
most dynamic societal, demographic, and cultural upheaval
in any twenty-year span of American history. It is important
to contrast the events that changed Chicago and America
during Daley's reign to try to understand the extent of his
national power and the instincts and experience he applied
to expand and retain it against the challenges of that period.

In retrospect, it is clear that Daley was far closer to being
historically unique than he was perceived as being during his
lifetime. While contemporary reporters properly assessed his
local dominance and joined in perpetuating his legend as
kingmaker, he was too often regarded as merely a natural

product of the Democratic organizations that had controlled northern big cities since the early 1900s. But those organizations—in New York, Boston, Jersey City, Philadelphia—were viewed as declining when Daley came to power. It was not immediately perceived that they already were dead. Nor was it at all apparent in the 1950s that only Daley, of all his peers, was able to perpetuate the dominance of the Democratic Party in Chicago by making it his personal instrument, one he constantly remodeled to sustain his many successes. It may have been only coincidence that by the 1960s there were no other Democrats—governors, mayors, senators—who could be considered rivals to his dominance over a single political entity.

But Daley was hardly a relic. The man so often characterized by intransigence was in reality more flexible than any of his predecessors or peers. If Daley, by accident or cunning, or both, had become a historical postscript, this was clearly recognized by all the men who would be or seek to be their party's leaders for twenty-five years. They wooed him, flattered him, and most times sat in awe of him. In that respect, he was singular as an icon of the political strength they all envied and implored him to share.

The *Chicago Tribune* library provided the bulk of the material quoted except where noted. *Chicago Tribune* staffers Al Peters, Mary Wilson, and Mary Ann Stenson were invaluable. A special debt of gratitude is owed Mary Knill and E. Philip Scott, of the Lyndon Baines Johnson Library, for their assistance in obtaining the information that portrays the personal relationship between the president and Dick Daley.

CHAPTER I

"The Rain Must Never Fall Till After Sundown"

SID HOLZMAN WAS UP EARLY AND OUT OF THE HOUSE BEFORE five. As he drove north from his South Shore home he was somewhat bothered by the heavy gray sky. Lake Michigan, to his right, was climbing with light swells and it had already begun to drizzle. It was not perfect election-day weather, but he felt comfortable with his predictions. He would be in his office by the time the first precinct captain called in the early numbers. Within an hour he would know what kind of turnout to expect. He had predicted the biggest vote since the FDR election of 1944, and he privately hoped the city might exceed its historic totals for Roosevelt in 1936.

Nine hundred miles east, where the Atlantic Ocean greeted America, John Kennedy was also up early, sipping orange juice and getting ready to go to the Hyannisport fire-house, where he would be one of only two men in the country to realistically vote for themselves for president. Three thousand miles to the west, the other man, Richard Nixon, was still asleep in the royal suite of the Ambassador Hotel on Wilshire Boulevard in Los Angeles. He would rise later and

be driven thirty miles to East Whittier to vote in the town
where he grew up. He had never heard of Sid Holzman.[1]

It was a bright, crisp November day in New England and
it would turn out to be a warm, typically sunny day in Southern California. It was also a warm, sunny day in Birmingham, Alabama, where Martin Luther King, Jr., was waking
up in his home, glad to be there after escaping a four-month
sentence to a Georgia chain gang. In southern Georgia, former naval officer Jimmy Carter was also getting up to go and
vote. His friend Wills Wright, a black man, was also going to
vote—for the first time. Across the country, a handsome,
undistinguished actor who now earned a living making commercials was about to rise for a day of riding and clearing
brush on his new Santa Monica farm. Ronald Reagan, who
had often voted for the Democratic ticket headed by Franklin
D. Roosevelt, would vote today for Nixon. It was hot in
southwest Texas along the Pedernales River, where Lyndon
Johnson would vote with mixed feelings. In Hope, Arkansas,
a fourteen-year-old wished he were old enough to vote. Young
Bill Clinton would have chosen Kennedy. Neither King nor
Carter, nor Reagan nor young Clinton had ever heard of Sid
Holzman.

In Chicago, Richard J. Daley was also up early. He was
having his poached eggs and getting ready to head downtown, a swift four-mile trip from the Bridgeport block where
he had lived his entire fifty-eight years. Daley and his wife,
Eleanor, would attend Mass at Nativity of Our Lord Church
three blocks from home. Then Daley would jump into the
official black Cadillac and head four miles northwest to City
Hall, where Sid Holzman was already scanning election numbers. Usually Daley had his policeman driver drop him off
on LaSalle Street, in the financial district, or on Michigan
Avenue so he could walk past the Art Institute and enjoy the
spacious parks that led to the vast lake that he believed also

belonged to Chicago. But it was going to be a very long day and a very long night, and he wanted to check in with Sid Holzman.

Daley knew who Sid Holzman was and how important he would become today. Holzman was the chief of the Chicago Board of Elections, which was charged with the proper conduct of all elections. It was also charged with ensuring that every one of the city's three thousand precincts was staffed with judges who would rule on the conduct of voting. Those rules would determine how many votes were allowed in each precinct. And those judges would properly count the ballots, certifying that each vote cast for John F. Kennedy was legal and valid—or if not legal, at least valid. For Richard J. Daley had planned for months to play the major role in the election of John Kennedy, and that wouldn't happen if Kennedy lost. It wouldn't happen if Kennedy failed to carry Illinois, with its 27 electoral votes, and Kennedy couldn't carry Illinois unless the Democratic margins in Cook County offset the traditional Republican and farm vote in all those counties that stretched four hundred miles south of Chicago to the Ohio River. It wouldn't happen unless the Chicago vote was so overwhelmingly Democratic that it offset the Republican suburbs of Cook County that surrounded the city. In all of those suburbs there were Republicans in charge of the elections, and each was doing what Sid Holzman was doing, except they were protecting the votes for Richard Nixon. And in the other 101 counties there were Republicans in charge of running elections. Daley knew that, but it didn't stop him from promising that Kennedy would win Illinois by five hundred thousand votes. He privately would have said five thousand rosaries if Kennedy could win the state by five thousand votes. But this was the day that Richard J. Daley planned to keep his promise and in doing so become a major political figure on the American national scene.

And Sid Holzman would become a footnote to history.

It was starting to rain in Chicago and most of Middle America. Holzman's experienced eye stared at the drizzle outside the window of his office in City Hall, a stumpy, ten-story building a block square surrounded by LaSalle, Washington, Clark, and Randolph streets in the heart of the Loop. He was confident. It was not the kind of weather that would hold down the vote. Holzman, a bantam of a man who had served with honor in two world wars, had been in charge of the Board of Elections since 1952 and would continue until his death in 1969. He was the biennial target of vote-fraud charges, which he tossed aside with good humor, and the perennial expert of the Democratic party in predicting voter turnout. Although city registrations had decreased to 1,931,000—about fifty thousand fewer than in 1956—Holzman was predicting a 95 percent turnout. The Cook County clerk had predicted a similar turnout in the Republican suburbs, where registrations had jumped by 161,466 over 1956. If either side failed to meet expectations, one party would gain a great edge.

Holzman began to collect samples of the voter turnout from each of the city's fifty wards shortly after the first voters arrived at 6 A.M. He would get a full report at 10 A.M., another at noon, and a third report at 5 P.M., an hour before the polls closed. After a quick first glimpse at the numbers, Holzman, who would puff on a cigar throughout the day and night, knew he was right. A few minutes later he made his first telephone call of the day to the Morrison Hotel, where Daley kept his office as chairman of the Cook County Democratic Party. Daley's party was generally regarded as the last powerful political machine in America, the organization that had delivered incredible numbers for FDR, aided Harry Truman's comeback win in 1948, and produced the Democratic presidential nominee of 1952 and 1956, Adlai Stevenson. Although Daley traditionally went to work at his fifth-floor

City Hall office on election days, he spent a great deal of time at the Morrison, making several quick shuttles between the hotel and City Hall. Late in the afternoon, he would go to the Morrison and remain there until after noon the next day.

Holzman reported the turnout would be 93 percent. He also called direct to the Kennedy headquarters at Hyannis Port, where a telephone bank had been set up on the porch of Robert F. Kennedy's home, the largest in the family compound. It was a short walk across the lawn from a smaller cottage where the candidate, his wife, Jackie, and their three-year-old daughter, Caroline, lived. The report of the big turnout in Chicago was greeted with relief by the Kennedy clan. Illinois was one of the key states, along with Ohio, Texas, Pennsylvania, Michigan, and California, that they thought they had to win.

Kennedy, nearly exhausted from an arduous campaign schedule, had made his last Chicago appearance the previous Friday to attend the Democrats' torchlight parade, a local tradition that began in 1932 when Roosevelt made his final election speech in Chicago. Daley had ordered the ward leaders to make certain the streets were lined from downtown to Chicago Stadium, where he had almost personally planted twenty-eight thousand Democrats. Labor leader Stephen Bailey, one of the mayor's closest friends, had promised that 650,000 union workers would provide the welcome. Ward leaders, including Claude W. B. Holman, one of the committeemen who belonged to Big Bill Dawson's black fiefdom, sent personal invitations to precinct workers designating the location of the buses that would take them to the stadium. Holman wrote, "I personally will receive you aboard the bus."[2] The precinct workers knew Holman would be taking names.

Besides the people lining the streets, Daley wanted the whole country to see how he conducted election rallies. He wanted Kennedy's last pre-election Chicago appearance televised. Daley had finally come to realize how powerful television had become in politics. After the first Kennedy-Nixon debate in Chicago—the only one that really mattered, as it turned out—Daley had told Kennedy aide Ken O'Donnell, "Get as many of these as you can, no matter what it costs." Now in the final days of the campaign, he wanted the nation the see how the Chicago Democrats welcomed their standard-bearer. He ordered an aide to arrange for network time so that Kennedy's thirty-minute speech at the stadium could be televised nationally. When the aide reported it would cost $125,000 Daley replied, "Go over to Mr. Kennedy at the Merchandise Mart, and he'll give you a check." The Merchandise Mart, owned by Joseph P. Kennedy and managed by his son-in-law R. Sargent Shriver, had been the setting of many meetings between the patriarch of the Kennedys and the mayor of Chicago. When the aide arrived, Kennedy wrote the check.[3]

The night of the torchlight parade, John Kennedy, hatless and coatless, rode in an open convertible, despite the rain, for two miles from Michigan Avenue to the stadium. He was awed by the crowd lining Madison Street the entire two miles. "I only hope they all show up to vote Tuesday," the tired candidate said to his host. Daley replied, "They will." There were no ifs or buts. Daley told reporters, "I promised him that Chicago would give a 500,000 plurality and last night's demonstration of party strength would stimulate the precinct captains to try to equal the record vote piled up by Franklin Roosevelt in 1936." Roosevelt had gotten a 553,386 plurality, a number Daley knew he could never match—but he had to get close.

Now, Tuesday, November 8, 1960, was here and Daley set about trying to find out if he would live up to his word.

He told reporters on Monday that Kennedy would carry Chicago by 600,000 votes, a boast neither he nor they believed—especially since in 1956, Dwight Eisenhower had actually gotten more votes in the city than Adlai Stevenson, the first time a Republican had carried Chicago since the birth of the machine in 1932. But Daley actually hoped for a margin somewhere near 500,000. If Holzman was right about turnout, then 1.8 million Chicagoans would vote. He wanted almost 1.2 million for Kennedy. Daley had also declared that Senator Paul Douglas would get a 600,000-vote margin and that his choice for governor, Otto Kerner, would have a 500,000-vote margin to take out of Chicago against Republican Governor William Stratton, who was seeking a third term.

Those would be historic figures, especially since the city's population was beginning to decline. The great exodus to the suburbs had begun and now, on the Southwest Side, not far from Daley's neighborhood of Bridgeport, whites were beginning to scatter as the growing black population spread into previously sacrosanct Irish, Lithuanian, and Polish neighborhoods. But on November 8, 1960, Daley wasn't concerned with the changing demography of his city or exactly where the blacks were moving. He was concerned with how they were voting.

The first reports he received from the South Side were good. U.S. Representative William Dawson, who had taken his black political machine from the Republican Party to the Democratic Party after Roosevelt's welfare programs came into being, controlled five key South Side wards. He also controlled the "policy" games, called "numbers" in the east. Again, this wasn't a day to deal with ethics. In 1948, after Truman desegregated the armed forces, Dawson's wards had been the decisive factor. The 3rd, 4th, 6th, 20th, and Dawson's home 2nd Ward had given Truman a 132,131 to 68,108 margin—nearly 65,000 votes of the total 320,000-vote Truman edge in the city. In 1955, it had been Dawson's wards that gave Daley his first mayoral triumph with even greater margins.

Dawson's committeemen were routinely checking in with good numbers. They wouldn't match the total vote of 1948, but instead of the two to one margin for Truman they were predicting three to one and even four to one totals for Kennedy. And better news. Douglas and Kerner were even running a few votes ahead of Kennedy.

On the West Side, the so-called river wards, where FDR had scored remarkable numbers in the 1930s and where Republicans and civic committees annually hunted for ghost voters and all sorts of other fraud, things were as Daley expected. The 24th Ward belonged to Colonel Jack Arvey, the former county chairman and mentor to Daley, who had become a national figure in the 1948 election when his surprise choices of blue-ribbon candidates Douglas and Stevenson had carried the ticket and Harry Truman to victory. Arvey then engineered Stevenson's 1952 nomination despite the candidate's Hamlet-like reluctance. The 24th was known nationally as "FDR's favorite ward," and even in the 1956 debacle had given Stevenson 21,019 votes to 3,951 for Eisenhower. Arvey was no longer the main man in the Cook County headquarters on election day, but he was part of the inner circle, and it was no surprise to him or Daley when his precinct captains forecast a 20,000-vote win for Kennedy.

The other river wards were sending in similar reports. Daley's own 11th Ward would be no problem, eventually providing Kennedy with 20,105 votes, compared to 6,052 for Nixon. As usual, the North Side committeemen were having difficulties. Although Daley's own re-election in 1959 had been a landslide throughout the city, the state and national contests evoked strong GOP support along the lakefront, where independents and reformers were hard to convince, and on the Northwest Side, where the second- and third-generation Poles and Germans tended to lean Republican. Alderman Thomas Keane, Daley's floor leader in the City Council, promised he would get a good vote for Kennedy in his 31st Ward. But the 45th and 47th would go to Nixon and the 41st Ward alone would produce 38,000 votes for the Republican, the largest single ward total in the city for either man.

State Party Chairman Jimmy Ronan, a Daley appointee, reported the downstate vote was also extremely heavy and that meant the Republicans, particularly in counties surrounding Cook, were likely to produce lopsided margins for Nixon. In Southern Illinois, some Democratic leaders, often at odds with Daley, were still afraid that the Catholic issue would cost Kennedy votes. Southern Illinois is more spiritually aligned with Missouri, and its political ties to Chicago had always been thin. Somewhere around Peoria is an invisible line that divides baseball fans along separate loyalties; north of the line are Chicago Cubs rooters, while everyone to the south is a St. Louis Cardinals supporter. House Speaker Paul Powell of Vienna was principally a fan of Harry Truman and had been a key player in Truman's 1948 upset over Thomas Dewey. On Truman's orders he had fought futilely to give the Democratic presidential nomination to Missouri Senator Stuart Symington. And he would have had a much easier time on November 8 if Symington, a neighbor and Protestant, had been the Democratic ticket leader or at least the vice presidential candidate. Lyndon Johnson's presence on the ticket, Powell said, would cost the Democrats 100,000 votes. But Powell could turn out votes, and the big Democratic precincts in Madison and St. Clair counties were expected to match the 1948 margins.

The question was whether Kennedy could cut into Nixon's vote in Peoria, Champaign, Decatur, Springfield, Bloomington, and Rock Island. Daley's inner sanctum, quartered in the Morrison, wondered how many votes the Republicans in nearby DuPage, Kane, Lake, and Will would either produce or steal for Nixon.

While the city was losing population, albeit a white population that did not have nearly the predictable voting habits of the blacks who were replacing them, the Republican strongholds were growing rapidly in population. Chicago had lost a hundred thousand people in the decade between 1950 and 1960, but the Cook County suburbs had grown by 750,000 and the leap was greater in DuPage County. In 1948, Dewey had clobbered Truman in DuPage County by 45,956 to 14,628. Just eight years later, the GOP candidate, Eisenhower again ran up a three to one margin, but his vote total was 91,653—double that of Dewey. The turnout in DuPage, then the most Republican county in the nation, could be as high as 175,000 and a three to one Nixon edge could gain him 80,000 or 90,000 votes, wiping away the entire lead from Dawson's black wards and Arvey's legendary 24th.

But Daley knew it would be late in the night before he could figure out what was going on in DuPage County. The Democrats and Republicans played a cruel game on election nights, taking turns holding back and releasing votes when they felt they needed a psychological edge or when they sought information about their opponent's totals. As one Democratic precinct captain told a reporter on a later election night, "We don't know how many we got until we find out how many we need."[4]

Kennedy's brother-in-law, Sarge Shriver, had been Daley's appointed head of the Chicago Board of Education until his resignation a month earlier to join the presidential campaign staff. At 2 P.M., he stopped by the mayor's City Hall office to say good-bye before heading to Hyannis Port to wait for the returns. "How does it look?" asked Shriver, who had been a possible Daley pick for the gubernatorial nomination in Illinois until Kennedy took the top spot on the ticket. "It's going to be very close," Daley said. "But we do have our poll-watchers downstate. That's the thing we have to worry about. They will certainly try to take the election, but we're ready for them."[5] By the time the polls closed, the downstate Republicans had begun their usual gamesmanship, announcing that the ballot counting had been halted and there would be no reports until after midnight. Daley stopped releasing his totals, hoping to keep in reserve an even larger batch of numbers than the GOP leaders were hiding.

But Daley, who had been back and forth on the telephone to Hyannis Port, told Kennedy aide Kenny O'Donnell that the big Chicago lead was being whittled away downstate. "Every time we announce 200 more votes for Kennedy in Chicago, they come up out of nowhere downstate with another 300 votes for Nixon. One of their precincts, outside of Peoria, where there are only 50 voters, just announced 500 votes for Nixon."[6]

By 9 P.M., things were looking good in Chicago. Daley was sending out reports that Kennedy would carry the city overwhelmingly. He was also buoyed by the national television coverage that showed Kennedy winning New York, as expected; Pennsylvania, a toss-up state where Daley's friend and ally, Governor David Lawrence, had been one of the final holdouts against the Kennedy candidacy; and Texas, where Lyndon Johnson's controversial presence on the ballot proved crucial. It was widely reported that Daley hadn't wanted Johnson in the second spot. Whether he believed a southerner would cut into Dawson's vote or whether he hoped to appease Powell and the other Southern Illinois Democrats, he reportedly had backed Symington. Now it seemed Kennedy had made the right choice.

Ohio was a loser, however, and now Illinois, Minnesota, and ultimately California loomed critically. Daley wanted to hold some of his votes in his pocket to have some weapons when the DuPage Republicans let go of their totals and he also wanted to provide a psychological edge for Kennedy. But most important, he did not want an Illinois triumph to go unannounced until it was no longer critical.

Daley released enough votes to persuade the news media that Kennedy would carry Cook County by 350,000 votes, a margin that would offset the Republican downstate totals. Television put Illinois in the Kennedy column and the *Chicago Tribune*'s Wednesday edition called him an apparent winner by 85,000 votes. But the Kennedy camp in Hyannis Port knew the fight for Illinois wasn't over. The DuPage numbers began to roll in. Nixon chalked up 101,000 votes. In Lake County, just north of Cook, he piled up 67,000 votes, 20,000 ahead of Ike's pace in 1956. At some point early Wednesday morning, Nixon moved ahead of Kennedy.

But at the Morrison, the downstate numbers didn't look all that bad. Nixon won Peoria County by only 6,000 votes. Kennedy had gotten a bigger Democratic vote than Truman out of Champaign and Springfield. He even nipped Nixon in Rock Island, along the Mississippi. And St. Clair County, with its large black population in East St. Louis, had an enormous 67,417 total for Kennedy. Daley had to smile when he saw the Winnebago County numbers. Kennedy had lost that Republican bastion, but by only 9,000 out of the 90,000 votes cast, a far better showing than any other recent Democrat had made. On October 28, Daley had made a rare trip outside Cook County for a campaign appearance. He went to Rockford, the second-largest city in the state and the heart of Winnebago County, ninety miles west of Chicago. His speech there was far more prophetic than he knew. "The approaching election is truly critical, for the 1960s will present problems that involve the survival of our nation."

At 3 A.M., Daley again called Hyannis Port and this time talked to Kennedy. Somewhat prematurely he greeted his candidate: "Mr. President, with a little bit of luck and the help of a few close friends, you are going to carry Illinois."[7]

For Daley, this was the message he had been waiting to deliver for a long time. It was a message he had probably dreamed about delivering ever since his first political convention at the Chicago Stadium in 1932, when Franklin D. Roosevelt was nominated. It was certainly the message he had been waiting to deliver since the Democratic convention in Los Angeles in July.

CHAPTER 2

"On the Atcheson, Topeka, and the Santa Fe"

THE SIXTIES. THERE WAS NOTHING ABOUT THE OPENING OF THE new decade that foreshadowed its historic, tragic, tumultuous impact on America. Nothing that stamped it along with the Twenties as the two definable periods of the century that changed essentially the way Americans behaved toward one another. There was nothing to foretell that the extraordinarily prosperous, comfortable postwar period's seemingly endless progression of upward mobility and technological luxury would be halted in a collision of cultures and a lasting dissolution of Americans' trust in the institutions that nurtured them: the White House, the campus, the family, City Hall, the corporations, the courts, the church.

There was "the bomb," but most Americans had given up on stocking canned goods in the basement and the Tuesday morning sirens were all but ignored. Color had come to television if not to mainstream America. The Japanese were very good at transistor radios but they hadn't yet stolen the steel industry. There was every reason to be optimistic about the Sixties, and no one could have been more satisfied than Richard J. Daley.

The fifty-seven-year-old Daley was about to complete his fifth year as mayor of Chicago. In those five years he had emerged from the relative obscurity of a minor office to symbolize the dynamism of a city that was rapidly shedding its Prohibition-era image and blossoming with new construction and new dreams of achieving the international reputation that its East Coast sisters enjoyed. The new forty-one-story Prudential Building had risen as a solid, square sentinel overlooking Michigan Avenue, the forebear of an architectural expansion that someday would create a Magnificent Mile to rival even the avenues of Paris for shopping elegance. In 1959, Daley had hosted the successful Pan-American track and field games, convincing everyone Chicago would make a fine Olympic Games venue. The queen of England came for a visit and Daley invited her to "bring the kids" on her next trip.

In 1960, Daley would cut ribbons almost as fast as he could count votes. He would open two new expressways, paid for by President Eisenhower's federal interstate highway program. He would dedicate a huge exposition center, pushed through the state legislature by the *Chicago Tribune*, which wanted it named for its late owner-publisher-editor, Colonel Robert R. McCormick. The city lighting program, started after World War II and funded by bonds initiated by his predecessor, was nearly complete and was the pride of neighborhoods. The city budget was growing at a record pace to take care of all the building and all the contracts that were personally handed out by the mayor.

In his first four years, Daley had convinced the business leaders and editorial writers that his apprenticeship in the Cook County Democratic Party did not translate into a renewal of the political corruption that was the hallmark of the 1930s and 1940s. The fears of a downtown overrun by gamblers and hookers had been allayed by the quiet but

firm moral tone that Daley used to run the city, to the disappointment of many of his fellow Democrats who had
chanted upon his 1955 victory, "Chicago ain't ready for
reform." Most important to Daley, he had become the undis-
puted Democratic leader of Chicago and Illinois. Any rivals
that existed before he took office had either died or aged or
accepted that they were no match for him. Any that seemed
to be rising challengers he dispatched by placing them in jobs
with lucrative rewards but doubtful political futures. Others
he crushed with masses of patronage workers who thwarted
their re-elections.

There was nothing at the beginning of the Sixties that
could have caused Richard J. Daley to look to the future and
see parts of his beloved city burning, the leaders of his party
murdered, the policemen who worked for him labeled
gestapos, the Michigan Avenue in which he took such pride
turned into a television studio where the anger of America
used Chicago as a stage and Richard J. Daley as a scapegoat.

What Daley could see were all the ribbons that needed
to be cut and the opportunity to expand his power far beyond
Lake Michigan. The 1960 presidential election was shaping
up as one of the most exciting in the century. For only the
second time in thirty-two years there would be no incumbent president running from either party. A score of Republican and Democratic candidates were already making plans
to seek the nomination and there were only a dozen or so
men in the country who could give it to them. Richard J.
Daley expected to be one of them.

On the second day of the new decade, the youngest of all
these aspirants, John F. Kennedy, announced he would run
for president. Daley knew Kennedy well. He knew his father
better. Joseph P. Kennedy had been the former ambassador
to Great Britain and chairman of the Securities and
Exchange Commission under Roosevelt, but Daley was far

more impressed with Kennedy as owner of the Merchandise
Mart, then the world's largest private office building, perched
on the north bank of Daley's own Chicago River. The senior
Kennedy was a powerful figure in the Democratic Party, and
his business influence in Chicago had caused him to take a
strong interest in the political affairs of the city. There had
been many visits between Kennedy and the various mayors
of Chicago, including Daley, who had first gotten to know
Joe Kennedy while Daley was in the legislature. It was no
coincidence that at his first Democratic Party fund-raising
dinner as chairman in 1954, the speaker Daley chose to spotlight was John F. Kennedy.

On the day following Kennedy's announcement, City
Hall reporters were surprised to hear Daley, usually taciturn
to the point of secrecy, make an uncharacteristically flatter-
ing statement:

"The Democratic Party is fortunate that it has such men
of high caliber as Senator Kennedy seeking the presidential
nomination. Kennedy's legislative career, his great war
record, and fine personal attributes make him highly qualified to lead our nation." Of course, with Daley, there was
always a caveat. "His campaign and the campaigns of other
highly qualified Democratic representatives seeking the presidential nomination will focus public opinion on the great
issues of our day."

As exciting as the presidential campaign of 1960 seemed
destined to become, Chicago reporters quickly checked the
tea leaves and decided this statement was clearly a step
toward endorsing Kennedy, whom Daley had supported for
the vice presidential nomination in 1956. Charles Finston,
political writer for *Chicago's American*, wrote, "It was noted
by local party powerhouses that Daley refrained from issu-
ing comment after Humphrey formally announced his candidacy 10 days ago."

Senator Hubert Humphrey of Minnesota, whose political fates eventually would intersect with Daley's own, was Kennedy's chief challenger in the early weeks of 1960.

Although Daley chose to say something about Kennedy's announcement, it was probably more of a courtesy than a commitment. Daley had long ago adopted a policy of never making a commitment. As the years went by and his stewardship of Democratic Party matters became a dictatorship, reporters and even Daley associates would marvel as he stonily made pronouncements of uncertainty about events over which he and he alone had total control. Yet those who went to seek his favor often allowed their ambitions to render them as gullible as the news media. Often a simple, "You'd make a fine candidate" from Daley was enough to spur total confidence that they were about to be anointed.

The Kennedys were not that naive. On September 23, 1959, Daley was the main speaker at the New York State Democratic Party dinner in Troy, New York. United Press International covered the dinner and reported that Daley hinted Adlai Stevenson might run a third time. Daley was quoted as saying he did not consider himself bound by Stevenson's contentions all that year that he would not be a candidate. Two days later, Daley told Chicago reporters he had been misquoted. But whatever he said, it made some Kennedy supporters nervous. While in New York, Daley had bumped into the mayor of Somerville, Massachusetts, John "Pat" Lynch, a member of the Kennedy clique. "How's our boy doing out there in Chicago?" Lynch casually inquired. "Who's our boy?" Daley innocently asked. "Jack Kennedy. Who else?" Lynch replied.

"I don't know how's he doing. I haven't heard from him in six months," Daley said.

The meeting took place outside a church where both men had attended Mass. Lynch became frantic. He called

Ken O'Donnell, the top Kennedy aide in charge of scheduling. "We don't tell lies at Mass," Lynch fretted, warning that Daley might not be for Kennedy. O'Donnell passed the information to Kennedy, who seemed unperturbed but agreed that he needed to touch base with the Chicago mayor soon.

As all other things were right in Dick Daley's world on the eve of the 1960s, even the Chicago White Sox, his boyhood passion, were conspiring to make his life perfect. Forty years after being the only baseball team in history to throw a World Series, the White Sox had finally made it back to the autumn classic (which, all other things being perfect, was still played in the daytime). Kennedy and O'Donnell were invited to join Daley for one of the games at Comiskey Park, but the senator didn't come away certain of the mayor's support.

"All he did was watch the game," Kennedy remarked afterward.[1]

Kennedy felt certain he would have Daley's support if he proved to be the strongest candidate, the person who would most help the Democratic ticket in Chicago and Illinois. Daley needed to get Senator Paul Douglas re-elected (and to keep him in Washington, where he was no threat to anything Daley wanted), to recapture the governor's mansion with a man who would take Daley's advice about the distribution of thirty thousand state jobs, and to defang State's Attorney Ben Adamowski so that any future mayoral challenge would not have either the fund-raising power of a county office or the political pulpit, not to mention the prosecutorial power that could ferret out corruption—not in Daley, of course, but in people close enough to him to taint the character he had carefully raised to personal impeccability.

If John F. Kennedy could do all those things, Kennedy knew, he would have every bit of support Daley could muster, which would be considerable. If not—well, there was Hubert Humphrey or Stuart Symington or Lyndon Johnson or even

Adlai Stevenson again. As much as Dick Daley may have atavistically yearned for an Irish-American in the White House he, like Kennedy, understood the imperatives of power, the most important of which was self-preservation. Personal relationships or ideology could dilute those imperatives, and on those occasions down the road when Daley was stricken by them it proved costly. But that was not the case in 1960.

Kennedy followed his World Series visit with a campaign trip to predominantly Republican downstate Illinois. In Springfield he ripped Eisenhower's farm policies, in Joliet he criticized the Republicans for mishandling the steel industry strike, in Peoria he called for financial aid for the elderly, in Decatur and Quincy and DeKalb, the heart of the farm belt, he asked for more government spending. He was appealing to Republicans but also taking the temperature about entering the April 12, 1960, Illinois preferential primary. And he was trying to determine whether Adlai Stevenson had any support in his home state.

Hy Raskin, a Chicago attorney who had worked in Stevenson's two presidential campaigns, was now the Kennedy point man with party regulars that he had cultivated in 1952 and 1956. He worried that Stevenson's fence-sitting on the 1960 nomination battle was hurting Kennedy. "When I ask Democrats whether they will be for Kennedy, they want to know what Stevenson will do. When I can't give them an answer, they are likely to say, 'Well, I'm going to wait and see.'"

The Kennedy trip was also meant to convince Daley and other Chicago Democrats that he was the man they needed at the top of their ticket. And Chicago Democrats were extremely nervous about the 1960 ticket. The Eisenhower landslide of 1956 had cost them all the critical state offices and, in most of their eyes, the more important county posts of state's attorney, recorder of deeds, and coroner. They wanted them back more than they wanted a Democrat in the White House. Before anything pivotal occurred on the national scene, the Chicago Democrats were going to choose their 1960 ticket. And many of them wanted Dick Daley to run for governor.

Almost as soon as the White Sox had lost the World Series, the rumors began that Daley would be the Democratic candidate for governor against William G. Stratton. Stratton had ridden Eisenhower's coattails to victory in 1952 and 1956 and was seeking an unprecedented third straight term. With Eisenhower no longer at the top of the GOP ticket, he was considered beatable. If Daley was seriously considering running, he didn't let anyone know. "You can't stop talk," he joked with reporters in October, making certain the talk would continue. When Stephen Mitchell, former Democratic National chairman and a foe of Daley and the Cook County Democrats, announced he would enter the April primary without the support of the party, Daley said, "I've never been opposed to a good primary fight. We had one in 1955. To use one word to describe it, it was lively." He was referring to his defeat of incumbent Mayor Martin Kennelly. At the same time, Daley ticked off the names of the loyalists he appointed to the slatemaking committee, which would begin interviewing candidates before the final choices were made in January 1960.

Slatemaking was one of the great rituals of the Cook County Democrats. Top party officials sat en banc and interviewed all the hopefuls. The aspirants and the committee members praised one another for days. From the 1930s to the 1970s, the newspapers followed the charade as though the many sessions, interviews, and responses had anything to do with who would actually be picked. Daley, and before him Jake Arvey and Pat Nash, would pick whomever they wanted

for whatever reason. Nash's and Arvey's choices may have
been made in concert with other local party leaders. Daley
listened to what others wanted, but in the end the choices
were his.

None of the Cook County Democrats ever publicly complained about this system, but the downstate leaders often
voiced their displeasure. After a month of wondering about
Daley's intentions in 1960, John Stelle, former lieutenant
governor who had sat in the governor's chair for a hundred
days in 1940, told Daley to make up his mind.

"I told him," Stelle told reporters on November 21,
" 'Why don't you run yourself or run Eddie Barrett and not
pull out of your pocket a Charlie McCarthy.' " Stelle added
that Daley would be a strong candidate downstate, but Daley
was furious at the reference to ventriloquist Edgar Bergen's
wooden dummy. For fifteen years, Republicans accused every
Democratic candidate for state office of being a Daley
puppet.

At the same time, the most powerful downstate Democrat, House Speaker Paul Powell, said he was not interested
in being governor or running for lieutenant governor on a
ticket with Daley. Powell and Stelle were also supporting
Symington in the 1960 presidential battle. Daley merely
responded that he had not had time to think about what he
might do in 1960. He said the question of a gubernatorial
candidate was "strictly up to the Democratic state central
committee."

There seems little doubt that Daley was giving serious
thought to running for governor. By the end of his career it
was part of the legend that he never wanted any political job
except the mayoralty of Chicago. But like any politician,
Daley was always interested in whatever job might be available that was better than the one he had. And Democrats
with long memories knew in January of 1960 that Daley

ɔoing to take Stelle's advice and slate County Clerk
ɪrd Barrett for governor. Barrett had been the Cook
ɔunty Democrats' choice against Stratton in 1952 (the nomination eventually went to Lieutenant Governor Sherwood
Dixon). But one of the people who had wanted that opportunity was Richard J. Daley. In 1952 there was also an opening for the Cook County Board presidency. Daley wanted that
too, but Arvey said no.

While the political reporters were trying to decipher
Daley's support of Kennedy in early January 1960, Daley was
making up his mind that he wouldn't run for governor—but,
of course, it would still be up to the slatemaking committee.
"The people still are urging me to continue as mayor, and
also to run for governor. It is an important decision to make,
and I will not make it until sometime before the committee
meets," he said. Two days later he said, "I am not a candidate for governor. I cannot leave unfinished the many projects we have under way and that we have initiated." On the
drawing board for 1960, Daley had $200 million worth of new
public construction, an amount that dwarfed the public
monies the governor could use to create improvements and
make friends.

And no matter who wound up leading the Democratic
ticket, the 1960 election would be a monumental battle in
Illinois. Despite his public statements about support from
the suburbs and downstate, Daley had to wonder how sincerely Powell and Stelle and former Senator Scott Lucas
would support his candidacy. He might have to agree to back
Symington to ensure the backing of the Southern Illinois
Democrats. And Symington probably was not strong enough
to ensure the critical victories needed by the Cook County
Democrats. Without those wins, Daley, as county chairman,
would be a far less effective political leader even if he did win
the statehouse.

He would not know for a few more weeks how wise a choice he had made. On January 9, the Democrats announced that County Judge Otto Kerner would be their candidate for governor. The Republicans promptly began portraying him as Daley's handpicked puppet, a charge he never fully eradicated despite serving two terms as governor. While reporters clustered in the lobby of the Morrison Hotel, Daley also pulled out of his pocket a candidate to run against Adamowski for state's attorney: Daniel J. Ward, a DePaul law school dean with no baggage, a man in the mold of Stevenson and Douglas. Daley was never opposed to doing the right thing if it was the right thing for the organization.

With the slate picked and no ribbons available to snip in January, Daley went off to Key West to do some fishing.

Back in Chicago, Ben Adamowski had come up with a prize catch. A small-time thief named Richard Morrison had been arrested and explained that he was able to carry off so many things from houses and stores because his accomplices were policemen assigned to the Summerdale district on the North Side. Morrison, labeled in the press as the "Babbling Burglar," implicated one captain and seven patrolmen from the District. Adamowski seized the opportunity to raise questions about widespread corruption throughout the police department and hinted that probably a lot more of the 204 cops assigned to Summerdale were in on the burglary ring.

Daley returned from Florida in virtual shock. After hemming and hawing for a few days, he fired Police Commissioner Timothy J. O'Connor, a holdover from the Kennelly era. He vowed total reform in the police department. For most of his career, when cornered, Daley would attack, especially the news media. But this time, he acted almost contrite. "This is the most shocking and disgraceful incident in the history of the Chicago police department," he admitted.

Despite newscasts and the headlines that kept Summerdale on the front pages for the next four weeks, it is probably fair to assume that neither Daley nor the citizens of Chicago were all that surprised. Although the moral fiber of the city had improved, it was still easy to bet on a horse or be picked up by a B-girl. No Chicagoan ever expected to receive a traffic ticket if he had a $10 or $20 bill to wrap around his driver's license. (Depending on the time of day, $2 or $3 for the officer's morning doughnuts would do as well.) Lawyers didn't make a living fighting DUI's in those days. No one ever got one. And the petty bribery, graft, and kickbacks that went on in Summerdale and every other district in the city were the same kinds of things policemen in most parts of the country were doing in the 1950s and 1960s. After all, there were no drug deals going down on half the corners on the West Side. Children weren't being blown away with nine-millimeter automatic pistols. The public and the police had reached an unspoken compromise. But Summerdale was serious. No one thought graft was organized. No one wanted to believe there was a conspiracy of burglars that might stretch through the entire department.

So Daley resorted to the same solution that worked so well in slatemaking. He named a blue-ribbon committee and made sure his choices controlled it. In late February, he named the chair of the committee, O. W. Wilson, a distinguished professor of criminology from the University of California, as his new top cop and changed the title from commissioner to superintendent, which sounded more politically independent. It was not his choice, Daley said; the committee had decided. By April Fool's Day he was being praised as the mayor who cleaned up the Chicago police department. Few remembered that he was also the mayor who had been responsible for it during the years the "burglars in blue" were busiest.

He had survived the first big crisis of his mayoralty. But it was probably just as well that he wasn't asking downstaters to vote for him while their newspapers were reminding them that Chicago was still a place where it might not be a good idea to ask a cop for directions.

––––––

On March 8, 1960, while Daley beginning to breathe a bit easier over the police department situation, John F. Kennedy won the New Hampshire primary. Hardly anyone noticed. Kennedy's only opponent was a ballpoint-pen manufacturer, who was defeated by a 9 to 1 margin with 43,000 votes.[2]

During the 1980 New Hampshire primary, Senator Edward M. Kennedy went to Manchester to speak at the Knights of Columbus lodge where his brother had campaigned in 1960. A few hundred reporters and a dozen or more television cameras tried to crowd their way into the tiny room where he would ask New Hampshire voters to choose him over President Carter. Theodore White, an owlish, gentle man and a superb journalist then working on *The Making of the President 1980*, was jammed into a corner. He shook his head, smiled, and said, "Twenty years ago, I was the only person here."

The presidential primary system that since 1972 has usurped from party leaders the choosing of a nominee was largely ignored for most of the century. Primaries were started in various states at the turn of the century on the heels of the Progressive movement led by Senator Robert LaFollette of Wisconsin. But they were often a party to which no one came. New Hampshire, having staked out the earliest primary date, got attention now and then. In 1952, Senator Estes Kefauver received a huge vote that may have prompted but more likely reinforced Harry Truman's decision not to seek re-election. In 1960, sixteen states held pri-

mary contests, but most were like the Illinois preferential primary, a "beauty contest" that did not bind any of the delegates to the Democratic National Convention in Los Angeles.
Such hopefuls as Lyndon Johnson, Symington, and the
inscrutable Stevenson were counting on a deadlocked convention where their respective power blocs would come into
play. But Kennedy knew he had to allay the fears of party
leaders that a Roman Catholic could not garner popular support for the presidency. He decided to enter seven primary
contests.

Hubert Humphrey had none of the strengths that the
other hopefuls enjoyed. His friends in the U.S. Senate would
certainly be for Johnson or even Kefauver. Harry Truman
was throwing his weight behind Symington, and Stevenson
had many admirers, including Daley's Pennsylvania coun-
terpart, Governor David Lawrence. So Humphrey chose to
run in five primaries. He and Kennedy would open the battle in Wisconsin.

On April 5, 1960, Kennedy won the Wisconsin primary
with 56 percent of the vote. His victory, Humphrey took
pleasure in noting, was built on the vote from the Catholic
areas in the southeastern part of the state. Humphrey won
in the Protestant congressional districts. Daley was most
interested in the turnout. He told reporters the heavy Democratic vote, more than twice as high as the GOP turnout,
indicated great interest in the coming election. He dismissed
suggestions that Kennedy could win only in places where
there was a heavy Catholic vote. "The people were voting for
the man," he said. But he studied the turnout and began to
realize just how much of a challenge his Democratic Party
faced in turning out a city vote that would match a large
turnout in the growing suburbs and downstate. At the same
time, the obvious excitement over the Kennedy-Humphrey
clash would be a plus for Democrats. Still, Daley wasn't

ready to publicly or privately give the nomination to Joe Kennedy's son. He and Truman had breakfast the day after the Wisconsin vote, and the former president urged Daley to consider his man, Symington.

Kennedy's people were disappointed in the narrow win in Wisconsin. They had hoped to overwhelm Humphrey and force him to abort his primary challenges, saving them the cost and risk of running in West Virginia, the next stop on the calendar and a state where 95 percent of the registered voters were Protestant. But Humphrey, ebullient over his showing in Wisconsin, charged ahead.

In the history of choosing presidents, the 1960 West Virginia primary became a milestone. Although the convention delegates that year remained under the control of party leaders, Kennedy's victory in West Virginia did exactly as he hoped. It persuaded Daley and many other politicos that he would indeed be a plus at the top of their local tickets. It raised second thoughts in the minds of people like Lawrence of Pennsylvania and Edmund G. "Pat" Brown of California, who had to begin conceding that the Catholic issue might not be as serious a detriment to their ticket as they had feared. Despite all the reports of the Kennedy family spending inordinate amounts of money in West Virginia, the simple fact was that Kennedy had won it. A Boston Irish-Catholic had gone into a border state and won. The Kennedy strategy was so apparent that although the other rivals for the nomination had disdained the primary route, they understood the value of the momentum he would receive by winning West Virginia. Although Humphrey's underfinanced campaign received last-minute help from all sorts of friends of Johnson and Stevenson, it was to no avail.

Daley noted the results. On May 11, the morning after Kennedy's win in West Virginia, Daley called a news conference. "It's another indication that Democratic primary

voters have spoken in an emphatic manner. It shows that people vote for the individual and not for his religion or his geo-
graphical qualifications. . . . If he continues to win primaries,
convention delegates following his series of victories cannot
help but be impressed," Daley stated. At the same time, in
suburban Libertyville, Adlai Stevenson issued a congratulatory message to Kennedy on his West Virginia triumph. But
in a telephone conversation with Arthur Schlesinger, who had
signed on with Kennedy after supporting Stevenson in his
two campaigns, Stevenson said he did not think West Virginia
settled anything. He said he believed Johnson and Symington controlled enough delegates to stop Kennedy from getting the nomination.[3]

The liberal and northern factions of the Democratic
Party were in a dilemma over Stevenson's posture all through
1960. His intellect, charm, and wit made him the natural
leader of those groups. Many felt a personal affection for him
that would linger all his life and far surpass their personal
feelings for Kennedy. But they all wanted a winner in 1960,
and Stevenson's refusal to say he wanted a third nomination
gave them the out card to join Kennedy. They wanted Stevenson's endorsement to push Kennedy over the top and they
also wanted Kennedy to be grateful enough to offer Stevenson the secretary of state's post in his cabinet. Stevenson's
view of world affairs was their view. They especially feared
that a Richard Nixon administration could be catastrophic in
terms of the Cold War.

Richard J. Daley wasn't part of this group. If he had any
concerns about who would be debating Khrushchev or meeting with Molotov, he never shared them. He also knew that
whatever Stevenson was plotting, he had few supporters
among the Illinois delegates. Most of the Democrats, especially the Southern Illinoisans like Powell who depended
heavily on the governor's office for patronage and favors, had

been disappointed by Stevenson's patrician manner during his four years in Springfield. And, like Daley, the Chicago bloc knew Kennedy could put over the county ticket. After all, Stevenson couldn't even carry the city in 1956. Still, the nomination wasn't certain. Too many powerful Democrats still yearned for Stevenson one more time. Eleanor Roosevelt and many others in the East were for him. Daley wanted Kennedy, but more than that, he wanted to be on the right side. Everyone assumed the West Virginia victory had locked up Daley for Kennedy. But the sixty-nine Illinois convention votes were too precious to take for granted. Lyndon Johnson went to Chicago shortly after the West Virginia vote and asked if Daley could support him at the convention in July.

Johnson later told Ken O'Donnell, the Kennedy loyalist who stayed on in the White House with Johnson, that Daley told him, "Lyndon, all of us out here like you. We think you've done a great job as our majority leader in the Senate, and you would make a fine president. But Jack Kennedy will get more votes for us in Illinois than you can get, so we've got to be for Kennedy." Perhaps Johnson, a kindred spirit in the realities of political power and its attendant obsessive secrecy, heard the usual complimentary platitudes and remarked mentally, "Bullshit." And then provided for posterity a translation that bolstered his own large ego. Or perhaps Daley implied that Kennedy now looked to be the strongest candidate, leaving unspoken the idea that if anything changed in a way that would be detrimental to Chicago Democrats, he could change. Johnson would have understood that and continued with plans to pursue the nomination just in case.

In June, Governor Lawrence of Pennsylvania came to Chicago to speak to the Loyal Order of the Moose convention. He and Daley had breakfast. "We always get together when he comes to town," was all Daley would tell reporters

about the meeting. Although the Catholic vote in Pennsylvania and Illinois was at about the same level, the chemistry
of the two states was different. Lawrence, four times the
mayor of Pittsburgh before moving to the governor's chair
in 1958, still believed Stevenson would be stronger at the top
of the ticket. Whether Daley argued Kennedy's cause sufficiently to reveal his ultimate support is debatable. They might
have talked about the Moose convention.

Daley obtained a private car to be attached to the end of
the Santa Fe Chief to take his wife, Eleanor, and their seven
children by train to Los Angeles for the Democratic Convention. They departed Chicago July 7 with Daley still mas-
querading about his choice for the nomination. "I'll tell you
after the Illinois delegation caucuses in Los Angeles. The
caucus is the place where you do your talking; then you do
your voting on the convention floor." He did predict the delegation would be united, which to Daley meant unanimous.

William Daley, the youngest of the seven Daley children,
was 12 at the time. "I'll never forget riding across the desert
and seeing these signs, 'Paddy Bauler and the 43rd Ward Welcome Mayor Daley,' " he recalled.

The Democratic Party met in convention on July 10,
1960, for the first time in Los Angeles, far from the Atlantic
Ocean, where the Boston, New York, and Philadelphia party
rulers had long dominated its affairs. Daley hadn't wanted the
Democrats to go to Los Angeles. He had taken his family to
Disneyland in 1959 and he saw no other reason to travel
halfway across the country when the Democrats could have
met where they belonged, in Chicago. Even after Los Angeles had won the convention, Daley and Arvey constantly
urged national chairman Paul Butler to reconsider. Among
other things, Los Angeles didn't have enough hotel rooms in
a central location. Delegations were spread all over Southern
California, which prevented the easy mixing of caucuses and

the neighborly gatherings of Democrats from similar regions. Also, the summer heat threatened to melt the delegates. Air conditioning was faulty in many of the hotels and didn't work very well at the Sports Arena, where the convention was held. The television networks, which had discovered in 1956 that political conventions were great theater, didn't want to travel to Los Angeles. Daley, who had become highly aware of television's impact, argued that the three-hour time difference between the East Coast and Los Angeles would deprive the party of many viewers during the evening events. But Los Angeles officials worked out most of the problems and the convention stayed there. Disgruntled, Daley promised himself he would bring the Democrats back to Chicago.

Four days before the convention began, Lyndon Johnson formally threw his hat into the ring. True to the roughneck politics of Texas, his aides immediately started a rumor that Kennedy suffered from Addison's disease and would not live out his presidency. The Kennedy camp issued furious denials. Stephen Mitchell, who had been trounced in the April Illinois primary by Kerner, was among those who thought the Johnson campaign had opened with "a low blow delivered at the last moment."

A welcoming committee complete with band was waiting on Track 8 near the Union Pacific station in downtown Los Angeles when the train carrying the Illinois delegation arrived on Sunday morning. Television crews were also on hand since Daley, Pennsylvania's Lawrence and California's Brown were the remaining big holdouts who hadn't publicly declared for Kennedy. But the Daley family slipped out of the back car and got off the train on Track 6. They walked two blocks to the Old Mission Church, where they attended 9 A.M. Mass. The welcoming committee included Cook County Assessor P. J. "Parky" Cullerton, Alderman Vito Marzullo of the West Side 25th Ward, State Senator William Connors of the 42nd Ward, U.S. Representative Dan Rostenkowski, and State Senator Marshall Korshak. The committee had hired a band, which caught up with the Daley family in the lobby of the Hayward Hotel and dutifully blared out verse after verse of "Chicago, Chicago." The Daleys were settled in the fifteenth floor penthouse suite. Like the other eighty-eight members of the Illinois delegation and assorted followers, they discovered the telephone didn't work, the elevators were slow, and July in Los Angeles was awfully hot. The Daleys moved out the next day to the Hilton.

It was more than the weather that made the 1960 Democratic convention different from the many that preceded it. The attendees were gathered to pick a president who would face a world of rapid change. New nations were being born before they could be named. Technology was changing the way people worked and lived. And the threat of whatever went on in the still mysterious Soviet Union foreshadowed the future. Author Theodore White wrote:

"The matters that concerned the delegates were many and diverse. But one could take their very presence in Los Angeles as symbolic. Almost all of those who had come from the East Coast had flown here on the new swept-wing jets, which now spanned the continent in five hours. . . . The continent had been cut in half. So much had America shrunk since 1956—so much had the world shrunk about America. So much had space itself shrunk, as man-made satellites now orbited the distant moon. It was as if the delegates sensed, if they did not know, that now halfway around the world missiles with hydrogen heads coded for Los Angeles, as well as Chicago and Washington and New York, were already in place." [4]

The headlines the Democratic convention participants left behind at home were similar to the ones that greeted them in Los Angeles. Congo Erupts . . . Khrushchev Threatens Austria . . . Castro Threatens . . . Russians Down Spy Plane. . . .

It was a brave new world and for many of the aging Democratic leaders it was a swan song. Carmine deSapio, leader of Tammany Hall, the New York party organization that had nominated Al Smith in 1928 and under Bronx boss Ed Flynn had given America four terms of Roosevelt, was not a player in 1960. Most of the New Dealers were left out. Daley sent Harry Truman a telegram pleading with him to attend the convention, but the elderly Democratic president, who understood that he would be regarded only as an interesting relic, stayed home. In four short years, the process had bypassed almost all the old bosses. Only the seventy-seven-year-old Lawrence would have a last hurrah and he almost bungled it with his dalliance over a possible late Stevenson candidacy. Eight years hence, none of them would be around, not the Harrimans or Stevensons, Rayburns or Russells, Browns or Farleys—even the Kennedys or Johnsons. From the last gasp of the era of brokered conventions in 1956 through the sea change year of 1960 to the chaotic divisiveness of 1968 to the television campaign of 1976, only one man stayed in the ever-changing circle of national Democratic power: Richard J. Daley.

On Sunday afternoon, July 10, in the Hayward Hotel, Daley was finally through saying he hadn't made up his mind, that he hadn't given it any thought, that he couldn't say anything until the delegation held its caucus.

Although Johnson, Symington, and the Stevenson forces were conceding that Kennedy had enough delegates to reach the magic 761 total needed to clinch the nomination, many of their older strategists remembered the conventions where front-runners missed out on a first-ballot nomination and fell into obscurity. With so many delegates not bound by law to

Kennedy, there was always a chance to deny him the first-ballot victory and hope a deadlocked gathering would turn to someone else. The Johnson, Symington, and Stevenson supporters were scurrying around trying to get votes away from Kennedy. It didn't matter where those votes went on the first ballot as long he stopped short of 761.

On the eve of the convention, Johnson's camp thought Kennedy had 420½ votes while their man had 408 votes. Johnson predicted he would climb to 600 votes on a second ballot and capture the nomination on a third. Stevenson's backers wanted Johnson to peak at 600, which would block Kennedy from the nomination and force a series of balloting that would create the deadlock Stevenson needed for a third try at the presidency. Critical to all the scenarios was the trio of states controlled by the three Irish bosses: Lawrence in Pennsylvania, Brown in California, and Daley. Larry O'Brien, Kennedy's campaign chairman, remembered, "We were actually in the convention or within a couple of days of it with some questions about what Daley's ultimate decision would be."[5] Johnson eyed the Illinois caucus and thought Kennedy would get 42 votes and Symington would hold 18, with 7 for Stevenson and 2 for Humphrey. Symington said he was confident of 17 votes from Illinois.

At 3 P.M. the eighty-eight delegates and alternates, empowered to cast sixty-nine votes—the fourth-largest block at the convention—closed the doors and began to caucus. In another of those oddities that used to frequent political conventions, Daley had been stuck in one of the Hayward's balky elevators with Stevenson as he headed for the caucus. When he reached the caucus room, he marched toward the podium to begin the proceedings. Near the front of the room sat Rostenkowski, the first-term congressman from the Northwest Side who was already becoming Daley's man in Washington. Daley stopped and said, "Danny, why don't you nominate

Kennedy?" Until that moment, Rostenkowski said, he had no idea who Daley was going to support. "I was for Kennedy, but if the mayor asked me to nominate someone else I would have nominated somebody else." But Daley didn't really let Rostenkowski put Kennedy's name before the caucus. "He went up and announced, 'And now the youngest congressman will introduce the name of the young senator,'" Rostenkowski recalled. After Rostenkowski's nomination, Daley went to the podium and made clear for the first time where he stood.

"The Democratic Party has always been the party of youth. I hope it will always be the party of youth. Jack Kennedy has a great record as a Navy commander. He was decorated for bravery. That's not all," Daley added between the interruptions of applause from the loyalists who finally knew when it was time to applaud. "He has a great legislative record and a long one. And his winning political record includes 1960, when he was willing to enter the preference primary and take his chances at the hands of the people. I'm for Kennedy."

Scott Lucas spoke for Symington: "I'm not trying to stop anyone in this convention. But I say Symington can win in November. If he is nominated, everyone on our state ticket will be elected. I'm not sure (of the state ticket winning) if it's one of the others for President." Lucas had gone into the caucus thinking he and Powell had secured at least 14 votes for Symington. The Kennedy camp had predicted Daley would give them 57 votes. When the caucus was over, it was a rout. The vote was 59½ for Kennedy, 6½ for Symington, two votes for Stevenson. Powell and the Southern Illinoisans kept their promise to Truman, except for John Stelle who switched to Kennedy as a favor to Arvey. The only remnant of the power Arvey had wielded in 1948 and 1952 was his post as Democratic national committeeman from Illinois. Daley, who in his career would annex almost any title that hovered within his reach, had considered taking that away, too. Instead he demanded that Arvey show some strength by converting Stelle. It was a tidy bit of revenge for Stelle's Charlie McCarthy remark of the previous November.

By the time Pennsylvania's Lawrence decided to abandon Stevenson and deliver 64 of his 81 delegates to Kennedy on Monday night, it hardly mattered. California's Brown, who also had a lingering lust for Stevenson, lost control of his state caucus, which split for Kennedy and Stevenson and earned Brown a lingering disrespect from other party chiefs. On Monday, July 11, Senator Frank Church delivered the keynote address to four thousand delegates, alternates, and any Democrat who could steal a credential to get into the Sports Arena. The convention was on its way toward nominating John F. Kennedy, but Richard J. Daley still couldn't savor the victory because Adlai Stevenson was the last man in Los Angeles to accept it.

Stevenson, who had vacillated for months on whether he wanted the nomination, arrived in Los Angeles on Saturday and was immediately trapped between two conflicting forces: those still trying to give him a third chance at the presidency and those insisting he nominate Kennedy to unite the party and enhance his own chances of becoming secretary of state. Stevenson demurred on the later, saying he had promised Johnson and Symington his neutrality, a characteristically apolitical approach for him. On Tuesday morning, he spoke to the Minnesota caucus but did not ask for the nomination. His most prestigious supporter, Eleanor Roosevelt, was working the telephones for him. On Sunday, she called Daley and asked if she could come and talk to him. Daley said that he would be glad to go to wherever she was, which turned out to be Pasadena, twenty miles from the convention hall. Daley, accompanied by his sons Rich and Mike, spent two uncomfortable hours with the widow of the president who had led the Democratic ticket to four great victories. Daley's natural reverence for women, especially older women and widows, made it difficult to refuse her wish. But he told her, Bill Daley said, "It's too late. We made our commitments. I asked Adlai over a year ago whether he would run. He told me no. We aren't budging."

Newton Minow, a Stevenson supporter in 1952 and 1956, recalled that Daley had visited Stevenson in Libertyville in the spring after the Kennedy primary triumphs and said, "Tell me if you're running—I've had trouble with the delegates before but I'll try if you're a candidate." Minow, who would become famous for calling television "a vast wasteland" during his term on the Federal Communications Commission during Kennedy's administration, also recalled that the week before the convention Stevenson called Daley in Chicago to find out what would happen if he now decided to enter the race. "Daley told him to stay out, he was already committed," Minow said. Shortly after Stevenson arrived in Los Angeles on Saturday, Minow told him again the Illinois delegation would be nearly 100 percent for Kennedy. "Really?" Stevenson asked, surprised. Minow was one of those hoping Stevenson would nominate Kennedy, but when Stevenson refused Minow loyally continued to work for his nomination.

Rostenkowski said, "Daley told me himself that he had gone to see Stevenson in the spring to find out what he was going to do. Stevenson told him he had no plans. 'Are you sure?' Daley asked him and then Daley said if he had any plans he ought to think about running in the primaries to show he still had strength. Adlai was amazed at that, Daley said."

On Tuesday, Stevenson, an Illinois delegate-at-large, decided to go to the convention floor and take his seat in the

Illinois delegation. The banners, "We Want Adlai," "Stick With Adlai," that had appeared Monday had multiplied. The chain dancing around the arena swirled faster. The television audience of the nation was focused on the Illinois delegation. Convention business was suspended as Stevenson shook hands with Daley, Arvey, and Joseph Gill, who had preceded Daley as chairman of the Cook County Democrats. Stevenson supporters clutching their signs crowded into the Illinois delegation, perhaps forgetting or unaware that there had only been two votes for their man there. Some of the Illinoisans shouted back, "We Want Kennedy, We Want Kennedy." George Tagge wrote in the *Chicago Tribune*, "Obviously hopeful for another nomination, Stevenson infuriated Illinois leaders. Their retaliation was deadly." Only one Illinoisan, Harold Pogue of Decatur, marched in the Stevenson demonstration with an Illinois placard. Joseph Germano, powerful Chicago head of the United Steel Workers, said the Stevenson demonstration was aided by the Communist Party.

As pragmatic as Daley was, the glory of his triumph in leading Kennedy to the brink of the nomination was chilled by Stevenson's presence. Stevenson had given Daley the choice Illinois revenue director's post when Daley needed an important appointment in 1948 and Stevenson's picture hung on the wall in Daley's office. More memorable and more personal, in 1955, when Daley was being characterized during his mayoral bid as just another machine hack, Stevenson had endorsed him over Kennelly, bringing to Daley some of the gloss of his own integrity and liberal intellectualism.

But Daley figured he had repaid that debt. In 1956, Illinoisans knew well that Stevenson was heading for another disastrous election and most of them, particularly the Paul Powell faction, wanted no part of him. But Daley prevailed in keeping the delegation united for Stevenson. Despite his assurances to Stevenson earlier in the year, it is doubtful

Daley could have lined up the delegation for him, but Stevenson had made that point moot by declaring himself out of the race. Now, with the nation watching and Daley anxious to share in the reflected glow of the Kennedy victory, Adlai Stevenson was standing by his side, a forlorn supplicant whose prayers would not, could not, be answered. Daley knew that the liberals would never forget this. Stevenson was led to the platform, where the man who had made so many memorable speeches in two losing campaigns spoke woodenly and deflated an audience that had been primed to start an old-fashioned convention stampede for him. The demonstration for Stevenson was still enthusiastic enough to shake the conventional wisdom. The Wednesday afternoon early editions read: "Kennedy Tide Ebbs . . . Kennedy Bandwagon Falters."[6]

On Wednesday, July 13, Adlai Stevenson decided he wanted to run for president again. He would allow his name to be placed in nomination by Senator Eugene McCarthy of Minnesota. He also decided he should see if he could round up any delegates. Minow warned him it was futile. "He just wouldn't believe it even though Daley had told him no." Stevenson telephoned Daley, who did not answer the call. Maybe Daley didn't want to answer or maybe he never got the message. The *Chicago Tribune*, which constantly described the Illinois headquarters hotel, the Hayward, as "inelegant," reported that telephone service was impossible. A high-ranking member of the Illinois delegation, State Senator Marshall Korshak, committeeman of the 5th Ward, was pressed into duty as a messenger between the hotel and the Sports Arena.

But Stevenson tried his old patron Arvey, who got the message and asked Daley on the convention floor to return the call. When Stevenson got Daley on the line he said he knew that the caucus had given him only two votes but he asked if that was because the delegates thought he was not a candidate. Daley told him that he had no support in Illinois. "Governor, you're going to look foolish running for this nomination because you'll get no support from Illinois. These delegates weren't for you in 1956 either, but I made them vote for you then. I can't do that again." Minow was with Stevenson at the time of the call. "He was genuinely shocked," Minow said. "It really affected their relationship for a long time."[7]

That blunt message was the death stroke for the Stevenson candidacy. Daley's honest remarks made it clear that Stevenson's earlier lack of interest had been a relief; Daley knew from the beginning of the 1960 campaign that he would not support another Stevenson bid.

Still, his brusque, swift manner of dispatch had hurt Stevenson, and Daley knew it. What is even more surprising is that he, too, was hurt by it. Fifteen years later, when Adlai Stevenson III was being mentioned as a presidential possibility, the pain in Daley's memory was evident. "If you do it," Daley told him, "I hope that nothing happens to me like what happened to me in Los Angeles."[8]

The relationship was repaired quickly. On the night of Kennedy's inauguration, the Daley family was leaving the ball to return to their hotel and found Stevenson without a ride. "My dad invited him in our car and they talked just like old friends," Bill Daley recalled. A year later, Rich Daley, who was in college at Providence, went down to New York with a bunch of friends and they all wound up staying with Stevenson at the UN ambassador's suite in the Waldorf Towers. "My dad never had a bitter feeling about Adlai. He really liked Adlai," said Bill Daley.

The day after Stevenson's final hurrah, Daley, angry at Stevenson and also seeking party unity, had joined those insisting that Stevenson nominate Kennedy. "I think he should. Didn't Kennedy make a nominating speech for Stevenson four years ago?"

Another Minnesotan, Governor Orville Freeman, wound up nominating Kennedy. Though his speech was lackluster, he had the winner.

"Let's go, Illinois," Daley shouted in the din following the nomination, and the fifty-eight-year-old mayor led the Illinoisans into the snake dance that circled the Sports Arena. Most of the delegates returned to their seats, sweating and rumpled, after a single circuit but Daley did another tour. Jack Arvey and Joe Gill stayed in their chairs. "We're just too old," Arvey said. Probably, but Jack Arvey had had 1948 and 1952. This was Dick Daley's convention. After the demonstrations halted, the roll call was taken. Kennedy collected 806 votes, Johnson 409, Symington 86, Stevenson 79½. Kennedy had 45 votes more than the required 761. The final tally from Illinois gave him 62 votes.

Moments after the roll call was completed, Daley and the other leaders who had supplied the numbers for Kennedy left the hall and walked to a model cottage that had been the Kennedy communications post for the convention. Their candidate arrived in a motorcade and went to the cottage, where he huddled with his brother Robert. Minutes later, Theodore White described, Kennedy allowed them to approach. "First Averill Harriman; then Dick Daley; then Mike DiSalle; then, one by one, in an order determined by the candidate's own instinct and judgment, he let them all congratulate him."[9]

Then everyone went to bed wondering who Kennedy would pick for his running mate. The vice presidential nomination in 1960 and for most previous conventions of the century was chosen for two reasons: ticket balance and payback. It had often been traded to secure the presidential nomination, as was the case with Franklin Roosevelt and John Nance Garner in 1932. In other years, the candidate tried to choose someone whose support he needed or someone who at least had the support of an influential bloc of Democrats who could deliver a vote. In recent years, the most influential vote getter has been television and the primary system has eliminated the need to barter the vice presidency. George Bush's selection of Dan Quayle in 1988 was a minor sop to the Republican right wing, but Quayle brought nothing to the ticket. In fact, recent polls indicate few running mates have any effect on the ticket—except in those rare years such as 1972, when the psychiatric treatment of George McGovern's choice, Senator Thomas Eagleton, forced him off the ticket and further debilitated one of the most inept campaigns in history.

But in 1960, the old school of thought regarding the vice presidential role still prevailed. The day after his nomination, John Kennedy invited Daley and the other kingmakers back to his suite at the Biltmore, where he discussed his decision to anoint Johnson as his running mate. Some said Daley was not pleased. He had been for Symington and he let Kennedy know it, the *Tribune* reported. Daley reportedly agreed, for once, with his Southern Illinois foes, Powell and Lucas, that Symington would be a plus for the state ticket. For Cook County he would probably be neutral, but Daley could not want a southerner like Johnson when he was going to depend so much on Bill Dawson's black wards. Daley would not, he explained, be able to deliver the huge Chicago margin that Kennedy needed to carry Illinois. But Kennedy had been battling with almost everyone else all day, starting with his top aides and labor leaders, and he had made up his mind. Daley reminded him how helpful he had been in getting Kennedy the nomination. "Not you, nor anybody else nominated us. We did it ourselves," Kennedy said.[10] Later Daley, like his peers Lawrence and DiSalle, agreed that if Johnson could carry Texas it would be worth the risk in the black and liberal neighborhoods.

That is one version of what happened. Rostenkowski has another version. "That morning I was with Daley when

Kennedy called. I could only hear one end of the conversation. I was for Symington. We had a Roman Catholic (Kennedy) at the top of the ticket, we had a Mason, Otto Kerner, for governor, and I thought if we got Symington, it would bring in Harry Truman, who was popular in Southern Illinois. I'm listening to Daley who says, 'Listen, you're the nominee and I don't care if you put Snow White on the back end of that ticket. You are going to get the credit or the blame for winning this election. If you think he's going to help you as the candidate, you do it. And I'll tell you something else, if you want Bill Dawson to put his name in nomination, I think I can talk Dawson into doing that.' Daley hung up the phone and said, 'It's Johnson,' and I shouted, 'No, No, No,' but he didn't say anything."

Why Kennedy really picked Johnson and who was for it or against it remain among the most interesting unsolved questions in American politics, especially given the consequences of that 1960 ticket. But Bill Daley said his father "absolutely believed it should be Johnson. He said all along Kennedy could not win the election without Texas. I think Johnson knew this and that was one reason for their friendship."

On Friday, Kennedy gave his acceptance speech at the Los Angeles Coliseum. Most of the Illinoisans were at Disneyland or Las Vegas or the beach. But the Daleys were there to hear the heralding of a new era:

"We stand today on the edge of a New Frontier, the frontier of the 1960s, a frontier of unknown opportunities and perils, a frontier of unfulfilled hopes and threats. . . ." Daley thought it one of the best speeches he had ever heard.

The Daley family left Los Angeles the next day and headed for the Grand Canyon. "He liked to see things, do things. He didn't like to sit by the pool, he always had us on the go, taking pictures, looking for bears or whatever. He really enjoyed those trips," Bill Daley recalled. On July 19 the Daley family arrived back in Chicago in time for Daley to attend funeral services for Al Horan, 29th Ward committee-man, who, with Arvey and Gill, had given Daley the chairmanship of the party in 1953. Dick Daley went to a lot of funerals for people who had helped him out.

CHAPTER 3

"The Town That Billy Sunday Could Not Shut Down"

JOSEPH B. MCDONOUGH, COUNTY TREASURER AND PROMI-
nent Democratic leader, died at 3:45 A.M. today at his
home, 551 W. Thirty-Seventh St. Death followed a gallant battle against pneumonia.

CHICAGO TRIBUNE, APRIL 25, 1934.

Chicago is famous for its gangland funerals, where the assassins were usually in the front row of marchers behind the cas-
kets of their victims. It also knows how to throw a farewell
party for its politicians. About fourteen thousand people
showed up to pray for Joe McDonough's eternal soul at the
Nativity of Our Lord, where the previous Christmas he had
passed out 5,600 baskets of food to the needy. The *Chicago
Tribune* reported that his funeral drew more mourners than
that of assassinated mayor Anton "Tony" Cermak the previous year. Governor Henry Horner and Mayor Edward Kelly
headed a delegation of officials who escorted the casket three
blocks from McDonough's home to the church. The newspaper printed a list of more than a hundred city, state, and
national officials who were honorary pallbearers. There was

a shorter list naming the eight men who actually lifted the casket. That may have been detailed reporting or a tribute to the fellows who did the lifting, since McDonough weighed more than three hundred pounds. They were called the active pallbearers: Hugh Connolly, James Doyle, George V. Curry, Charles Karleskind, Edward J. McAvoy, Stephen Bailey, Joseph O'Connor, and Richard J. Daley. It was certainly not the first wake or funeral that Daley attended and it would not be the last.

Joe McDonough was a typical machine politician of the 1920s. He was a rough-and-tumble, glad-handing personification of the Tammany Hall/James Michael Curley school of spoils. The Irish political organizations that influenced northern big-city politics from the 1890s to the 1930s were built on providing jobs, housing, food, and funerals for the new immigrants and all those already here still trying to break the Anglo-Saxon grip on economic dominance. These "machines" grew as one-man fiefdoms, ward leaders who controlled a single section of a large city and formed various alliances to obtain patronage and graft. The struggle for control of the wards was often an intramural ethnic battle: Irish versus Irish, German versus German. In New York and Boston, the Irish achieved control of the Democratic Party by sheer numbers. In Chicago, the numbers favored at first the German-Scandinavians, later the Polish, and in the reign of Richard J. Daley, the blacks. But somehow the Chicago Irish politicians, invested with the same skills, affinities, and determination as their East Coast cousins, emerged as minority rulers.

The success of Irish politicians in America has been traced to many mystical and practical origins. Supposedly their fey Celtic nature endowed them with persuasiveness through song and speech that propelled them to success in an arena where words were more powerful than swords. They emigrated from a tiny nation free of the nationalistic strife that was so divisive in other European ethnic groups. They suffered cruelly under the British Empire, but they understood it was not the English armies that caused thousands to die in the famine of the 1850s; it was British policy. It was not fire and iron that forged the British decision to refrain from feeding a starving nation; it was oratory. And the oratory claimed that no matter what natural events or circumstances contrive to oppress a people, they must lift themselves through their own perseverance and will rather than through government intervention. The bitter memory of that policy drove many Irish politicians to argue that the government's foremost role is to help people.

The Irish did arrive first and they did speak the language. The prejudices ("No Irish Need Apply") were as strong against them as against succeeding immigrant groups, but the Civil War offered many of them an opportunity to shed blood for their adopted country and remove some of the second-class stigma. It is ironic that while the Irish battalions and regiments would become some of the most heralded of the Civil War, a century later (with scant exceptions) African-Americans were not permitted to demonstrate their patriotic fervor in World War II. It was not until after that great triumph that Harry Truman issued an executive order to integrate the armed forces—a decision that would play a key role in the political career of Richard J. Daley.

Roger Sullivan and George Brennan were the first bosses who tried to unify the Democratic Party in Chicago, but they were stifled by the rivalry of progressive Mayor Carter H. Harrison and later by the reign of William Hale Thompson, the ornery, pugnacious Republican who is second only to Daley in Chicago's list of memorable mayors. Thompson held the mayor's office from 1915 to 1923 and again from 1927 to 1931. Part of his political success stemmed from Al Capone's intimidating support, but he also won his three terms because the Democratic machine was in its infancy.

Sullivan helped give it stature during the marathon Democratic National Convention of 1912. He played a decisive role
in throwing the nomination to Woodrow Wilson (mostly to
spite Harrison, who was supporting another candidate). After
his death in 1922, Brennan took over the party with the goal
of putting a machine candidate into City Hall. His rival for
party control was a West Side Bohemian alderman, Anton
Cermak.

McDonough was one of the feudal ward leaders of the
time. He was elected alderman in 1917 from Bridgeport and
re-elected six times. He was also the ward committeeman
from 1918 until his death. He loved the racetracks, restaurants, and a piece of the action. Once entrenched in the
council, McDonough was caught in the battle for party control between Brennan and Cermak, who knew his ambition
to run Chicago could never succeed unless he split the Irish
factions. No one knows what Cermak offered McDonough
to join his side, but it was enough. In the years that McDonough was serving the public he had time to own a saloon,
become vice president of a fledgling automobile sales company, own a real estate firm, and benefit financially from all
the public excavating and Teamster operations in the ward.
His obituary confessed "he was no angel," but also heaped
praise on his ability to build playgrounds and defend salaries
for the police and fire departments, whose ranks were already
swelling with Irish names. In 1930, McDonough was elected
country treasurer. In the depths of the Depression, he initiated the idea of paying property taxes in installments. As the
stories describing his funeral attest, McDonough was a popular figure in the Chicago of the 1920s. But in terms of the
city's history he is best remembered as Richard J. Daley's
"Chinaman," his "rabbi," his "clout"—political slang for
patron.

Daley was born May 15, 1902, in a two-flat at 3502 South
Lowe and spent all his life on the same block. He was the

only child of Michael Daley, a sheetmetal worker who was born in County Wexford, Ireland, and his wife, Lillian Dunne Daley. Daley went to grade school at Nativity of Our Lord. Like most of the other male students, he was an altar boy. It was in that role that he was introduced to funerals and requiem masses as well as weddings. Altar boys become more realistic about these passages than others who do not experience the more practical aspects of the ceremonies. The funeral director would generally give altar boys a nickel or dime after the funeral mass. Depending on the state of the bridegroom's hangovers, the tip at a wedding could be as much as a quarter or even a dollar. And altar boys, somber as they might appear waving incense toward the casket, also got the day off school. In addition to his religious duties, Daley sold vegetables with his friend Ed Cunningham on Saturdays, and he delivered newspapers. "I used to make fifty or sixty cents a day selling newspapers," he would recall.

Daley went to DeLaSalle High School, run by the Christian Brothers. He took a commercial course, typing and bookkeeping, to prepare for a career as a white-collar worker and avoid both the stockyards, with their stench and blood, and the "cars," the buses and trains where the post of conductor or motorman was the route of upwardly mobile Irish lads of the 1920s. The only other possibilities were the police and fire departments and, of course, politics. Daley decided on the last alternative. After graduation he worked in the yards—in an office dealing with ledgers, not in the pens slaughtering steers and hogs with a sledgehammer. Like most young men in their first jobs, Daley wanted to be the boss. His early ambition, he said, was "to be another P. D. Armour."

He joined McDonough's organization, working a precinct in the mayoral and aldermanic elections of 1919 and the presidential election of 1920. This was probably a baptism of political reality for young Daley. The Democratic candidate that year was Ohio Governor James Cox, and the Democrats who nominated him knew that after eight years of Woodrow Wilson and America's involvement in a war that was highly unpopular in the isolationist Midwest, Cox was doomed. Not that the young Daley or any other precinct captain in Chicago cared about Cox or the presidency. The deciding factor was that he was no help to the local ticket—the only thing that mattered—and the Democrats were swamped in 1920. This drubbing, of course, did not harm McDonough's status, since aldermanic and mayoral elections were set in odd years precisely so the national elections would not affect their outcome. (In the heyday of the Chicago machine, when FDR was at the top of the ticket, the odd-year strategy would have been moot. But Daley must have said a private prayer for his political ancestors when he thought about what would have happened to him if his first mayoral election would have been held in conjunction with the 1956 Eisenhower landslide instead of a year earlier.)

Despite the 1920 presidential election, Daley quickly demonstrated the diligence that would distinguish him in every job he ever held. He performed his precinct duties well enough that McDonough rescued him from the private sector forever by appointing him 11th Ward secretary. It was the beginning of a political apprenticeship that, like the military, would take Daley step by step to the top of Chicago's political ladder. The job also entailed being McDonough's personal secretary, an eye-opening experience. It was in the ward that Daley first discovered the intricacies of patronage and formed the habit of knowing exactly who had every available job and why. That probably wasn't difficult in 1922, when the ward had only a few hundred patronage employees. What was amazing was Daley's detailed knowledge of thirty thousand patronage workers a half century later.

Daley was also spreading his fledgling political wings in the Hamburg Social and Athletic Club, the Bridgeport organization that served as a social mecca for the stockyard neighborhoods and a political arm of the Democratic Party. Everyone with a taste for life in the public trough was a Hamburger; Daley joined in his teens. In 1923, the Democrats' reform candidate interrupted Big Bill Thompson's frolic through City Hall, and Brennan and Cermak, the rival bosses, split up the jobs among their troops. There was a job downtown for Daley and he began his fifty-year-plus odyssey between Bridgeport and City Hall.

The Roaring Twenties were in full swing when Daley arrived at City Hall to work in a small office behind the council chambers. He was assigned menial tasks: fetching coffee and rolls, providing newspapers, typing a document now and then, probably striding in that rapid, signature pace across to the Sherman House or one of a dozen nearby speakeasies to pick up an alderman's winnings or deliver an order for a case of Al Capone's best illegal whiskey. Although Daley's responsibilities were so minimal that he immediately began attending night school to earn a law degree, and although his personal proclivities, shy manner, and moral tone suggest that the hedonism of the 1920s did not interest him, nevertheless he was a man of his time. Growing to manhood in that robust era, in a cloistered family and church existence, endowed Daley with many of the traits that biographers would later cluster as the nature of a political boss. But in reality, they were simply the nature of his time.

Learning that the police could be used to reward friends and punish enemies, that City Hall offices could be used to provide jobs and harass opponents, that neither the public nor the church was bothered by the illegalities of booze or bookmaking, became part of the morality of Richard J. Daley. None of these things was specifically banned by the Baltimore catechism. The Ten Commandments did not mention kickbacks. Throughout Daley's career, journalists and political analysts, as well the Democratic cohorts who watched him the closest, observed an amazing contradiction in the man to whom no political corruption could be connected and the legion of thieves he tolerated around him. Daley would slice a political ambition into oblivion if he knew a person was an adulterer. That violated the Sixth Commandment. Mail fraud, however, wasn't on the list.

Daley's reputation would suffer greatly in the 1960s for what was perceived as an a racist attitude in his handling of the impossible civil rights turmoil. Some biographers have hinted that his membership in the Hamburgers proved his involvement in the 1919 race riots, when thirty-eight blacks were killed and five hundred injured after a black teenager tried to go swimming at a whites-only Lake Michigan beach. The Hamburgers and an even more violent Irish group, Ragen's Colts, were blamed for much of the bloodshed. But there is no reason to believe that Daley took the risk of being involved in something potentially damaging to his reputation or to his future. Certainly Daley may not have foreseen a role in public life in which participating in a riot would be a liability, but even as a boy and a young man, he demonstrated the inordinate ability to control himself and most situations he encountered. In the same fashion that he would distance himself in later years from any embarrassing actions of those close him, he undoubtedly refrained from any personal involvement in the violence, though he knew who was involved and probably was in agreement with their sentiments. After all, he was born in 1902. There were not many white men born that year with the vision to foresee that unless African-Americans were given equal opportunities, the city that Daley would rule sixty years later would be glutted by a core of people who were hopelessly unemployed, permanently disenfranchised, and (worst of all from a pragmatic viewpoint) a perpetual drain on city resources.

As late as Daley's first mayoral term, blacks in Chicago were invisible after dark in the night life of the Loop and

Rush Street. Blacks had their own night life, their own shopping, their own church. Chicago was as segregated as any southern hamlet. Daley lived in an era where no one of any political stature thought African-American people deserved anything more than the right to breathe and wait on tables and send their children to schools—as long as white kids didn't have to go with them. It wasn't until Roosevelt's coalition of the 1930s that African-Americans began to be considered for their votes. Fewer than 10 percent of Chicago's more than three million residents in the 1920s were African-Americans and those few who voted were still casting ballots for Lincoln in the Republican Party. If Daley's vision of race relations was formed by a turn-of-the-century attitude that was universally racist and leavened only later by an understanding of the value of African-Americans' votes, it doesn't suggest that he was less sensitive than most political leaders of a similar vintage and no more in conflict with the Christian ritual he practiced daily than the leading bishops of his church, who segregated seating at Catholic churches and schools in the south well into the 1960s. What would happen to Richard J. Daley in 1968 was far more telling than whether he privately reveled in the Hamburger involvement in the 1919 riots.

Daley's membership in the Hamburgers was social and political. He saw the opportunity to build his first political base and, following in McDonough's footsteps, he was elected president of the Hamburgers in 1924. He probably thought it a far more significant post than it now seems. He held on to it for fifteen years. In the 1920s, Bridgeport and the other Chicago neighborhoods were more like nations in a world that began and ended with Chicago. Bridgeport politics were dominated by the Irish, but the ward of more than sixty thousand people was filled with Lithuanians and Poles and Czechs, a smattering of Serbs and Croats, a few Ukrainians, and some leftover Germans and misplaced Italians who should have been up north on Taylor Street. To the south-west was an enclave of Poles and to the south was another Irish pocket called Canaryville. To the east the African-Americans migration had settled in along South Shore. In that foreign area north of the river, there were Andersonville for the Swedes, Streeterville for the carriage trade, and Logan Square for another group of Poles. To the northwest were the Germans. Along Maxwell Street and extending west into what would be the renowned 24th Ward were the Jews, merchants of all manner.

A boy born in Bridgeport might never travel to these neighborhoods until well into his adult life. Adventurous youths who made the trek often wound up in brick-and-stone battles with local youths exercising territorial imperatives. As the immigrants clustered in the various neighborhoods, the shops and smells reflected their heritage. There was enough alien experience in a long bus ride to satisfy anyone that whatever existed in the larger world already existed in Chicago. It was real and definable and an alluring prize for someone with the ambition to rule it. But in his and the century's twenties, Richard Daley was content to shuffle among City Hall, night classes at DePaul University, and the center of his life then, Bridgeport, where there were softball games and a saloon on every corner where you could discuss the White Sox and the Democrats. At one of those softball games in 1929 he was introduced to nineteen-year-old Eleanor Guilfoyle, a secretary who came from a large Irish family in Canaryville. They kept company for seven years before their marriage in 1936.

If Daley's career during the 1920s was plodding, the Cook County Democratic organization was blossoming. Two landmark events occurred in 1928. The Democrats, nominated Al Smith, the governor of New York and a Catholic, for president. It was a dull convention in, of all places, Houston. There was not much to argue about, because once again the party leaders accurately sensed an autumn disaster. But with their eye on the far more important local ticket, the big-city Democrats were not so distressed. Although Smith lost big in the South, the rural Midwest, and the West, he was, briefly, a political standard-bearer for the largely Catholic inner-city dwellers. The nomination of a Catholic was undoubtedly a major topic of conversation in the Bridgeport saloons, and while Daley would have known there was no chance of Smith's election, he took pride that one of his own had reached so high on the national political scale.

The second coronation was more meaningful. Tony Cermak had left the City Council and had been elected president of the Cook County Board of Commissioners, expanding his political base and forging further alliances with the North Side Germans and such Irish defectors as McDonough. The reason for his popularity was simple: He had a lot of jobs to pass out. In 1928, George Brennan died and Cermak took the machine away from the Irish. But he rewarded his friends, and McDonough become Cook County treasurer in 1930. It was a Democratic sweep and Richard Daley's career got another shove. Since McDonough never spent any time in any office he held, Daley, as deputy county treasurer, functioned as the boss. It was a great opportunity to learn from Cermak and other party leaders where county funds should be deposited, how to make friends with bankers who were happy to contribute to the party during election seasons, and exactly where public funds were disbursed. Daley learned some interesting things. He also had access to payrolls. For someone with his affinity for detail and the kind of knowledge that truly translated into power, a list of every patronage job in the county was like a map to Solomon's treasure.

In 1934, having crammed forty-five years of living into his three-hundred-pound body, McDonough died. Pat Nash now held the party chairmanship and had installed former

Sanitary District engineer Ed Kelly as mayor to succeed Cermak, who was killed in 1933. It took a quick act by the Illinois legislature to alter the city ordinance that said a member
of the council had to succeed to a vacant mayoralty, but that
was of little consequence to everyone except an alderman
named Frank Corr, who got to be mayor for thirty days
while the legislature acted.

McDonough's death held all sorts of opportunities for
Daley. He could have been appointed to the county treasurer
post. But Nash put in his cousin, Thomas A. Nash, boss of
the 19th Ward and a criminal lawyer who specialized in
defending mob figures, including Capone. Daley could have
been bounced as deputy treasurer by the new regime, but he
had managed to be loyal to McDonough and Cermak without alienating the other side. He was retained.

The job Daley really wanted was McDonough's post as
11th Ward committeeman. The committeeman, then and
through all the years of Daley's regime, was the key political spot. Patronage, contracts, favors from all the city and
county offices held by the party emanated from the county
committee. Aldermen, state representatives, and congressmen, unless they also held the committeeman position,
served at the whim of the committeemen. Few committeemen chose to run for alderman also. Several of them found
more obscure spots on the Cook County Board or in the legislature, where reporters were too bored to get as excited as
they could be when observing the carving of the pie in the
City Council chambers. But since the spoils were so lucrative, the next best thing to being a committeeman was to be
an alderman. That's why Tommy Doyle, a graduate of the
Hamburgers, quit Congress in 1930 after four terms in the
House to succeed McDonough as alderman. Doyle, who was
the president of the car dealership of which McDonough was
the vice president, was not going to get the committeeman's

post too. Nash and Kelly, like all bosses, were careful about consolidating strength in their subordinates. Hugh "Babe" Connolly, who had helped Daley lift the McDonough casket and who was eleven years older than Daley in both age and 11th Ward seniority, got the job. Daley would have to be content with running the treasury and the Hamburgers.

> Alderman Thomas A. Doyle, congressman from the Fourth District from 1922 to 1930 and a member of city, state, or national legislative bodies for twenty-one years, died yesterday in his home at 3537 Lowe Avenue.
>
> *Chicago Tribune*, January 30, 1935.

It wasn't long before Daley and his friends had another wake to attend. Doyle's death at age forty-eight, left open the aldermanic slot. Connolly, a former speakeasy owner who went legitimate after Prohibition, was now the committeeman, with the power to appoint Doyle's successor. He appointed himself. But Daley was now clearly the no. 2 man in the 11th Ward. He had, after eleven years of night school, obtained his law degree the previous year but he had no great ambitions as a litigator. He never practiced law for a single day. What he wanted was an office.

> State Representative David E. Shanahan, Republican leader and dean of the Illinois legislature, died at 3:38 o'clock yesterday afternoon in the Mercy Hospital after a long illness. He was 74 years old on September 7.
>
> *Chicago Tribune*, October 19, 1936.

Although Bridgeport has given five mayors to the city of Chicago,[1] its only native rewarded by a statue (which stands majestically in an alcove off the second-floor rotunda of the state capitol) is David Shanahan. He served Bridgeport for forty-two years in the legislature and was speaker of the house for five terms. But hardly a word has been spoken of him in Bridgeport since his death sixty years ago. He was a Republican. There were quite a few words spoken about him immediately after his death, however. On his deathbed, Shanahan took a bride, Helen Troesch, who was his secretary. He also signed a new will leaving $200,000 to her. The will was contested by Shanahan's spinster cousins, Mary and Margaret Flynn, and Bridgeport tongues wagged happily over the whole affair. Daley would not have been surprised: if there was any dalliance between Shanahan and Troesch prior to the nuptials, he would have known about it and chalked it up to the moral deficiencies one could expect from Republicans. What he was worried about was Shanahan's seat. With only two weeks between Shanahan's death and the 1936 general election, there was no time to appoint a substitute candidate whose name would appear on the ballot. Daley organized a write-in campaign and got 8,267 votes. Robert E. Rodgers, a Republican also running a write-in, got 3,978 votes. Richard Daley finally had an office.

(On the day Daley was sworn into the legislature, the Republican leader asked on which side of the aisle he wished to sit. "Over there," Daley murmured, bobbing his head toward the Democratic side. "Go on over then," the Republican leader said. "We don't want you over here.")

Michael J. O'Connor, deputy country controller for several years and an authority on county tax matters, died in the Passavant Hospital yesterday after a brief illness. Mr. O'Connor was 65 years old.

CHICAGO TRIBUNE, DECEMBER 10, 1936.

O'Connor died one day before Edward VIII gave up the throne of England. While most of the world speculated on the royal succession, one man on the 3500 block of Lowe

Avenue speculated on the O'Connor succession. A few days later, Michael J. Flynn, county clerk, announced the appointment of Richard J. Daley to the deputy controller's post, which paid $6,000 a year. Flynn noted that Daley had served four county treasurers faithfully.

> State Senator Patrick J. Carroll, Democrat, who represented the 9th district at Springfield for 28 years died in his home at 3542 South Hermitage Avenue last night after a long illness.
>
> *CHICAGO TRIBUNE*, JANUARY 16, 1938.

The primary election was scheduled for February 1, 1938. Daley swiftly filed petitions to get on the ballot. He got 16,231 votes. His eight primary opponents garnered a total of 14,792 votes. In the November election Daley trounced his GOP opponent, Anthony Benkowski, by 33,486 to 12,013. He was now Senator Richard J. Daley.

Daley served eight years in the Senate and became its minority leader, responsible to Mayor Kelly for taking care of Chicago interests in the face of the dreaded Republican majority and governor. Legislators who spent the muggy spring nights in Springfield cavorting in saloons or establishments where young women could be met did not run into Daley. Except for walks through Abe Lincoln's old neighborhood and his daily visit to Mass, Daley was tucked away in his room studying bills for the next day's session. He rarely made speeches in the state senate, relying instead on his knowledge of pending legislation and its nuances. Many of his new colleagues would play roles in his future: Abraham Lincoln Marovitz, Thomas Keane, Paul Powell, Vito Marzullo, Benjamin Adamowski.

As a freshman lawmaker in 1937, Daley was only one of the many Democratic loyalists to the Kelly-Nash organization. But in his deputy controller's position, he had his first

distasteful brush with the news media. A tiny story appeared
in the *Chicago Tribune* on December 7, 1937.

> Richard J. Daley, assistant county controller, yesterday
> averted a threatened county board wolf scandal. It came
> about when the board's finance committee voted to pay
> a $10 bounty—the first in five years—to each of two
> huntsmen. Commissioner Daniel Ryan, chairman of the
> wolf bounty committee, warned that the pelts should be
> examined. "Once," he said, "the county was accused of
> paying a wolf bounty on five police dogs."
>
> "Having served with the state legislature last year,"
> interrupted Mr. Daley, "I consider myself an authority on
> wolves. I will certify that the pelts on which we are pay-
> ing belonged to two timber wolves."
>
> Recipients of the bounties are Peter Jepson, Cicero,
> who shot his wolf at 79th Street and Cicero Avenue, and
> Ralph Roesner of Palatine, who shot his in Palatine
> Township.

On December 11, 1937, the *Tribune* printed the following
letter to the editor.

> Chicago, Dec. 8—On Tuesday, Dec. 7, a news article
> appeared in your newspaper where I was directly quoted
> as having said the following:
>
> "Having served with the state legislature last year,"
> interrupted Mr. Daley, "I consider myself an authority on
> wolves."
>
> I emphatically deny that I made this statement and I
> trust that you will make the necessary retraction through
> the medium of your newspaper.
>
> > Richard J. Daley
> > Representative, 9th Senatorial District

There is no record of the *Tribune*'s correction nor any record that Daley ever again wrote to a newspaper seeking one. Undoubtedly Daley made the remark, displaying the wit he would rarely expose again until the dwindling years of his career. Although reporters were capable in those days of creating quotes to spice stories, it is unlikely anyone would have taken the trouble to improve a three-paragraph brief. Daley learned for the first time that as a public figure he had no assurances that anything he said would remain private. He learned the lesson well and for forty years rarely said anything that could be mistaken for a criticism of a fellow Democrat or even another politician. His rule didn't include the usual campaign diatribes against Republicans in general, reformers in particular, and the year 1968 in total. But that early embarrassment was the beginning of a long and hostile relationship with the media. Daley never trusted reporters. A very private man, he couldn't understand why anyone would have a job that pried into other people's affairs. A very suspicious man, he regarded even the most innocuous question as some form of entrapment that he should avoid or criticism he didn't want. He needn't have worried. Only his own occasional televised outbursts would ever harm his image. Nothing reporters ever wrote or said impeded the career of Richard J. Daley.

Dan Rostenkowski remembers that Daley would often caution, "Watch that guy. He's probably writing a book."

His career in Springfield, of which little note has been made, was remarkable for its purposeful or accidental prescience. In his eight years in the state senate, Daley handled all sorts of bills that became a blueprint for the early years of his mayoral administration. His New Deal allegiances were most apparent in his introduction in 1939 of a state income tax of 2 percent. Daley proposed it to protect the poor from the regressive sales tax. The bill died and it was not until

1969 that Illinois enacted an income tax. Four times Daley pushed through a bill that would allow Cook County residents to appeal their property tax rates directly to the county assessor without requiring a lawyer to go through the court system. At the time, only corporations were allowed direct appeals. The first two times the bill passed, the Illinois Supreme Court ruled it unconstitutional. Republican Governor Dwight Green vetoed it once. Finally, in 1943, Daley got it passed. "I hope that the Supreme Court will say this time, for the sake of small home owners, that we have a constitutional bill. I followed the court's adverse opinions closely in drafting this bill." The court agreed with him.

Daley was also busy doing the bidding of Mayor Kelly. Kelly, who had been an engineer at the Sanitary District when Nash chose him to succeed Cermak, may have been the guiding light behind all the legislation that Daley pushed involving future building projects. A slum clearance proposal, passed in 1939, was the starting block for the ribbons Daley would cut at the Cabrini-Green and Robert Taylor housing projects. It also created the Public Buildings Commission, which could raise private funds through bonding power. In later years, Daley would, of course, chair this commission and use it to reshape downtown Chicago.

Another of his pet projects involved seeking $20 million from the state's treasury surplus to finance superhighway construction in Chicago after the war. In the bill was an appropriation for $100,000 to pay for initial consulting fees. Daley learned about pinstripe patronage early in his career. Daley was also involved in partisan legislation, fighting futilely in 1943 to win a redistricting that would give Cook County control of the legislature and divide the congressional seats evenly between Cook and downstate.

In 1942 he won his second senate term, despite his Republican opponent's attacks against him for being a double dipper—holding two public jobs simultaneously—and for not being in the armed forces. Daley was thirty-nine at the time, with four children—hardly a candidate for the trenches. But he was very youthful in appearance, always neatly groomed and sporting slick dark hair. The *Chicago Tribune*, which didn't see a lot of good in most Democrats in those days, had written in 1942: "With an eagerness that makes his facial expression younger than his 36 years [sic], Senator Daley has been one of the most active junior legislators. This has given him quite a record of accomplishment for his two years as a representative and four years as senator." In fact, Daley omitted his age in the Illinois Blue Book of government because he considered himself too young for a position in leadership. But Kelly, who took over the party chairmanship when Pat Nash died in 1943, orchestrated Daley's election as minority leader that same year. One of the losers for the post was Representative Paul Powell, who would be both a valuable ally and a constant annoyance to Daley for another quarter century.

Daley was enigmatic to most lawmakers. He quickly built a reputation for honesty. His loyalty was to Chicago and the Chicago Democratic organization, not to his wallet, which was unusual in Springfield. That was the era when many legislators spent their time dreaming up "fetcher" bills, proposals that would threaten various interest groups and prompt lobbyists to surface with cash-filled envelopes or at least a week of free dinners to ensure that the bill would die harmlessly in a committee, where it was intended to disappear from the start. If Daley was involved in any of the quid pro quo maneuvers that typify legislative activity, he had higher motives than a thick steak.

His fellow lawmakers also noticed that Daley had a quick temper and a long memory. In later years the whispers around City Hall were that Daley had a credo: Don't get

angry, get even. But he often did both. During a 1943 debate
on giving Kelly emergency funds, Republicans charged Daley
had cut deals with some Republicans, promising them slight
challenges in the city elections in exchange for their vote on
Kelly's money. Daley sulked silently for the rest of the day
and petulantly refused to vote on a routine $50,000 bill that
he had cosponsored. Daley was fiercely partisan, attacking
any Republican administration bill that had politics linked to
it. His brusque, accusatory style of rhetoric, replete with non
sequiturs, was on early exhibit in Springfield. When Republicans proposed a resolution to look into the civil service situation under "Kelly's corrupt regime," Daley leaped to the
floor and said, "A meeting was held in the office of a state
director for the purpose of coercing state civil service
employees, who were threatened with the loss of their jobs if
they didn't contribute to the Chicago (Republican) campaign
fund."

Daley was ironically involved in one measure of a
prophetic nature. In 1943, the Republicans approved, over his
opposition, a new state office for a director of revenue. Daley
warned that such a department would "subtly and cleverly
take over the taxing machinery of every local government."

He also got passed a request from Kelly to allow the
mayor of Chicago to fill any vacancies that might occur in
the offices of city clerk and city treasurer. Most of the vacancies in those days were caused by the Grim Reaper. Neither
Kelly nor Daley could not have foreseen the number that
would be caused by federal grand juries.

Although Daley was not in uniform, the war years were
extremely busy ones and his family was growing. The Daleys'
first daughter, Patricia, was born in 1937. She was soon followed by Mary Carol, Eleanor, Richard, Michael, John, and
William, the last born in 1949. When not in Springfield or
in his county office, Daley fretted over things in the 11th

Ward, where Connolly continued as alderman (which Daley didn't care about) and as committeeman (which he did). Daley continued to attend softball games, funerals, and weddings and to stop for a beer with all the 11th Ward Democrats who were beginning to realize that the senator was held in great favor by Mayor Kelly. They assessed his chances for greater things and considered what his ascendancy could mean to them.

In 1945 the war ended and millions of Americans began looking for new jobs. Richard J. Daley was one of them. Kelly, lambasted daily by the newspapers and civic groups for the continuing corruption of his organization and the decay of Chicago's downtown, was in trouble in the party. The committeemen sensed he was on his last legs and prepared to stop him from seeking another term. The prime mover was Thomas A. Nash, Daley's old boss as county treasurer, who wanted to grab the reins of the machine that had been built by his late cousin. Nash was allied with Alderman John Duffy, who ran the council's finance committee—a prime source of patronage. Another patronage boss, County Assessor John Clark, was also eyeing Kelly's power, and most of the committeemen didn't like the idea of Kelly holding both the chairmanship and the mayor's office.

What Kelly needed was to elect men loyal to him to the key county patronage posts in 1946. Sheriff Michael Mulcahy, a Kelly man, couldn't succeed himself, but Kelly wanted to run him for county treasurer. County Clerk Michael Flynn, one of Kelly's closest friends, would be unopposed for a third term. Nash wanted to run Duffy for sheriff and the increasingly powerful Polish bloc wanted Alderman Joseph Rostenkowski of the 32nd Ward to get the spot. Nash shouted and ranted at the slatemaking session in Kelly's office, but in the end he cast the only vote for Duffy. There were no votes for Rostenkowski. Kelly had lined up all the rest for

Richard J. Daley. Organized labor came out strongly for
Daley, as it always would. The names on the committee
would be aligned with Daley for thirty years: William Lee of
the Chicago Federation of Labor, William McFetridge of the
Flat Janitors Union, Stephen Bailey of the Plumbers, Emmett
Kelly of the Meatpackers. Daley's old friend, Ben
Adamowski, who had quit his post as majority leader of the
Illinois House to serve in World War II, returned to his law
practice and chaired a lawyer's committee for Daley.

Daley was nominated without opposition in the April primary, only a few weeks after Jackie Robinson signed a con-
tract with the Brooklyn Dodgers. Daley campaigned as a
New Deal Democrat, not because he believed in Roosevelt's
vision of government but because he mistakenly thought
Roosevelt's coattails were sticking out of the grave. "I still
believe in those policies for which Franklin D. Roosevelt was
the great spokesman," he proclaimed.

His opponent was Elmer Michael Walsh, who used an old
theme: "D is for Daley and also for double on the payroll.
He draws one salary as state senator and another as deputy
county controller. He is another example of how the present
city and county administrations fail to give the public value.
Nephews, aunts, uncles, and even cousins of cousins have
been uncovered feeding upon spoils of the Kelly machine."

Like Americans everywhere, most of the Cook County
voters were tired of the war, the New Deal, and the Democrats. The Republicans swept just about everything in the
fall elections of 1946, and Daley was among those who were
swept out. One consolation for Kelly, and ultimately Daley,
was that Mike Flynn squeaked by to a third term as county
clerk.

But the terrible whipping of his ticket was the beginning
of the end for Kelly. Jacob Arvey, former councilman and
24th Ward committeeman, returned from the service with the
rank of colonel (a title he used the rest of his life) and was

prevailed on to take over the chairmanship of the party. His first job was tell Kelly he was through. Kelly at first agreed to step down, then recanted, like so many politicians Daley would observe trying desperately to escape the axe. Arvey recalled, "He asked me to reconsider. I said I can't. I've burned my bridges. If you want to run I'll vote for you, but I'll have to resign as chairman of the county committee because I've given my word and I have to keep it."[2]

Arvey then picked Martin Kennelly who, like Kelly, was a native of Bridgeport. Kennelly had been head of the regional Red Cross, was a successful moving van company executive, stayed active in civic affairs, and had an outstanding reputation, which he improved upon in his campaign by pledging civil service reforms to end the corruption of patronage. The committeemen treated this as necessary campaign rhetoric and figured that the silver-haired naif, Kennelly, would occupy himself by passing out keys to the city while they continued to pass out jobs. But Kennelly's election and his disdain for patronage would play a vital role in the future of Richard J. Daley. Daley was not officially consulted about the dumping of Kelly in December 1946 because despite his service in the legislature and his county position, he was not a member of the exalted Democratic Central Committee.

In January 1947, only three months after losing his election for sheriff, Daley decided to win one. He organized the precinct captains in the 11th Ward and dethroned Hugh Connolly for the post of committeeman. He then informed Connolly that when his aldermanic term ended the next month he would not be reslated. When Arvey took over as chairman, the party meetings were moved from Kelly's office back to Democratic headquarters at the Morrison Hotel. In those days the hotel stood where the Chagall mosaic now graces First National Plaza, one form of art replacing another. At the January 1947 meeting, Committeeman Daley took a chair in the room. He would remain there for twenty-nine years. County Commissioner Dan Ryan, who was aligned with the Nash-Duffy forces, observed, "Daley figured to be a pain in the ass, having so much ambition and being in with Kelly."[3]

Daley has been characterized as having great patience in his climb to ultimate authority, but his activities in the late 1940s and early 1950s prove that was hardly the case. And they also seriously question the other myth that the only thing Richard Daley ever wanted was to be the mayor of Chicago. That may have been what he wanted most, but in practice he wanted just about anything he could get.

Former Corporation Counsel Barnet Hodes will withdraw his name from favorable consideration for U.S. district attorney here, it was reported last night. . . . The political grapevine favors someone else—possibly Richard J. Daley, formerly Democratic minority leader in the state senate, who insists he is not an aspirant.

CHICAGO TRIBUNE, MAY 20, 1947.

Democratic leaders were reported late last night to favor Richard J. Daley to step into the place of William J. Touhy, stricken state's attorney, in the event he is not able to fight his way back to health. . . . Daley, 41 years old, is highly regarded not only by Touhy but by Mayor Kennelly and former Mayor Kelly.

CHICAGO TRIBUNE, DECEMBER 4, 1947.

Mayor Kennelly's blanket approval of three men yesterday left it up to Democratic slatemakers to choose a candidate for state's attorney from among John S. Boyle, Richard J. Daley and Judge Cornelius Harrington.

CHICAGO TRIBUNE, JANUARY 9, 1948.

Rivalries seething in the Democratic organization came to the surface yesterday but Cook County Chairman J. M. Arvey got his wish: unlimited authority to appoint slate-making committees. Soft-spoken but persistent Richard J. Daley (11th) attempted for nearly an hour to change the setup to one more to his liking: He is an aspirant for president of the Cook County Board. Observers concluded that unless Mayor Kennelly should interfere strongly for Daley his chances of getting the spot he wants are slight. Daniel Ryan, veteran county board member, now is deemed to lead the race.

Chicago Tribune, December 9, 1948.

Richard J. Daley probably can have the county clerk's spot on the Democratic ticket if he wants it. . . . If Daley prefers to run for county treasurer, Democratic state chairman George Kells might agree to go for clerk instead. Daley, young, 11th Ward Democratic committeeman, was bitterly disappointed three weeks ago when the organization refused to slate him for president of the county board.

Chicago Tribune, January 6, 1950.

Richard J. Daley said yesterday he is "available" for the governor nomination left open by Gov. Adlai Stevenson's race for the Presidency. "I'm available," Daley said. "Many people have suggested that my background of legislative leadership and as a state revenue director would fill the bill. It is not only a question of picking the best candidate most likely to win Nov. 4, but the one who will be the best governor."

Chicago Tribune, July 29, 1952

In the years between 1946 and 1952, Daley offered himself for every office except president, U.S. senator, and mayor
of Chicago. Chicago Democrats weren't certain that even the
ambitious Daley saw himself as presidential timber, but no
one doubted it was only a matter of time before he asked to
become mayor.

Daley didn't get the slating for state's attorney that he
wanted in 1948, but it turned out to be a very good year.
Arvey, mindful of the fate that befell Kelly after the 1946 dis-
asters, knew he needed to produce a winning ticket—but all
the polls were forecasting a Truman defeat. Arvey knew his
rivals, Nash, Duffy, and Ryan, were giving him a free hand
in choosing candidates so they could blame him for the
inevitable November losses. Arvey followed the same strategy he had used in 1947, when he surprised everyone with
Kennelly, who retained the mayor's office for the party by
300,000 votes when it had looked like a Republican year. In
fact—and some of the wiser Democrats knew it— Kennelly,
for all his disdain of the machine, may have saved it. A
Republican mayoral victory in 1947 would have leveled the
playing field in Chicago politics and might even have fore-
stalled Daley's arrival.

Arvey knew he needed more blue-ribbon types to stop
independent defections to the Republicans. He decided to
slate Paul Douglas, a maverick alderman and University of
Chicago professor who had joined the Marine Corps after
Pearl Harbor at the age of forty-three. Douglas was anath-
ema to the committeemen; they went along, assuming he
would be trounced and out of their hair in the council, where
he was too shrewd at sensing when deals were being made
to profit the aldermen rather than the public. Arvey's choice
for U.S. senator was Adlai Stevenson, grandson of a vice president, a Princeton man and lawyer well respected for his
intellect and involvement in public affairs. The party didn't

know much about him but what they knew they didn't like, and their fears were eventually confirmed. But they also doubted he could win.

Arvey thought the ticket could win but he also knew he wouldn't solidify his power with the ward bosses if he gave them a Democratic governor who wouldn't share the spoils. Before the slatemakers gathered for the ritual at the Morrison Hotel in January 1948, Arvey had changed his mind. He realized that if by chance Douglas captured the governorship, his high principles would make him impossible to work with and the committeemen would have a difficult time getting their share of the patronage, "Douglas was an advocate. He'd take a position and he'd hold to it tenaciously, stubbornly. [He] couldn't compromise."[4] So Arvey pulled a switch. He ran Douglas for the U.S. Senate and Stevenson for governor.

Although the pollsters had given Thomas Dewey the presidency and predicted huge Republican victories, Illinois Democrats sensed something different. The colorful Paul Powell, a staunch Truman man, summed it up: "The Democrats can smell the meat a-cookin'."

Stevenson and Douglas galloped to victory with enormous margins, helping Truman narrowly carry Illinois. Stevenson, only the fourth Democrat elected governor since the Civil War, won by more than 570,000 votes; the Chicago Democrats gave him a plurality of 520,000 in Cook County. Truman won the state by only 33,612 votes, and Democrats everywhere credited Arvey's inspired ticket of Stevenson-Douglas with providing the coattails for Truman. Democrats swept everything. Arvey's famous 24th Ward provided Truman with a 26,497 to 3,530 edge. The rookie committeeman from the 11th Ward was also impressive. Daley's ward gave the Democratic ticket leaders 23,000-plus votes compared with 7,000 for the Dewey ticket. Arvey thought Daley ought to be rewarded and told Stevenson so.

On December 21, 1948, Daley was appointed state director of revenue, the office he had argued in the state senate
should not be created. "I need him in my show," Stevenson
told reporters. The *Chicago Tribune* noted, "Daley . . . is
expected to be an ace on Stevenson's staff in helping guide
the legislative programs over the hurdles ahead."

The revenue department was a graduate course for Daley.
After his years as ward secretary, city council clerk, and
deputy county controller, he had mastered the flow chart of
jobs and dollars directly controlled by the mayor and the
county board president. Now he got the map to the state treasury. Daley's later skills at appropriating and spending public funds for the many things he wanted to build to glorify
Chicago were helped immensely by his knowledge of state
taxing and spending. Daley never idled his hours wondering,
as many of his peers would have, how to divert some of those
millions that crossed his desk in various ledgers. He was content, even thrilled, to discover where it came from and how
it could be spent. He was completing an MBA in government
that Harvard could never match. But he was still not on the
electoral ladder that he wanted to climb.

In 1949, Arvey convened the slatemakers to choose the
1950 ticket, which would be headed by the re-election bid of
Scott Lucas, majority leader of the U.S. Senate. The key
county offices the party wanted were county board president
and sheriff, the two posts the GOP had captured in 1946 when
Daley was the losing candidate for sheriff. Arvey, as the
chairman who had led the 1948 sweep, was the key figure in
slatemaking, but he didn't have the consolidated power that
Kelly had held as both chairman and mayor from 1943 to
1947. Stevenson, now the governor, could play a role and
Kennelly, despite the grumblings he had stirred among ward
bosses during his first eighteen months in office, had a voice
in matters. Daley decided he wanted to be slated for county

board president. The favorite was supposed to be commissioner Dan Ryan (who years earlier had fretted that the county might pay wolf bounties on dog pelts). Ryan was a close friend of Kennelly's. Meanwhile, the Nash faction was ready to make a move. John Duffy, who had left the City Council's powerful finance chairman post in 1946 to run for county commissioner, was also planning to seek the nomination for board presidency.

Uncharacteristically, Daley opposed Arvey at a county committee meeting. Daley wanted Arvey to place both Stevenson and Kennelly on the slating committee. He also wanted them to appoint committeemen who were aspirants, meaning himself. Arvey said that neither the governor nor the mayor wanted to serve on the slatemaking group because "I know that the mayor and the governor don't want to be pictured as political bosses."

State Senator William "Botchy" Connors of the 42nd Ward spoke against Daley's motion and had a somewhat different take from Arvey. "What the hell does Stevenson know about ward committeemen? You're likely to get three or four members of the Chicago Crime Commission on the ticket if you let these guys [Stevenson and Kennelly] name the candidates."

Daley lost his motion and Duffy won the nomination. Daley's departure from the role of a "go along" loyalist could be traced to his understanding that none of the top party leaders—Arvey, Stevenson, or Kennelly—had or wanted the power to punish. It would have been easy for Daley to play off Stevenson's loyalty against Arvey's chagrin. And he knew that Arvey, always threatened by the Nash-Duffy 19th Ward alliance, needed Daley himself for future battles. It may also have occurred to Daley, if not to Arvey, that Duffy was going to make a grab for the nomination and position the 19th Ward to dethrone Arvey and leave Daley in the political cold.

Besides, having denied Daley one job the party now owed
him another.

> County Clerk Michael J. Flynn died last night in Michael
> Reese Hospital, where he was taken yesterday after suf-
> fering a heart attack Monday night in his home. He was
> 75, and had been county clerk since 1934.
>
> *CHICAGO TRIBUNE*, JANUARY 4, 1950.

Less than two weeks after the slatemakers turned Daley
down for the board presidency, they met again. Daley
appeared at the Morrison Hotel and told the slatemakers
about his thirteen years of experience as deputy controller,
his loyalty as senate minority leader, his stint as state revenue
director, and his ability to crank out 11th Ward votes for
Democrats. Stevenson said he was "very pleased to see
Daley's great qualifications recognized." The governor later
sent his campaign fund a check for $250.[5]

Kennelly reportedly telephoned Arvey to get in line. On
January 9, 1950, Daley was slated for county clerk. The new
post paid $15,000 a year. In February, the county board
appointed Daley to fill the vacancy in the office, which meant
that the millions of county forms that Cook County residents
would fill out between then and the November election would
carry the name Richard J. Daley, county clerk. The year 1950
would be a good one for Daley. It would be a nightmare for
his mentor and friend, Jake Arvey.

Arvey had decided he wanted a law enforcement man to
run for sheriff. He ran Captain Dan "Tubbo" Gilbert. The
announcement shocked the liberals and appalled Senator
Douglas and Governor Stevenson. In the summer of 1950, an
ambitious senator from Tennessee named Estes Kefauver
brought his Senate committee, which was investigating organized crime, to Chicago. One of the people called to testify

was Dan Gilbert. Kefauver, who thought he might need the help of the Chicago Democrats in seeking the 1952 presidential nomination, promised to keep Gilbert's testimony secret. But the *Chicago Sun-Times* got a copy of it and printed Gilbert's tale five days before the election. Gilbert, known ever after as the "world's richest cop," told the Senate committee, "I have been a gambler all my life." Through gambling he had accrued, he admitted, assets of $360,000 in securities and a net annual income for 1949 of $45,000—five times his salary.

Gilbert was trounced. Scott Lucas was defeated for the U.S. Senate by a blustery congressman, Everett McKinley Dirksen. John Duffy lost the county board presidency, which put a crimp in the 19th Ward's desire to control the party and the mayoralty. The only Democrat who survived was Daley, with a 147,000 plurality over Nicholas Bohling. Bohling, the 7th Ward alderman, was not well known and campaigned on the same theme the Republicans always used against Daley: "He is owned by the machine. They rule him and they would rule his office. . . . He was an errand boy, the mouthpiece of the Kelly-Nash-Arvey machine in the legislature." Bohling's attack didn't work.

Daley now had a county office. He was on the ladder. He also had his own patronage to cultivate friends, though he wasn't yet ready to punish enemies. And he had another graduate course in politics. The clerk's office controlled the election machinery in nearly nine hundred suburban precincts. If in his ruling years Daley often showed disdain for the suburbs, no one should have assumed he didn't know anything about them—especially how to squeeze every possible vote out of them.

Arvey was distraught. "I blundered," he would say later.[6] He had cost the party a U.S. senator (Lucas would bitterly fight the Cook County party at every turn for the rest of his

life) and he had blown the two most powerful patronage
offices in Cook County. He resigned the chairmanship of the
party. It was too early for Daley to move, and Duffy, just
beaten, couldn't round up enough support to fight for the job.
So all sides tacitly agreed on a caretaker. The choice was
Joseph Gill, age sixty-six, committeeman of the North Side
46th Ward and for nearly two decades the custodian of the
patronage-rich office of clerk of the Municipal Court. Gill
and the Municipal Court's bailiff, Al Horan, committeeman
of the 29th Ward, had been Arvey supporters. Neither man
had higher aspirations, and the party cruised on automatic
pilot through the 1952 election year. Illinois Democrats loyally supported Stevenson in his hopeless run against Dwight
Eisenhower and satisfied themselves by re-electing John Boyle
as state's attorney, keeping that potentially threatening job out
of the hands of the Republicans.

Gill, a diplomat rather than a leader, wanted out of the
chairman's spot as quickly as possible without suffering the
scorn that had been heaped on Arvey. Arvey, Gill, Horan,
Arthur X. Elrod (Arvey's 24th Ward disciple), and Thomas
Keane (31st Ward) were going to support Daley. They also
tried to enlist the support of the Germans, Paddy Bauler of
the 42nd Ward and Charlie Webber of the 45th. P. J. Cullerton of the 38th Ward on the Northwest Side was lining up
with the Duffy forces, who were backing Judge James
McDermott, a former 14th Ward alderman. Alderman
Clarence Wagner of the 14th Ward, who had succeeded Duffy
as finance chairman, was for McDermott. So was Tom Nash's
powerful 19th Ward organization. The Arvey forces thought
they had the votes for Daley and on July 8, 1953, the *Chicago
Tribune* ran a story with the headline: Daley Slated as Democrat County Chief.

The newspaper and the Daley forces were premature.
The following day, Daley, who was vice chairman, read Gill's
resignation letter to the fifty ward committeemen and thirty

committeemen representing the townships in Cook County outside Chicago. When he finished, Wagner jumped up and praised Gill's stewardship, then made a motion that no action be taken on a successor for two weeks. "We need time to look over the situation," he said. Gill rose and said, "Now the question is whether you should keep this old guy on two weeks more. I say, accept my resignation today and you can postpone action on my successor. I'd say do it within a week."

"Two weeks!" shouted Nash. Gill agreed.

The Nash-Duffy strategy was for Judge McDermott, recently elected chief justice of the Superior Court for a third term, to resign from the bench. Wagner would quit as 14th Ward committeeman to allow McDermott a seat on the county committee, and McDermott would run against Daley. Nash, Duffy, and Wagner all had too many enemies to take the spot but McDermott, a respected judge, might swing them the votes. They needed time and Wagner's power as finance chairman to twist some arms.

An auto crash at 60 m.p.h. killed Ald. Clarence P. Wagner (14th), powerful Chicago political leader, near International Falls, Minn.

Chicago Tribune, July 11, 1953.

On July 21, 1953, Judge McDermott withdrew as a candidate for county chairman and canceled the plans of the 14th Ward Democrats to name him a committeeman as Clarence Wagner's successor. The Democratic Central Committee then elected Richard J. Daley chairman. Daley rose and thanked McDermott for "putting the unity and harmony of the party first. I have made no deals or commitments to anyone, nor will I."

The *Tribune* wondered about the political sagacity of this move: "Daley has frequently been mentioned as a likely candidate for mayor in 1955. Some observers say he didn't want the party leadership post because it would hurt him in this quest, but he finally had to go after the chairmanship or suffer greater damage to his mayoral chances with the Nash-McDermott group in power."

Now Daley had the party, but Kennelly still had the jobs—even if he didn't know what to do with them. Daley had seen what happened to chairmen who didn't control the mayor's office. Even the cordial relationship between Pat Nash and the man he anointed mayor, Ed Kelly, made Kelly the primary figure. Still, as the *Tribune* story showed, there was such stigma of corruption attached to the Democratic Party post that the public was considered unlikely to pick a mayor who held the party office. At the same time, the ward committeemen were even more reluctant to place the two most powerful offices in the city in the hands of one man. Two days after his election, Daley appeared on television to pledge his support to Kennelly. He said he planned to seek re-election as county clerk and would support Kennelly "if the mayor is interested in being a candidate." Daley described Kennelly as "an honest man who has tried to do a good job for Chicago but who has been obstructed and criticized, sometimes unjustly." Daley also said he favored an open primary for mayor in 1955. He added, "I don't believe in bossism."

CHAPTER 4

"East Side, West Side, All Around the Town"

IF DALEY HADN'T CARED FOR BOSSISM, HE WOULD NOT HAVE enjoyed his first Democratic National Convention, held in 1932 at Chicago Stadium. It had been thirty-six years since the Democrats had met in Chicago; they traveled like outcasts to St. Louis, Denver, San Francisco, Baltimore, or Houston in those long years when only Woodrow Wilson broke the GOP clutch on the White House. It was Daley's first opportunity to study kingmakers and there were plenty of them around: Ed Flynn from the Bronx, William McAdoo from California, Sam Rayburn and Tom Connally from Texas, Tom Pendergast from Kansas City, James Farley, who was masterminding Roosevelt's campaign, and of course the hometown tandem of Cermak and Nash.

Roosevelt, who had succeeded Al Smith as governor of New York, was the clear favorite for the nomination, but he was far short of the required number of delegates and there were numerous strategies to nominate a dozen other people. Smith had not been considered in the running, but as so often happens with patrons and protégés, Roosevelt had

ignored him after becoming governor and now Smith was
back in the race, if not to secure a second nomination, at least
to deny Roosevelt. All sorts of deals had been offered,
rejected, and made by the time California agreed to go for
Roosevelt if the speaker of the house, John Nance Garner of
Texas, was chosen as his running mate. Garner was another
of those reluctant candidates but unusual in that he really
didn't want to be president and told his Texas boosters to take
the deal.

Cermak, hoping to emulate the crucial role that Roger
Sullivan had played in 1912, refrained from joining the bandwagon until the outcome was certain. But Daley learned
something he would never forget. Cermak, to the skepticism
of reporters and Roosevelt aides such as Farley, kept insisting he could not reveal where Illinois' forty delegates would
vote until the state party caucus. Illinois wound up joining
the Roosevelt bandwagon, although Cermak personally didn't
like the aristocratic governor of New York and had been
holding up his endorsement on the chance that something
better might come along. That did not escape the eye of Roosevelt supporters. Daley would not have been privy to the
Cermak inner circles but he certainly was interested enough
to see how the game was played.

He also may have had his first chance to meet a man
whose career would be inextricably linked with Daley's in any
history of big-city political organizations: James Michael Curley. Except for their Irish heritage and their will to achieve
power, the two men were not very similar. Daley was incor-
ruptible. Curley flaunted his graft. And neither Daley nor any
other politician of any era could match Curley's flamboyance.
His presence at the 1932 convention was a typical expression
of the Curley style. After supporting Roosevelt in a losing
primary cause in Massachusetts, he arrived without delegate
credentials but somehow (and with Curley one could assume

it was via a cash transaction) he obtained credentials from the delegate of Puerto Rico and was transformed into Alcade Jaime Miguel Curleo.[1]

In the same crowded aisles of the hot, smoky Chicago Stadium where Daley was running errands for Joe McDonough and other council chiefs, a lanky young Texan was bringing in beer and hot dogs to the Garner boosters. Lyndon Johnson, an aide to millionaire Richard Kleberg of the fabled King Ranch, was, like Daley, getting his first lesson in national presidential brokering. After Roosevelt's election, Cermak, at the insistence of his Irish cohort Patrick A. Nash, tried to mend fences with the president-elect and went to Florida to join him in a motorcade. An assassin's bullet intended for Roosevelt struck Cermak, who died of the wound. Control of the Cook County Democrats was returned to the Irish, who concluded that was the way God wanted it.

In those Depression years, the business of the Democratic conventions offered little suspense. FDR accepted another nomination in Philadelphia in 1936 and proceeded to another triumph. He wanted another term in 1940 and everyone knew it. But he was leery about breaking the two-term precedent without making it appear that he had no choice. Roosevelt spent the spring and summer encouraging a variety of people to run for the presidency with the unspoken implication that he would not seek a third term. He did nothing to discourage his good friend, Postmaster General James Farley, who had been the principal strategist in Roosevelt's first triumph, from entering the early primaries. But later he was quoted as saying Farley should not be the party candidate because he was Catholic. When Vice President John Nance Garner informed Roosevelt he also planned to run in primaries, Roosevelt did not object. He whispered to everyone that his personal choice was Secretary of State Cordell Hull, but he never told Hull.

As a result, when the Democrats gathered in Chicago Stadium on July 15, they were utterly confused about what to do. The party bosses—Flynn of the Bronx, Frank Hague of New Jersey, Pendergast of Kansas City, and Mayor Kelly—had not flashed any signals. Daley was in Chicago Stadium on July 16 as the nation's Democrats speculated on whether Roosevelt's refusal to declare his nomination was sincere. They sat stunned when Senator Alben Barkley of Kentucky announced he had a message from Roosevelt saying that the president had no desire to be nominated. Then he added, "He wishes in all earnestness and sincerity to make it clear that all of the delegates to this convention are free to vote for *any* candidate."

At that point, the loudspeakers boomed, "We want Roosevelt. Everybody wants Roosevelt." Soon all the delegates took up the cry. The snake dancing began around the stadium as the loudspeaker voice urged on the crowd. The demonstration went on for more than an hour, and the next night Roosevelt was an overwhelming first-ballot victor. The voice on the loudspeaker may have seemed to be a divine intervention to the uninformed delegates, but it belonged to Kelly's superintendent of sewers, Thomas Garry.

Another kingmaker from Chicago was born. And young Richard Daley learned another lesson. In politics, refusing to reveal your hand until the final bet was not called lying. It was not a sin. If the man who was revered as a moral force for transforming the federal government into an ally of the poor, the jobless, the elderly, the homeless, the widows, and the sick could deceive a country about his political intentions to enable him to continue his just and kind rule, it obviously was good politics, not immoral behavior. There is no doubt that Daley greatly admired Roosevelt and no doubt that he would imitate him.

Daley was a delegate for the first time in 1944 but this time, with American troops fighting their way through Normandy, FDR didn't keep anyone in suspense. He announced for his fourth term a week before the Chicago convention. The guessing game centered on the vice presidential nominee, especially since most Democratic leaders knew Roosevelt was in bad health. The party didn't want Henry Wallace again, but there was tremendous pressure from the powerful CIO and other unions to support the vice president. In the White House, Mrs. Roosevelt was also pressuring the President to keep Wallace, who shared her pro-labor, pro-welfare views.

As he had with his own candidacy in 1940, Roosevelt played games with everyone. It became clear to the party bosses that the vice presidential nomination—which they accurately believed meant the presidency itself—was up for grabs, so they all began angling to become kingmakers. Ed Kelly elbowed his way to the front of the line. Roosevelt was trying to figure out which way to lean without angering the key elements he would need in the November election. Although he was aware of his weakened health, he approached the selection of a running mate as though all the man would be required to do was preside over the Senate. Two weeks before the convention, he convened his own gathering in a smoke-filled room at the White House. Kelly, Flynn, and Democratic National Chairman Bob Hannegan were in the group. Roosevelt suggested Supreme Court Justice William Douglas as a possible nominee. Hannegan and the others wanted Senator Harry Truman of Missouri. Another possibility, Roosevelt said, was James Brynes, the South Carolinian who headed the Office of War Mobilization.[2] Nothing was resolved. Wallace still thought Roosevelt might keep him. Truman thought Roosevelt didn't want him.

Kelly developed a favorite-son strategy for Senator Scott Lucas. Hannegan and Flynn believed this was camouflage for Kelly's eventual swing to Truman. But even Kelly had no idea where to go.

As convention week loomed, the only three candidates appeared to be Wallace, Brynes, and Truman. Hannegan arrived in Chicago on Saturday, July 14, 1944, and got a double-barreled surprise. Truman, giving up the ghost, had agreed to nominate Brynes. And there was a rumor that Kelly was now supporting Brynes to create a deadlock that would turn to his favorite-son candidate, Lucas. Kelly may have heard the same rumors. He telephoned Brynes to tell him he would be the candidate. Kelly also held an Illinois caucus on Sunday at the Morrison Hotel and virtually told the delegates that the dreaded Wallace was out of the picture. "The President is with us. He's for the kind of fellows we are—organization fellows." That eliminated Wallace, a progressive reformer. Then Kelly tipped his hand on Truman by praising Hannegan, whom Kelly had helped elect to the national chairmanship. He gave Hannegan the finest endorsement the Chicago Democrats could want. "You will get anything and everything you ask for with Hannegan in there," Kelly declared.

On Monday, July 16, Truman met with Sidney Hillman of the CIO Political Action Committee, representing the most powerful bloc of Democratic voters in the country. Hillman told Truman flatly that if Wallace was unacceptable to the convention, the only other candidate who would receive labor's support was Truman. That put the Missouri senator back into the race. Hillman would be the subject of the 1944 campaign's most memorable slogan: "Clear it with Sidney." This was the remark Roosevelt made to Hannegan about the vice presidential choices. The Republicans used it throughout the fall to depict Roosevelt as a tool of the labor unions, but all it did was remind union members to vote for Roosevelt.

Kelly, who now abandoned Brynes and any pretense of a deadlock, announced his personal support for Truman while at the same time pledging to keep his promise to nominate Lucas as a favorite son. He also followed the pattern of his predecessor, Cermak, by not disclosing how the Illinois delegation would vote. On the day of the nomination vote, Kelly said, "The president likes Truman and thinks he would add strength to the ticket. The president told me himself." But he again left everyone confused when he went ahead with his promise to nominate Lucas. The furious CIO delegation, which had expected Kelly to back either Wallace or Truman, now thought the mayor of Chicago was double-crossing them and was trying seriously to get the nomination for Lucas.

Kelly said, "The world wants our sad-faced president to continue to carry the heavy burden which he alone is capable of bearing. We believe our great senator, Scott Lucas, can help him carry the burden, and I present his name with that in mind." The union leaders staged a huge pro-Wallace demonstration during Kelly's speech and the labor delegates practically booed him out of the stadium.

On Friday, the roll call began. Wallace led on the first ballot with 429½ votes, with 589 needed for the nomination. By the end of the second ballot, Truman had leaped to 447½, against 373 for Wallace. During the second ballot, the Illinois delegation, still pledged to Lucas, left the stadium to caucus and have a drink at the 27th Ward Democratic headquarters across the street. A messenger ran over to tell Kelly that the other delegations were now changing their votes and the stampede had started for Truman. The police halted traffic to let the delegates rush back into the stadium and send Kelly to the microphone with Truman standing at 586½ votes, two shy of nomination. Kelly voted 55 Illinois votes for

Truman to put him over the top. It seemed that Kelly had missed his chance to be the pivotal force in Truman's nomination, although he was there for the official victory.

The *Chicago Tribune* commented: "The irony of all the futile dashing around was that Kelly had been for Truman all the time. Kelly could afford to take this in good humor. He is a pal of National Chairman Robert Hannegan of Missouri, Truman's sponsor. Moreover, the mayor's role in the many conferences paving the way for Truman was generally recognized. . . . If Sen. Truman should eventually succeed to the presidency, the sky would be the limit on rewards to Kelly's organization."

Whatever goodwill emanated from Truman's White House to Kelly didn't last long. Just eighteen months after Truman became president upon FDR's death in April 1945, Kelly was replaced as county chairman by Arvey and subsequently dumped as the party's mayoral choice. But delegate Daley again found much to observe and learn in the 1944 helter-skelter over the second spot. If nothing else, he should have learned to never leave a convention floor during a roll call. It is not known what Daley thought about Truman's nomination, but his old foe Paul Powell, whose political tentacles crossed the Mississippi River into Missouri and hobnobbed with the Pendergast machine (which had sent Truman to the U.S. Senate), was delighted. One minor event also caught Daley's notice in 1944. A few days before the convention, Kelly hosted the delegation at the Blackstone Hotel, where he was re-elected without opposition to his post as a member of the Democratic National Committee. Kelly now had three party titles: ward committeeman, county chairman, and national committeeman. To date, Daley had none.

In 1948, the last thing the Democratic Party wanted was Harry Truman as its presidential candidate. The southerners boiled at his efforts to pass civil rights bills. Liberals thought he was too conservative and conservatives thought he was too pro-labor. Labor was upset that he never went far enough. The Democratic coalition of southerners, liberals, big-city bosses, and labor chiefs was being shredded. Truman's approval rating was just 36 percent, and Democratic leaders, spoiled by sixteen years of White House control, expected him to withdraw gracefully so they could go about the business of finding a winner. He didn't. For the first and only time in the twentieth century, it appeared that a sitting president who wanted another term would be rejected by his party. Even in 1932, the Republicans had grudgingly renominated Herbert Hoover without opposition. In later years, the power of the presidency became so great, and the nominating system so expensive, that unless an incumbent stepped aside, there would be no way he could be denied renomination by a gathering of party leaders. In fact, in future years, there would be no party leaders.

That was not the case in 1948. The problem for the Democrats, who were certain that Truman could not win, was that the party was so divided ideologically that an alternative choice was almost impossible. The big-city leaders and the liberal wing would not tolerate a southerner like Richard Russell of Georgia or Strom Thurmond of South Carolina. Neither northern or southern pols wanted anything to do with the progressives who were threatening to run Henry Wallace on a third-party ticket. The South would not tolerate anyone from the North, the Midwest, or the West who would not swear an oath to white supremacy. A great white hope was needed and one was out there: Dwight D. "Ike" Eisenhower, one of the biggest heros of World War II.

And once again Richard J. Daley had a close look at American political history. His patron, Colonel Jake Arvey, had bet his political career on a state ticket that included Adlai Stevenson and Paul Douglas. Now Arvey, like Mayor

Kelly in 1944, was angling to be the kingmaker. Arvey, Mayor William O'Dwyer of New York, and James Roosevelt, representing the Roosevelt family's inability (like the Kennedys a generation later) to accept that they no longer owned the White House, formed the leading triumvirate in the "Draft Ike" movement. Eisenhower had issued a General Sherman–like statement in March and gave no indication of retreat. But as the Democrats headed for Philadelphia and the July 12 convention opening, Arvey persisted. He sent telegrams to every delegate asking them to attend a preconvention caucus on July 10 "to choose the ablest and strongest man available" as the party's nominee. The telegram did not mention Eisenhower but said, "It is our belief that no man in these critical days can refuse the call to duty and leadership implicit in the nomination and virtual election to the presidency of the United States."

Eisenhower did. He did it again and again, as late as July 9, when he told the Democrats to "accept my refusal as final and complete, which it most emphatically is."

Unable to speak with all the egg covering their faces, Arvey and O'Dwyer issued a joint statement: "It is our feeling that in the absence of a demonstrated mandate on behalf of any of these men [possible candidates other than Eisenhower] from the people themselves, it is in the best interests of our country and our party that our democracy unite for President Truman."

A reporter asked Arvey if he would predict a Truman victory. He was not exactly the voice of optimism. "I hope he'll defeat [Thomas] Dewey. Ask me that November 1 and I'll give you an honest answer." He also refused to say that Truman would be nominated on the first ballot. It was a dismal show for a kingmaker. The Democrats were in such disarray that on the eve of the convention opening, there was even talk of Mayor Kennelly becoming a favorite-son candidate.

But there was no one left to seriously challenge Truman, who was nominated on the first ballot, with Senator Russell of Georgia an insignificant second.

The Democratic fireworks were just starting. On July 14, the platform battle over the civil rights plank erupted. The majority report had been drafted by southerners and carefully avoided any specific promises about Negro rights. The minority plank, carved by Michigan Governor G. Mennen Williams and Mayor Hubert Humphrey of Minnesota, was far more liberal.

Humphrey gave the 1948 convention its historical oratory: "To those who say that this civil rights program is an infringement on states' rights, I say this, that the time has arrived in America for the Democratic Party to get out of the shadows of states' rights and to walk forthrightly into the bright sunshine of human rights."

The convention floor exploded and Arvey saw his chance both to regain some stature with the party's standard-bearer and to help his Illinois ticket with the increasing number of black voters in Chicago. At his signal, the seventy Illinois delegates began marching around the convention hall, leading a demonstration that resulted in the passage of the minority report, which specifically endorsed Truman's order eliminating segregation in the armed forces. Arvey invoked the unit rule to ensure a unanimous vote from the delegation, although Senator Scott Lucas had been a sponsor of the majority report. Neither Hubert Humphrey—whose eloquence on that July night propelled him to a distinguished Senate career, the vice presidency, and the doorstep of the White House—nor Daley, who had joined in the first vote that would lead to two decades of civil rights redresses, could have imagined how their careers would converge twenty years after they left Philadelphia with an underdog presidential candidate and a new message for America. The convention ended with Truman, his running mate, Alben Barkley of Kentucky, and Rayburn waiting at the podium for the applause to end. A flock of pigeons had been released in the convention hall, signifying peace, and several flew over the platform. One was overcome by heat and fell dead at the feet of the president. Another landed on Rayburn's bald head, and the Democratic gathering of 1948 was over.[3]

The 1948 convention was an extraordinary political event. Several other events occurred in the Illinois arena that were hardly extraordinary but worth noting for Daley. His old friend from Springfield, Ben Adamowski, now a city corporation counsel, got into the limelight by being chosen to give a seconding speech for Truman's nomination. Mixing up his political parties, Adamowski compared Truman to Lincoln as "a man of the common people." Daley had to be jealous. He was probably daydreaming during Mayor Kennelly's rousing ovation, imagining the day when he might lead the Illinois delegation and have the spotlight of the nation on him.

Arvey's performance may have baffled Daley, whose loyalty to presidents was unremitting. His trademark refusal to criticize other politicians when they were caught in a flare of criticism from the public or the media was multiplied geometrically when it came to the president. Daley even refused to be critical of Richard Nixon while he was in the White House. On the other hand, Arvey was doing what politicians do: trying to win elections, trying to save his local ticket. Daley understood that; in fact, it was the imperative that marked his political reign. Years later, Arvey said that Truman forgave him for his attempts to draft Eisenhower. "He called me the next day [after the Arvey-O'Dwyer statement] and we had a talk, and from that time on he and I were close friends. If there was any bitterness in his heart about what I had done for Eisenhower, he certainly never showed it."[4]

Truman, however, had written in his diary that O'Dwyer and Arvey were "double-crossers. . . . But they'll get nowhere—a double dealer never does."[5] Still, four years later, when Truman flew to Chicago to celebrate Adlai Stevenson's nomination, the person he took to dinner was Jake Arvey. These were the kinds of practical politicians Daley saw and emulated. The Trumans, the Arveys, and the Richard J. Daleys of American politics understood that their personal power was almost inseparable from the Democratic Party. If at times they (and later Kennedy, Johnson, and Humphrey) had trouble distinguishing between themselves and the party, it was understandable. If they couldn't tell whether their strength came from the Democratic Party or they were the strength of the party, it was because nothing separated their own power from the party's power, and they depended on each other for victory. Ideology was an issue for administration, whether it concerned dropping an atomic bomb, lighting alleys, defying the Soviet Union, building public housing, or arguing against the Vietnam War. Ideology did not allow for treason against the party or the power.

Arvey's decision to dump Truman was a classic example of the head overruling the heart. Arvey, born in Chicago's Jewish ghetto in 1895 of immigrant parents from Russia, was proudest of his support for Israel and his lobbying to obtain recognition of the Israeli state. Yet at the very time that Truman courageously recognized Israel, Arvey was begging Eisenhower to take the Democratic nomination. Surely Daley, who himself would attend many Israeli bond dinners where Arvey was often honored, understood the conflict that his mentor endured, just as he understood that recognizing Israel was not going to carry Cook County the way Ike could.

The 1952 Democratic convention returned to Chicago, this time in the International Amphitheatre just around the corner from County Clerk Richard J. Daley's home. For the first time since 1932, the Democrats faced a truly open convention. It would also be the last truly open convention of the twentieth century, even though many of the smartest

Democrats would not believe it for another thirty years. Truman had made it an open convention by declaring on March 29 that he would not be a candidate. Unlike 1948, the 1952 aspirants were plentiful and had excellent credentials. Richard Russell of Georgia was back, with a more moderate outlook on civil rights. Estes Kefauver of Tennessee had pulled a surprising vote in the New Hampshire primary. Robert Kerr of Oklahoma was the "log cabin" candidate, the first since Lincoln to boast that he had been born there en route to his oil millions. Averill Harriman of New York, worldly diplomat and White House troubleshooter, was available; so was lovable, aging Vice President Alben Barkley. The man who kept saying he wasn't available had been alternately the favorite and the dark horse throughout the year, Adlai Stevenson of Illinois.

The Chicago Democrats should have focused on Stevenson's candidacy when the convention opened on July 21, but as usual in the raw world of the ward committeemen, what caught their attention were the seating arrangements. Up front, right in the middle, squarely in front of the podium and television cameras was the host Illinois delegation. Seated in the front row was Arvey, national committeeman who was up to his usual behind-closed-doors maneuvering to nominate Stevenson. Next to him was Joe Gill, the Democratic county chairman and head of the Illinois delegation, and next to him was County Clerk Daley, who had been chosen as secretary of the delegation. The committeemen knew this convention was Arvey's swan song as a power broker. He was no threat to them. They knew Gill was a caretaker who wanted to get out of the chairmanship and was therefore of no consequence. Mayor Kennelly once again had a brief moment of glory delivering the welcoming address, but the committeemen already knew he had no future. For most of them, he had no past. They knew Daley was the one to watch.

Richard Daley, age 50, was at last in the inner circle. His old boss and friend Stevenson could be the titular leader of the Democratic party. If nominated, he might become president of the United States. Few Democrats at the Amphitheatre, even Arvey and Daley, really thought that would happen. Arvey's failure four years earlier to persuade Eisenhower to take the Democratic nomination proved doubly troubling now that Ike had been nominated by the Republicans and seemed a sure winner in the fall. But the Democrats had left Philadelphia in 1948 convinced that Truman couldn't win, and he had surprised them. Anything could happen. Arvey was desperately trying to vindicate his reputation in his last chance to be a party powerhouse. He had consulted with Truman about Stevenson and had become as frustrated as the president with Stevenson's reluctance to declare himself. So Arvey was playing a cat-and-mouse game. A "Draft Stevenson" committee had been set up at the Conrad Hilton Hotel. Arvey declared that he had no role in it, that he was taking Stevenson at his word. Yet Gill and other party leaders (no doubt including Daley) noticed that everyone in the draft organization was close to Arvey, including U.S. Rep. Sidney Yates, whom Arvey had sent to Congress. Arvey did seem convinced that Stevenson really would not accept the nomination. At one point he promised Barkley the support of the Illinois delegation.[6] But others believed that was a ruse, using Barkley to create a deadlock and hoping that Barkley's age would prevent a stampede to him.

At 4 P.M. on Sunday, July 21, the Illinois delegates gathered at the Morrison Hotel for their caucus. Stevenson, a member of the delegation, addressed them. "I just don't want to be nominated for president. I just couldn't . . . wouldn't . . . didn't want to be a candidate. I have no ambitions, no fitness either mentally, temperamentally, or physically for the job as president. . . . What I personally wanted is to run for governor. I ask you to abide by my wishes and not to nominate or vote for me should I be nominated. I also urge all your friends."

Arvey told the caucus he would do whatever Stevenson wished, so Illinois would not nominate its own governor. But, he added, if someone else nominated Stevenson he personally would vote for him on the first ballot. "When that happens I consider I am relieved from any promise I have made not to further his candidacy. He cannot take away from me my right to cast my ballot as I wish to cast it." The delegation cheered, for a lot of reasons. There is no doubt that many of them wanted to see their man win the nomination. They were politicians and trained to put winning first.

There certainly were those who thought Stevenson in the White House would be less bother to them than Stevenson in the state mansion. Some historians discount the feudal nature of committeemen that would motivate their reasoning in that manner. But all through the spring and summer of 1952, when Stevenson's candidacy was peaking, there is no record of any party leader exclaiming dismay that the Democrats could lose the governorship if Stevenson were nominated for president. Contrast that with modern history, when in 1995 some California Republicans threatened to boycott any presidential aspirations of Governor Pete Wilson because the lieutenant governor was a Democrat. Chicago Democrats were not at all pleased in 1980 when Alan Dixon abandoned the secretary of state's office to the Republicans to run for a vacant U.S. Senate seat, and although the secretary of state's post has a nice chunk of patronage jobs it is hardly the governor's office. It is not out of the question that Botchy Connors, Paddy Bauler, Charlie Webber, and others were not thinking of saving the world from the bomb when they enthusiastically supported Stevenson for president just to get rid of him.

Another group saw Stevenson's move as an opportunity that would open the slot for governor. Former Senator Lucas,

Secretary of State Edward J. Barrett, and Lieutenant Governor Sherwood Dixon were on this list. Still another group in the surly delegation—Arvey and Gill did not have the muscle Kelly had used to impose solidarity in previous years—didn't want Stevenson at all. Paul Douglas had pledged his support to Kefauver and had about a dozen compatriots.

After the caucus, reporters asked Stevenson if he would accept a draft in the event of a deadlock. "Show me the deadlock first," he replied. Arvey later said, "Everybody thought it was an act, but it wasn't an act at all. That night after the caucus Stevenson came to my apartment and said, 'You got me into this, now get me out.'"[7]

Arvey did no such thing. The *Chicago Daily News* reported, "Arvey was in a ticklish situation. If he worked outwardly for Stevenson, the governor might suspect that the draft was being arranged. He continued to avoid seeking votes, but he did the next best thing. He made himself available all over town. He was always on the convention floor, available to talk to anybody. . . . He always left the door open wide enough that his questioner had no doubt that Adlai could be had."

The convention opened on Monday, July 22. As host, Governor Adlai Stevenson delivered a superb speech that convinced all the fence-sitters this was the man to take on Eisenhower and the Republicans. The nominating process began on Thursday; Indiana Governor Henry Schricker placed Stevenson in nomination, setting off the traditional dancing and demonstrating. At the conclusion, a floor fight occurred that had all the ingredients of the legend that surrounds that period in America, when chicanery and deals and tactics and strategy melded into the politics that produced presidents. Convention Chairman Sam Rayburn, the Speaker of the House from Texas, gaveled for a roll on whether to seat the Virginia, Louisiana, and South Carolina delegations,

who were refusing to accept a loyalty pledge to support the
nominee of the convention. The northern liberals had created this rule to prevent another Dixiecrat walkout like the
one Strom Thurmond led in 1948. Illinois voted 45–15 against
seating the southern delegations. Other northern states,
assuming Arvey was acting in Stevenson's best interests, followed suit. It was only a matter of completing the roll call
before the rebellious delegations were unseated.

President Truman, watching on television in the White
House, called Rayburn on the platform and told him he
wanted the southern delegations seated.[8] Rayburn sent mes-
sengers scampering after Arvey, who had taken Gill to the
Stock Yard Inn restaurant in the Amphitheatre complex.
Arvey now grasped what Truman had understood immediately. If the three states with 64 votes walked out of the convention, the total required for nomination would be reduced
and Kefauver, who figured to have almost 500 votes on the
first ballot, would be within striking distance of the nomination. Moreover, the southern states that were about to be
banished figured to switch to Stevenson rather than Kefauver or Harriman now that Barkley had dropped out. Arvey
quickly sent Gill to switch Illinois' vote to 52–8. That
stemmed the tide, and other states followed until the vote to
seat the southern delegations passed 615 to 589. Television
commentators called it an Arvey-Dixiecrat alliance and
forced Stevenson to deny any personal role in the Illinois
switch. Harriman and Kefauver made last-ditch efforts to tar
Stevenson as the puppet of the big-city bosses, Dixiecrats,
and the national committee.

The vote on nomination took place Friday, July 25. On
the third ballot, after midnight, Stevenson was nominated.
Jake Arvey got his absolution. Stevenson picked Senator John
Sparkman of Alabama as his running mate and began one of
the most thoughtful and inspiring presidential campaigns in

history. But Stevenson had barely stepped off the nominating platform when another campaign began among Illinois Democrats.

Ambitious Illinois Democrats didn't wait until the roll call to start scrambling for the new vacancy on the state ticket. Lieutenant Governor Sherwood Dixon obviously would be considered. Scott Lucas would be a choice of the downstate bloc. Edward J. Barrett, sometime enfant terrible of the Democratic Party, was appropriately the first hustler. Barrett ran against the Cook County organization as a brash youth in 1930 and was elected state treasurer. He again challenged the organization candidates in 1940 and 1942 for the offices of state auditor and secretary of state, losing narrowly in bitter primaries that party leaders blamed for the subsequent GOP general election victories. Barrett, running again for secretary of state, was the party's top candidate in the April 1952 primary, gathering more votes than Stevenson. Now he felt ready to take Stevenson's place on the ballot.

Barrett began lining up his support during the convention. One of the first people he buttonholed was Daley. "On the national convention floor on July 22, in presence of witnesses, several downstate delegates, I asked Daley whether he would support me. Without any hesitancy, Daley answered, 'Absolutely,' and we shook hands on it," Barrett told the *Chicago Tribune*. "He said I should be the man and that he would be with me."

By the Monday morning after the convention, there was a new candidate for governor.

"I'm available," Daley told reporters at his county clerk's office. "Many people have suggested that my background of legislative leadership and as state revenue director under Governor Stevenson would fill the bill. It is not only a question of picking the candidate most likely to win the November 4 election, but the one who will be the best governor. The nominee for governor should campaign on an intelligent discussion of the issues."

Except for the flabbergasted Barrett, most people viewed Daley's announcement as a surprise only in the sense that it was thought he had another goal. In listing the available candidates even before Stevenson's presidential nomination, political writer George Tagge of the *Tribune* included Daley. "(He) has excellent relations with the governor and is vice chairman of the Cook County Democratic organization . . . but he has long had his eye on the mayoral nomination in 1955."

In writing of Daley's availability, Tagge noted that Daley "had been considered a backer of Barrett." Daley's declaration for governor, only forty-eight hours after the conclusion of the national convention, illustrates how hard his political instincts drove him. The man who always wanted to be mayor was like any other ambitious politician; he wanted to be whatever was available. Daley knew Stevenson would have a great deal to say about his possible successor, and Daley was on good terms with Stevenson. He knew that Arvey and Gill still controlled enough of the Cook County party to help him get that endorsement. And Barrett's headlong demand for the vacant ticket slot was an opportunity for Daley to be seen as a compromise choice. Stevenson would probably want Dixon but the Chicago ward leaders, Arvey in particular, might demand another choice as a reward for his unsolicited but now appreciated efforts to give Stevenson the presidential nomination. Stevenson would never stand for Barrett. Daley's chances of winning the office, if nominated, looked good. Stevenson would be at the top of the ticket and the Republican candidate for governor, William G. Stratton, was a former congressman at large who hadn't seemed to excite anyone.

And Daley had to be influenced by the previous week's experience. The ebb and flow of power permeating political conventions of that era could infuse even cynical reporters with impossible scenarios. One loud outburst from the gallery could elevate some obscure governor or senator, for a brief moment, to the doorstep of ultimate political success. And for a politician in America, no matter how obscure his current office, ultimate success always resides at 1600 Pennsylvania Avenue.

Imagine Daley watching his patron Jake Arvey, a cagey Jewish lawyer from the West Side of Chicago, maneuver to move Stevenson to the final hurdle to the White House. Daley's view of Stevenson, now the national leader of the Democratic Party, would not be one of awe. Daley never held anyone in awe. Stevenson, too, had been a patron and Daley recognized his great intellect. But he would also recognize that Stevenson had no great political skills, that he had not manipulated and contrived or built alliances and isolated enemies. He had merely been in the right place at the right time. The right place had been the governor's mansion. And if that worked for Adlai Stevenson, who could say it wouldn't work for Richard J. Daley? It is conceivable that Daley, having watched the sloppy efforts of Kefauver and Harriman, concluded that he was as capable of capturing a presidential nomination as any of those heralded Democrats he had finally seen from an insider's view. Daley was only fifty years old. A term or two as governor would make him the perfect age to run for national office in four or eight years. It might never happen, but the governor's office might hold a promise that being the mayor of Chicago would not.

Daley also knew from recent experience that nothing was certain about his future in the Cook County party. He knew that the Nash-Duffy-Wagner clique would not simply hand him the chairmanship without a fight. And despite the grumbling about Kennelly, it was not altogether clear in the summer of 1952 that the incumbent would be tossed aside in 1955 or would go quietly. That was Daley's plan, but he had seen

how quickly Arvey had lost what seemed like unchallenge-
able control after 1948. He had seen how Ed Kelly, holding
both the mayor's office with its patronage power and the
party chairman's post, had been swiftly dethroned. Even a
losing gubernatorial bid wouldn't hurt. Daley would still be
county clerk and he still could maneuver for the chairmanship and a statewide candidacy might even be a plus when
he ran for mayor. The opportunity to jump into the race for
the vacated ballot spot had no down side. But three days after
Daley became "available," he was not.

"I am not, and was not, a candidate for the nomination
for governor," he said on Thursday, July 31. "Governor
Stevenson had indicated his choice to be Lieutenant Governor Dixon to succeed him in carrying on his great program."

He also denied ever making a commitment to Barrett.
Stevenson wanted Dixon and the party went along. Al Horan,
the 29th Ward commiteeman and Daley's friend, probably
explained it to Daley just the way he did publicly. "Stevenson is the no. 1 Democrat in the nation and all of us realize
it would be embarrassing to him if the Illinois organization
didn't respect his wishes."

Daley's blatant contradictions of his own statements were
another of his trademarks. He never showed any public
embarrassment over changing his position and denying things
he had said. In many instances, little notice was paid to his
inconsistencies. But some of them would shade his legacy.

———

Four years later, Adlai Stevenson and the Democrats were
back in Chicago, but this time it was different. Their host
was Mayor Richard J. Daley, chairman of the legendary Cook
County Democratic party, chairman of the Illinois delegation, and chairman of just about anything he wanted to be
in Chicago. Daley's first year as mayor was filled with

announcements and projects and openings. The Congress
Expressway heading directly west from the Loop, was built
with appropriations that Daley had initiated years earlier
when he was the state senate minority leader. A $675-million
building plan was unveiled. Daley named five of Chicago's
top civic and corporate leaders to join him on the Public
Buildings Commission, which had been created while he was
in the Senate. Then the five bluebloods voted him chairman
of the commission that would plan a new downtown anchored
by a new Civic Center that someday would bear his name.
As mayor and chairman, he handpicked the state Democratic
ticket for 1956 and drew charges of "bossism" from his own
party.

He also began to display the petulance that flared whenever his city was criticized and the childish fantasies he often
indulged in without ever revealing whether he was serious or
just being silly. When John Kelly, father of actress Grace
Kelly, said a "mob from Chicago" had robbed guests of jew-
elry while they were attending her wedding to the prince of
Monaco, Daley snapped, "If the wedding were held in
Chicago, I'm sure none of the guests would have been
robbed. I don't think Chicago hoodlums were involved. If
they were, it is because they were driven out of Chicago by
the good work of the Chicago police."

A few weeks later, after one of his rapid walks through
downtown, Daley decided Chicago needed innovative transportation. He said it might be a good idea to have gondolas
on the Chicago River. "You would bring in the experts from
Venice to operate them," he said with a straight face. He also
wondered, as he would increasingly over the years, about how
"nice it would be if youngsters could fish on the banks . . .
or you could do it during the lunch hour."

When the Democrats from all over America arrived at the
International Amphitheatre on August 13, 1956, Daley greeted

them with a speech that would have made George Babbitt proud. "Chicago is the supermarket of the world," he declared. He said Chicago grew to be the nation's second-largest city because it was the center of inland waterways and land transportation. "With the opening of the St. Lawrence Seaway, history will repeat itself. We are the only inland port that joins the two great inland water routes—one leading to the Mississippi and the Gulf ports, and the other through the Great Lakes and to the sea. . . . In this metropolitan giant of the Middle West can be found all the diverse interests of the nation." He boasted of the management–labor harmony that existed in Chicago because of "a recognition of the right of the working man to share in industry's increasing prosperity." And he spoke more than he knew when he said Chicago represented "every shade of thought, every economic level, and every tension of urban living." The delegates gave him polite applause and then he set about the business of the convention.

There was something different this time, too, about Adlai Stevenson. This time he had asked for another nomination. Not everybody wanted to give it to him. Harry Truman, ignored by Stevenson during the 1952 campaign, wanted Averill Harriman. But the former president was just that, and only a few people remained loyal to his wishes.

Certainly not everybody in the Illinois delegation wanted Stevenson, but Daley was loyal to his old boss and wanted to make certain he was not embarrassed by lukewarm support from his home delegation. Daley presided at the usual preconvention Sunday caucus at the Morrison Hotel, but when he quickly discerned that Stevenson might get only as few as 20 of the state's 64 votes, he decided not to poll the delegates. Democrats said Harriman would have gotten as many as 20 votes out of Illinois and that would have provided him with strong ammunition to wage a floor fight.

Daley, for perhaps the only time in his career, had played his cards early. He had been on record all summer as being for Stevenson. He said the primary results showed the people wanted Adlai Stevenson as their next president. "I think the ticket should be Stevenson and Kefauver." Now he spent the first two days of the convention cajoling and threatening to get Stevenson's Illinois totals to respectability. Once again his downstate nemesis, Paul Powell, was working with Scott Lucas and John Stelle against Stevenson. So were some of the Chicago delegates, including the militant labor leaders who wondered about Stevenson's stand on communism. But one by one Daley got most of them. He wasn't able to make it unanimous. By the roll call on Thursday, August 16, Daley was able to take the microphone and give Stevenson 52½ votes. Harriman got 8½, mostly from the Powell contingent's loyalty to Truman. Still, Daley had kept the Illinois disaffection for Stevenson under wraps until it didn't matter. Stevenson won easily on the first ballot. Never again in the twentieth century would it take more than one ballot to nominate a presidential contender in either party.

But Stevenson created another swatch of convention history. He announced that he was throwing open the choice of a running mate to the convention, setting off one of the most frenetic twenty-four-hour skirmishes in American political history. It was the first time in the century that a presidential candidate failed to endorse his running mate to the convention, and most Democrats didn't know what to do. It also was past the time when the vice presidential nomination was considered "not worth a bucket of warm piss," as Jack Garner had said. Roosevelt's death and Eisenhower's heart attacks had too recently put to rest the theory that a vice president was merely someone who yawned in the Senate and attended funerals deemed too minor for the chief executive.

Moreover, in 1956, most Democrats doubted Eisenhower could be beaten and figured Stevenson would disappear after a second loss. The vice presidential nomination, in this new era of televised campaigning, could be a stepping stone for someone to take over party leadership. Everybody suddenly wanted it or wanted to stop someone else from getting it. Stevenson's decision gave a national television audience a textbook view of politics that previously had been reserved for a few hundred party loyalists and the newspaper reporters who tried to make sense of what they did. Now it was a wide-open scramble and all America could watch—even if few really understood what was happening. America's top Democrats didn't get much sleep that night. The candidates for the no. 2 spot were Kefauver, Kennedy, Humphrey, and Al Gore of Tennessee. Lyndon Johnson and Sam Rayburn were for anybody but Kefauver. Tammany Hall was trying desperately to get New York Mayor Robert Wagner into the race. Minnesota was splitting between Humphrey and young Eugene McCarthy. Daley wanted Kennedy, whose nominating speech for Stevenson was one of the best Daley had ever heard.[9] Mayor Lawrence of Pittsburgh wanted anybody but Kennedy, whose antifarm positions would hurt Democrats in Pennsylvania. Kennedy and Humphrey were certain that Kefauver would win it. Kefauver was so unnerved by Stevenson's decision he almost went home. A third Tennessean, Governor Frank Clement, who had opened the convention with a rousing country fair speech, was a dark horse and a bitter enemy of Kefauver's. But the Tennessee delegation was committed first to Gore.

The balloting for the Democractic vice presidential nominee began on a hot Friday afternoon in August and the vapor of the adjacent stockyard draped over the International Amphitheatre. Rayburn gaveled the roll call at 12:45 P.M. Daley had been marshaling support for Kennedy in Illinois.

At a Friday morning caucus, the Illinois delegation was split 36½ for Kennedy, 11½ for Kefauver, 3½ for Wagner, and 2 for Stuart Symington of Missouri. One of the Wagner votes was from Jake Arvey, who was doing a favor for Tammany Hall's deSapio. Daley expected Arvey to switch to Kennedy whenever he asked. One of the Kefauver votes was from his senate colleague, Paul Douglas, who told Daley he would not switch to Kennedy. He never did. On the first ballot, Daley had worked the Kennedy count up to 46 votes. Kefauver had led the first ballot with 483½, followed by Kennedy with 304, Gore 178, Wagner 162½, Humphrey 134½, and scattered votes for another eight candidates.

Then came the second hectic ballot. Rayburn turned the gavel over to Senator Warren Magnuson of Washington and stood at the rear of the platform to take a break from peering into the mass of banners and the din of screaming delegates. From the beginning Kennedy's strength increased at a rate that had veteran Democrats predicting his nomination. It appeared a classic convention stampede was under way. The first big switch was early. Arkansas gave 16 votes to Kennedy. Then, with more and more votes switching to Kennedy, everyone looked to the big delegation from New York that had been loyal to Mayor Wagner on the first ballot. The Amphitheatre erupted with a roar when New York gave 96½ of its 98 votes to Kennedy. The official tally was Kennedy 559, Kefauver 479½. Then the states that had passed voted, and Kennedy moved to 647½ votes, only 39 shy of victory. Daley had now pushed Kennedy's total in Illinois to 49.

At that point, Kennedy seemed unstoppable—but he was stopped. Only it has never been made clear exactly how or why or who was responsible for keeping the Massachusetts senator from the vice presidential nomination. A score of state delegations were screaming for recognition. Hale Boggs of Louisiana, a staunch Kennedy supporter, moved near the podium, where Rayburn had reclaimed his gavel. "As far as I can see," Rayburn said to Boggs, "it's a fielder's choice."[10]

"Tennessee! Indiana! Missouri! Florida! Tennessee! Tennessee!" the tumult continued. Rayburn recognized Tennessee. Would the Kefauver feud with Clement now push 32 votes into the Kennedy column and decide the nomination? Is that what Rayburn expected? Or had he changed his mind after voting for Kennedy in the Texas caucus? While he was standing in the glare of lights on the platform, did Rayburn decide the young, handsome Massachusetts senator was too popular on the convention floor and would surely emerge as the party leader at the expense of someone like Rayburn's protégé, Lyndon Johnson?

In a meeting to discuss the vice presidency on July 26, when the subject of a Catholic on the ticket came up, Rayburn had told Stevenson, "If we have to have a Catholic, I hope we don't have to take that little pissant Kennedy."[11] Or was the aging speaker too confused to think anything through, with shouts coming constantly from all directions? The chairman of the Tennessee delegation yielded to Senator Gore, who rose and said, "I respectfully withdraw my name and support my distinguished colleague, Estes Kefauver."

Rayburn blanched. Bill Haddad, a Kefauver staffer standing at the foot of the platform, said, "I'll never forget the look on Rayburn's face as long as I live. He was so shocked, he really lost his composure for a moment."[12]

Weeks earlier, after Kefauver withdrew from the presidential race, the Tennessee delegation had voted to support Clement (the keynote speaker), Gore (its favorite son), and Kefauver, in that order. Regardless of personal enmity, Gore and Clement kept the bargain. The switch gave Kefauver 527½ while Kennedy was holding at 647½. Now Rayburn had to make another choice and again dozens of voices beseiged his ears and dozens of banners waved in his face. The southern states were leaping up for Kennedy, who they felt was more sympathetic on the civil rights issue than Kefauver. The farm states wanted no part of Kennedy because of his vote backing Eisenhower's farm bill. Daley, sitting in front, had five more votes to give from Illinois. Lyndon Johnson had personally asked the governor of Oklahoma to switch from Gore to Kennedy. Rayburn recognized Oklahoma, which delivered 16 votes to Kefauver.

If Rayburn was trying to push Kennedy over the top, he apparently had no idea where he should look for help. He chose the best he could get. House Majority Leader John McCormack of Massachusetts was standing at the foot of the podium shouting, some reported, "Missouri, Missouri," in the belief that Missouri was switching from Gore to Kennedy. McCormack said later he was shouting "Kentucky!" Rayburn recognized Missouri, which threw 32 more votes to Kefauver. Then Michigan switched to the Tennessean and the landslide was on. Daley finally got to add his five votes, bringing Kennedy's Illinois total to 54½. But it was too late to stem the tide.

McCormack's role has long been a subject of speculation. He and Kennedy had engaged in a bitter battle over control of the Massachusetts delegation in the spring of 1956, and the young senator's rising star must have nettled the veteran congressman. Yet he had eagerly made a seconding speech to nominate Kennedy the previous night. It might have been in McCormack's best interests to put Kennedy on a ticket headed to a defeat of embarrassing proportions and even worth the gamble that a surprise victory removing him to the obscurity of the vice presidency would return Massachusetts' Democratic control to McCormack. In later years, Daley said privately that he believed Stevenson didn't want Kennedy on the ticket and telephoned Rayburn with orders to stop Kennedy. But at the moment not even Daley, who had a front-row seat, could offer any explanation. Obviously disappointed, he could only tell reporters what was painfully obvious from the viewpoint of a Kennedy loyalist: "Rayburn recognized the wrong people."

CHAPTER 5

"When Irish Eyes Are Smiling"

ON DECEMBER 1, 1954, MARTIN KENNELLY ANNOUNCED HE would seek a third term as mayor and said he hoped the party leaders who had begged him in 1947 to run for the office would appreciate the fine job he had done for them. In reality, although the high-minded Kennelly made no boasts about it, his victory in 1947 had taken a veneer of dirt off the Democrats. But he had virtually been excluded from party affairs after Daley became chairman in 1953. This was in stark constrast to 1950, when Kennelly was consulted over the county ticket and pushed the selection of Daley as county clerk, or 1952, when he participated in discussions about Stevenson's successor as governor. When Daley held the traditional precinct captains' luncheon before the 1954 elections, the mayor wasn't invited. "Kennelly's not a committeeman," Al Horan simply explained, without explaining why Kennelly had been at every other previous captains' luncheon. Daley had used up a lot of words in denying that he would be a candidate for mayor. On October 21, 1954, he had vowed to put the record straight. "Let us get the record straight once and for all. I am not and never was a candidate for mayor. I am definitely a candidate for the important office of county clerk."

But by now the reporters had Daley pretty well figured out. They had already learned, as one of his future press secretaries would demand, to report what Daley meant, not what he said. As the Democrats moved past the 1954 elections, the speculation was strong that Kennelly would not run in 1955 and that Daley would be the party choice. That was the way Daley wanted it to work. Daley's strategies in fulfilling his ambitions never changed. He never wanted anyone to know exactly what he was planning even when, as in 1955, it was obvious to everyone. Part of this was simply smart politics, not revealing your hand to the other guy until you were sure you had a winner. But part of it derived from the other side of Richard J. Daley, the daily communicant whose every triumph was sealed with a pledge to "walk humbly with my God." When he insisted on the pretense of being "drafted" for whatever he had carefully orchestrated, it was as though neither God nor anyone else would be able to peek deep inside and view the powerful pride that drove his ambitions.

Kennelly's decision to seek a third term interfered with this scenario. More upsetting was his vow that he would run in the February 22 primary. Daley had no doubts whom the party would slate for mayor, but he was not so certain about facing a tough, probably bitter primary fight and then having to defeat the Republican candidate in April. It would help that his old ally Ben Adamowski had already announced for mayor and, like Kennelly, planned to run in the primary with or without the organization's support. That would split the Democratic vote three ways. Of all the committeemen, only Frank Keenan, the newly elected county assessor, was a staunch Kennelly supporter, volunteering to serve as the mayor's campaign chairman. Daley knew the 19th Ward bloc led by Nash would privately be against him, but their power to form alliances had declined since Daley assumed the chairmanship.

Daley was also disturbed by Kennelly's timing. He originally planned to begin the slatemaking session on December 28 so there wouldn't be time to put together an effective anti-organization movement before the February 22 primary. Daley knew that the newspapers would defend Kennelly and the business interests would give him financial support, but he also knew it would take time to organize campaign workers and precinct judges, people to staff the voting booths to make sure the other side wasn't taking the ballot box home to count. He was right about the newspapers. The *Chicago Tribune* editorialized:

"Mr. Daley is no hoodlum, but if he runs he will be the candidate of the hoodlum element. He will also be the candidate of those who wish to load the city's offices once again with political payrollers and thus undo the great work of Mayor Kennelly in giving the City a real merit system of appointments and promotions. Mr. Daley will also be the candidate of those who want to see the city purchase of supplies and the contracts let in the good old-fashioned way, with a nice percentage for the politicians."

Kennelly had started a system of centralized purchasing, which the committeemen abhorred and there was no doubt that with his departure the committeemen expected to see the last of Stephen Hurley, president of the Civil Service Commission.

Daley's response to Kennelly's announcement was predictable. "I expect the Democratic mayoral primary to attract the most able men in our great city. Thus far we have two candidates of high caliber—Benjamin S. Adamowski and Mayor Kennelly. I have been asked as chairman of the Democratic party just whom the Democratic party will endorse. Obviously, I cannot answer that question because I do not

know. The Democratic party will meet and discuss all candidates, and it will select the best candidate."

The *Tribune* noted that John S. Clark, the retiring county
assessor, might be the organization choice if Daley chose not
to run (indicating the *Tribune* still hadn't figured out Richard
Daley). Of course, there were plenty of people who wanted
to run. Eddie Barrett, the former secretary of state, said he
was ready. But the field was pretty crowded.

On December 3, Adamowski opened his headquarters,
denouncing the slatemakers and saying he would not appear
before them. Adamowski had quit his city corporation counsel post in 1950, charging that Kennelly was still controlled
by bosses. He intended to run a campaign that outreformed
the reformer.

In mid-December, Kennelly opened his headquarters and
the captains of business and industry paid their respects.
The Democrats did not. Daley said he had to take the kids
to see Santa Claus. On December 15, 1954, Mayor Martin
Kennelly left City Hall and walked to the Morrison Hotel,
where the twelve-member Democratic Party slatemaking
committee was interviewing candidates. Reporters stopped
Kennelly on the third floor in front of the adjoining doors
leading to party headquarters. "Which door do I go in?"
Kennelly asked. "Did you ever read the story of the lady and
the tiger?" a newsman replied.

When Kennelly entered the party chambers, he was
aware of the hostility facing him. The slatemaking committee appointed by Chairman Daley included Barnet Hodes of
the 5th Ward, who was Jake Arvey's law partner; Alderman
Joseph Rostenkowski of the 32nd Ward, the leading Polish
politician; State Senator William Connors of the 42nd Ward;
former party chief Joe Gill; and the most formidable, William
Dawson, the black boss of five South Side wards who had
argued vigorously against giving Kennelly a second term four

years earlier. Kennelly, in his lofty reform manner, had done nothing in his City Hall tenure to ingratiate himself with Dawson, whose party finances depended on support from the various mob leaders who ran the highly profitable "policy" games in poor black communities. Kennelly read a statement to the slatemaking committee. It took, he said, three minutes and fifty-six seconds.

Kennelly said to the committee chairman, Gill, "You invited me, I'll be glad to answer any questions." There was no reply. Kennelly asked, "Is there anything you want me to explain?" Gill said, "No." Kennelly looked from one dour face to another. "I presume it's unanimous?" he asked. Dawson quickly replied, "It's unanimous."

Later Kennelly said, "I knew what he meant. He didn't have to elaborate. The word was 'out.' Dawson won't stand for Kennelly again. Obviously, Dawson was in control. But, as I turned to go, I saw the county clerk, almost hidden on a sofa. That's the kind of committee it was—he picked it!"

Daley told reporters that since his office was right next door to the slatemaking committee room, "I pop in and out when I have time." Asked again if he were a candidate for mayor, Daley said, "That's up to the committee. I would await the decision of the committee." Another reporter asked, "Would you like to see the slatemakers do the same kind of job they did in 1947 and 1951 when Kennelly was endorsed?" "I wasn't chairman then," Daley said with the finality of a trapdoor on a gallows.

On December 20, the committeemen of the fifty city wards met to select their mayoral candidate. Al Horan forecast the outcome. "It's so near unanimous that it's pathetic. The only one who has spoken for Kennelly is Thomas Nash." And even Nash didn't vote for the incumbent mayor. The vote was 49–1 for Daley. Keenan cast the lone ballot for Kennelly, earning the lasting enmity of Richard J. Daley.

Reporters asked Daley why Kennelly had not been slated a third time. The reply, always abrupt, defying any rebuttal, was classic Daley. "He failed."

Kennelly called it a "phony draft" and set the theme of his primary campaign by declaring, "The question is whether the people of Chicago will rule or be ruled by the willful, wanton inner circle of political bosses at the Morrison Hotel." What Kennelly and many others didn't realize was that the circle of bosses had become quite small. There was only enough room in it for one man.

If the newspapers knew a lot about Richard Daley by then, few of the voters did. It is hard to imagine after the three decades in which his name became synonymous with Chicago that a Daley campaign ever had all the trappings of photo events and baby-kissing that lesser political figures engage in to make themselves known and adored. The many later campaigns of Richard Daley were marked by a precision of orders: a half-million signatures filed promptly and without challenge for the nominating petitions; a half-million votes delivered promptly on primary election day; another half-million delivered in the general election; a few huge dinners in one of the downtown hotels; a few stops in the black churches and at some of the giant Polish banquet halls on Milwaukee Avenue; a feigned ignorance of any issues that were raised; a refusal to acknowledge any opponent by name; an occasional brief, rapid denunciation of any criticisms; and certain victory an hour after the polls closed—or even before they closed.

But in 1955, Daley was only the county clerk, another Irish guy from Bridgeport, a rather portly, neatly dressed, and most of the time soft-spoken fellow who talked about saving the taxpayers money. Now there was a different Daley to behold. He was in the black wards, he was marching in parades, he was stopping shoppers and dropping in at bars and churches and rallies all over the city. Certainly Daley saw places in 1955 that even he, the biggest booster and most ardent lover Chicago ever had, had never seen before. And he began the pattern of orchestrating endorsements that always overwhelmed his opponents. On January 4 the Chicago Federation of Labor, headed by his good friend William Lee, endorsed him. On January 7, the state CIO endorsed him. The All-Chicago Committee for Daley was formed by former assessor John Clark. In early February, he got his most important endorsement. Adlai Stevenson, the titular national leader of the Democrats, surprised his many liberal and reform friends by abandoning the reform mayor and supporting Daley. But Stevenson knew that Daley was a superior administrator, far from the machine hack the newspapers were painting him. He also knew that without Daley's involvement, Arvey could never have manipulated the 1952 convention that gave Stevenson his place in history. And Stevenson wanted another run at the presidency to vindicate himself. He knew Martin Kennelly could not help him.

Still, Stevenson seemed tortured between ideology, which he adored, and pragmatism, which he envied but rarely emulated. "I have not taken sides in Democratic primaries anywhere in the country and I had intended to follow that practice in the Democratic primary for mayor. . . . But I am moved to say—emphatically—that the continual attacks on Dick Daley are, in my opinion, unfair and misleading. . . . Aside from my personal respect and friendship for him, I think Dick Daley's contributions as a political leader and a public official commend him highly to the confidence of the voters of Chicago." Paul Douglas also endorsed Daley at Arvey's request. Douglas would not, however, endorse him in the general election against Robert Merriam, a kindred Hyde Park–University of Chicago progressive.

If Chicago was getting its first chance to see and hear Daley, he was getting his first taste of rough campaigning, personal campaigning. In his previous election forays his opponents had limited their charges to accusing him of being a double dipper and a tool of the machine. Since he was both, Daley didn't argue much. No one paid much attention, and the rhetoric had no impact on the outcome of the election. Now, Martin Kennelly was going on television charging that Daley would turn loose the worst kind of corrupt influences on the city, that he was backed by the "dark dictatorship" of William Dawson, and that the Democratic party wanted to get control of the city's schools and turn them into a patronage haven. Daley, who would always wear the chip of personal integrity on his shoulder, fired back. "There are many false charges and malicious remarks being made about us," he told a rally of committeemen on January 28, exhorting them with a charge that would be his eternal refrain. "Where is the proof? Where are the facts behind the rumors? I have not heard of the facts because there are no facts!"

And he could be humble. "We've all made our mistakes, but in my entire political life no one has ever been able to point one finger of criticism at me." And he could put words in places they were never intended to be. "I do not wish to walk in the toga of one who has never sinned."

Four thousand of his friends and neighbors in Bridgeport set off aerial bombs and marched up Halsted Street with the Daley family to a huge rally at the Lithuanian Hall. He laid out with remarkable prescience the program he would implement and keep running for twenty years. "Everyone wants his neighborhood to have good police protection, frequent garbage collection, adequate sewers, speedy public transportation." He also promised more housing, which ultimately proved to be a mixed blessing. But most of all he forecast the style that marked every decision, every plan, every dream he would ever have: "This is the spirit I will bring to the mayor's office, a spirit of getting these things done for the people, not in the distant future, but right now!"

Daley also did what for him would be a rarity: He appeared at a public forum with his opponents. And he did what would become commonplace: He got mad and shouted. Kennelly, Adamowski and Daley appeared February 6 at a women's gathering at Temple Sholom on Lake Shore Drive. Adamowski got him mad first. "The hocus-pocus is over. [Daley] can't deny that he picked the committee to run him for mayor." Daley's face got red. Kennelly followed by saying. "They gave me three minutes and fifty-six seconds to tell about what has been done in eight years, how the city government has been improved."

Daley leaped up and bounced to the microphone. "The mayor took two minutes. He could have had all day if he wanted it! Nobody stopped him! He could have had all afternoon!" he shouted. Kennelly returned to the microphone and described seeing Daley sitting on the sofa in the room. Daley again leaped up and went for the microphone but was blocked by the woman moderator. He sulked silently through the remainder of the session.

Kennelly spent a lot of his radio and television time attacking Dawson. "Dawson's leadership in the 'dump Kennelly' movement is a cover-up for his real motives, which are his interest in his purse, not his people." Kennelly charged that Dawson wanted him out because Kennelly refused to permit open gambling in Dawson's wards.

While Kennelly was attacking Dawson, Daley was cultivating him. Dawson had been named vice chairman of the Democratic committee and Daley always referred to him as the "distinguished congressman," which might have raised some eyebrows at the Hamburg club.

One of the great ironies of Daley's career is that in the 1940s and 1950s, regardless of what he might have had to tell his priest in confession, publicly he was on the correct political side of the race issue. And he was there at the right time.

His alignment with Arvey and Gill in the 1940s put him on the progressive side of the county's party structure. It was the more polished, urbane Nash-Duffy-McDermott wing that was trying to seize control of the county organization to retain the status quo of payoffs and kickbacks. Arvey's anguished ouster of Ed Kelly in 1946 was based on race. Kelly had supported allowing Negroes to share in the new federal public housing plans being drawn up Washington. Since everyone assumed the low-cost housing would be put in the deserving white neighborhoods, and since the committeemen who saw great opportunities in any construction project would go to great lengths to make sure these buildings were erected in their fiefdoms, Kelly was in effect promoting integrated neighborhoods. The white backlash, even in a city that was less than 15 percent black, was loud. It gave the Nash bloc a political reason to insist on dumping Kelly and it also coincided with the emotions of their constituents. The issue of public housing and Negroes remained quiet during Kennelly's terms. But in Dawson's mind, neither he nor his people needed any additional excuses to exile the mayor.

In 1955, however, Kennelly played the race card. Not only did he attack Dawson for the racketeering whose illicit profits trickled down to the Dawson organization, but he also raised the specter of the machine taking over the school system and dealing with its problems in a way that would please Dawson—integration. In the early 1950s, the Chicago schools were vastly overcrowded. Ten thousand pupils went to classes in shifts. There were not enough classrooms, especially in the South Side wards where Dawson's voters lived. And there were no integrated schools. Daley accused the Kennelly campaign of "raising the question of racial tension in the community, (spreading) a deliberate, fraudulent lie." Uncertain of how much white backlash was out there, Daley reassured a 19th Ward white audience. "I'm a kid from the stockyards. I'd never do that," he said.

Whether Kennelly's tactic was the inadvertent stumbling of a political naif, which he was, or whether the shrewder Frank Keenan saw a possible wedge into the ethnic and racist strongholds of the organization, the bid to win white backlash votes failed. Only few of Chicago's whites had begun to feel the threat of neighborhood blockbusting. The competition for jobs that always spurred nationalist and racial rivalries was diminished by a booming manufacturing economy that could employ everyone who wanted to work. And for the politically devoted, the organization had control of thirty thousand jobs that were given, outside of Dawson's bailiwick, exclusively to whites.

But there was a backlash. It came from the previously docile black community. Not all the black vote was deliverable to the machine. There was a middle-class and religion-based liberal element that saw the machine as just another form of plantation rule. There was also some lingering Republican sentiment among older black voters. But these patches of resistance had no money to hustle precincts on election day or jobs to promise for corralling votes. Kennelly should have realized that the antimachine vote did exist. He had narrowly carried four of the five black wards in his 1947 victory, winning big only in the 20th Ward. By 1951, with Dawson already making snorting noises about him, Kennelly lost two of those wards, a clear indication that anyone opposing the Democratic organization's candidate could find some relief among black voters. But Kennelly's race-baiting killed any hope of that. The *Chicago Defender* editorialized on its front page a defense of Dawson and a repudiation of Kennelly, comparing his tactics to those of Hitler and Mussolini.[1] Daley was the beneficiary of this enormous miscalculation.

Kennelly clearly did not have the appreciation of his city's black population that Daley did. Kennelly hobnobbed with the owners of the State Street stores, not with the people who shopped there or scrubbed the floors. He moved out of

Bridgeport as fast as success could take him to a luxurious lakefront apartment. He undoubtedly thought of blacks as custodians or domestics, and unlike Daley and his friends at the Hamburg club, never regarded them as a threat, socially or economically. In many ways, he was like many urban northerners, content to nod sympathetically at the oppression of blacks in the South and smug in the belief that places like Boston, Pittsburgh, Cleveland, Detroit, and Chicago were true havens of equality (despite a flare-up of rioting every twenty years or so).

In 1954, America was bursting with new housing, new cars, new television sets, new jobs, new opportunities. There seemed to be enough to go around. Only the threat of nuclear war, which seemed so unimaginable that no one could imagine it for very long, interfered with the march to the greatest prosperity any nation would ever know. Gasoline cost fifteen cents a gallon and Eisenhower was promising to build a network of superhighways that would let every steelworker, store clerk, mail carrier, and bricklayer drive his children to some new magic world called Disneyland, which had been conjured up out of acres of California orange groves. Detroit was making cars whose engines poured out power and speed that ate up miles and gasoline long before anyone dreamed Rachel Carson would reinvent the word "environment" or that America did not own all the oil in the world. For those with really small incomes, American Motors came out with the Rambler, the first compact car, in 1954.

For people who stayed up late, NBC inaugurated "The Tonight Show," with Steve Allen, an old Chicago lad, as the host. America watched Phil Silvers and Ernie Kovacs and Jackie Gleason and Lucille Ball, and although neither Dick Daley nor his twenty thousand precinct workers knew it, the evenings when they could solicit votes in the local saloon or drop in unannounced at some good Democratic household were coming to an end. Television was shoving them out of the parlor. In 1954 Americans watched grainy kinescopes of a messianic senator from Wisconsin investigating the United States Army. On the day Martin Kennelly announced he would seek a third term, the U.S. Senate censured Joseph McCarthy. But he had created havoc. J. Robert Oppenheimer, the theoretical physicist who directed the Manhattan project that built the atomic bomb, was denied forever his security clearance, a victim of McCarthy's witch hunts.

There were also newsreels of the French army surrendering a place called Dien Bien Phu to a group of soldiers wearing coolie hats who called themselves the Viet Minh. The junior senator from California, Richard Nixon, had argued vigorously in the Senate for American intervention to help the French hold onto their colony in Indochina. The junior senator from Massachusetts, John Kennedy, had argued just as vociferously not to get involved. Most Americans neither knew nor cared where French Indochina was. In 1954, Ernest Hemingway won the Nobel Prize. Daley would never claim Hemingway, whose first job was in Chicago and whose first stories were written there. Hemingway, after all, was from Oak Park, one of the "country towns" on the other side of the street from Austin Avenue.

In 1954, Willie Mays made the most famous catch in World Series history. Eugene McCarthy won his fourth term in Congress. Martin Luther King, Jr., was appointed pastor of the Dexter Avenue Baptist Church in Montgomery, Alabama. The Democrats won back control of the Congress they had temporarily lost in the Eisenhower landslide of 1952. Lyndon Johnson of Texas became Senate majority leader. In 1954, the United States Supreme Court handed down its opinion in *Brown v. Topeka Board of Education* and changed America forever.

The country had lived a hundred years after Lincoln's Emancipation Proclamation with the understanding that by law blacks and whites were equal but they would exist separately: in separate houses, separate towns, separate stores, separate churches, separate restaurants, separate seats, separate schools. The Supreme Court ruling ended that, and the southern political leaders erupted in a pledge of defiance. The symbolism of Orval Faubus defying the U.S. Army in Little Rock played on the nation's televisions. George Wallace stood at the gates of the University of Alabama saying no. Federal troops were needed to escort James Meredith to class at the University of Mississippi. The volcanic venom from Little Rock, Montgomery, Atlanta, and Jackson drowned out the quiet unrest that was being felt in the North, where the liberals and big-city bosses, out of respective fervor and common political sense, hailed the court decision.

But the true impact of *Brown v. Topeka* would be in the North. *Brown v. Topeka* was not merely a landmark ruling. It was a wake-up call. If Martin Kennelly, leader of the nation's second-largest city, had not seen what was happening to his community, he could not be blamed. Hardly any white people saw it. And no one told them about it. The nation's media, now swelled by the new journalists of television, completely missed the mass migration of blacks from the South. No one stood at Chicago's Randolph Street station and counted as the Illinois Central's trains arrived with thousands and thousands of black people who had paid $10 or $12 for a ticket to leave the Mississippi Delta and the Arkansas cotton fields and move to Chicago. They came in the early 1950s at the rate of a thousand a day. But after *Brown vs. Topeka*, everyone began counting. School integration might have to be carried out at the point of a bayonet in Little Rock, but it was not going to be that easy in Boston and Chicago. Suddenly, northern cities were no longer enclaves of white European immigrants. Almost overnight they had changed. And the Democratic Party of Cook County had also changed.

When Cermak and Nash created the modern machine in 1930, Chicago had fewer than 150,000 blacks among its more than three million residents. Most of them voted for the party of Abraham Lincoln; their participation in local elections was Republican but not critical. In Cermak's 1931 mayoral victory, he got only 25 percent of the black vote, the same number Roosevelt gathered the following year. But the New Deal began to change black voting habits. In 1936, Roosevelt doubled his vote among Chicago blacks and Ed Kelly won 57 percent of their vote in 1939. During the 1940s, blacks in Chicago still moved toward the Democratic Party nationally but began to drift locally. Roosevelt, after a strong integration stance in 1944, jumped to 63 percent with black voters but Kelly had slipped in 1943 to only 53 percent. Truman's integration order of the armed forces and the Hubert Humphrey–inspired civil rights platform of 1948 brought 75 percent of the black vote to the Democratic president.

But Chicago blacks, who could see what they were getting from the New Deal, could also see what they were not getting from the local organization. Kennelly got only 51 percent of their vote in 1947 and barely broke the 50 percent mark in 1951, losing two of the black wards. And the black population was no longer viewed as unimportant. It was doubling every decade, up to 250,000 in 1940, representing 7 percent of the city total; up to 500,000 in 1950, 14 percent of the city total; and to nearly 30 percent, or 900,000 blacks in a population of 3,480,000 in 1960. In 1955, there were more than 800,000 black people living in Chicago, almost one-fourth of the population. If Daley was like Kennelly and most other northerners, he was probably unaware of the metamorphosis of the cities in terms of the dramatic social and political changes that would mark the remainder of the century. But he could count. Daley had spent most of his adult years counting. He counted jobs, salaries, revenues, taxes, expenditures, bills, amendments, ordinances, committees, commissions, delegates, and votes. Above all he was a master at counting votes. And Bill Dawson had them.

As February 22, 1955, approached, Daley had whipped the county loyalists to a frenzy, creating the impression that the world as they knew it would end unless he was nominated and elected. And many of them thought it would. Another Kennelly term could only lead to more and more jobs placed in the dreaded civil service category, more backroom gambling operations closed, and more city contracts awarded on honest bidding, in the open. Very few of the committeemen had a personal passion for electing Daley mayor. Some of them clearly did not twist too many arms for him. And many of them, particularly on the North Side, would be hard-pressed to carry Daley in the ethnic wards and in the wards that traditionally voted Republican in state and national elections and turned to the Democratic ledger only in city balloting. In light of the citywide landslides of his later years—losing only a liberal lakefront ward here and there—it is hard to grasp that in the 1955 primary, Daley, the greatest mayor Chicago ever had, the greatest kingmaker Chicago ever had, the greatest vote getter Chicago ever had could only win five wards north of the river.

But that was enough. As the party faithful and the handful Daley would allow to become his personal inner circle trooped to the Morrison Hotel on February 22, 1955, it was quickly apparent that remnants of the old machine and the advance guard of the new machine were producing for the man who would rule all the Chicago machines for the next twenty years. The committeemen from the river wards were always the first to report their vote count, probably because they often knew before the polls opened what it was going to be. Arvey's famous 24th delivered 13,607 for Daley, better than 3–1 over the two opponents. Al Horan's 29th provided 11,176 for Daley, 4,000 for Kennelly, and 400 for Adamowski. Harry Sain's 27th was huge: 12,772 for Daley to 1,720 for Kennelly and about 200 for Adamowski. Daley's own 11th was faithful with 13,487 cast for its Bridgeport native. Kennelly had pinned his hopes on a big turnout, one that would rival the record 1.4 million vote in the 1939 mayoral primary when Kelly turned back a challenge from State's Attorney Thomas Courtney. (Courtney, of course, was rewarded with a judgeship.) But the pattern of an enormous drop-off between presidential and mayor elections that always benefited the organization held and only 746,000 people voted.

Now Dawson's five wards came in and the significance of the black vote was clear. Dawson had delivered 59,000 votes to Daley and 13,450 to Kennelly, a 45,000 swing that along with the river wards and the 11th provided Daley with a 100,000-vote edge. Everywhere else he ran no better than even. He carried 27 wards to 19 for Kennelly and 4 for Adamowski. He wound up with 364,539 votes, in contrast to 264,775 for Kennelly and 112,072 for Adamowski. Even if Adamowski had stayed out of the race, Kennelly would have had to get all his votes to win, which couldn't have happened. Adamowski's totals were strictly from the predominantly Polish wards, and if he hadn't been on the ballot, committeemen such as Joe Rostenkowski surely would have made stronger showings for Daley. Even more remarkable was that the river wards were no longer immigrant Jewish and Italian bastions. By the mid-1950s their populations were black, and so were parts of a half dozen other South Side wards, including the 7th, 8th, 16th, and 17th. And there were pockets of black residents living in Hyde Park and along the lake. Some had begun moving into the 25th and 26th Southwest Side areas and middle-class blacks were eyeing homes in the 34th Ward. The Democratic machine that the Irish and Bohemians had built could no longer give a majority of the vote to a Democratic candidate for mayor. By 1955, only a candidate who won the black vote could win—and that was Daley.

The suspense was over by 7 P.M. Jake Arvey, Joe Gill, and Al Horan were out front accepting congratulations. Daley remained in his office scouring the ward reports. Out front they were singing, "When Irish Eyes Are Smiling." State's Attorney John Gutknecht and Judge Richard Austin, head of the criminal courts, stuck their heads in to congratulate Daley. It was allowed. The state's attorney handles vote fraud charges. The criminal courts are where vote fraud cases land. At 7:30 P.M. Horan predicted a 125,000-vote victory. Daley said, "It's too early." At 9 P.M. Kennelly appeared on television and conceded. Fifteen minutes later a Western Union messenger showed up with a telegram from Adamowski: "Congratulations on your nomination." At 9:32 Daley came out of the inner office and gave his first major acceptance speech, which sounded exactly like all his future postelection analyses would sound. "In typical American fashion, the people have spoken . . . ."

The Daley family was still up when Dick arrived home after midnight. Eleanor Daley's shout could be heard by reporters following the nominee. "Here he is, kids!" The six children at home (Patricia, the eldest, was a postulate at the Sisters of Mercy Novitiate in Des Plaines) all hugged their dad, who promised: "When you get home from school this afternoon we'll go fishing at the sports show over at the International Amphitheatre. Tell your mother not to fix anything for dinner. We're going to bring home some trout."

But Daley wasn't the only winner celebrating, and as he studied the returns he was thinking about the general election. Four men wanted to become mayor of Chicago in 1955 and all of them were Democrats. Three ran in the party primary and the fourth, Robert E. Merriam, a reform alderman from the traditionally maverick 5th Ward, decided to run as a Republican. He easily got the party's nomination and with strong support from liberals and independents figured to make a race of it against the Democratic organization candidate. Merriam, 36, began making all the usual machine and corruption charges, and Daley gave as good he got. "I never before have been the object of such vicious abuse as I have received in this campaign," he told a luncheon rally on March 20 (apparently forgetting the abuse he had complained of the previous month). "[Merriam] says I would corrupt the city—that I corrupt the neighborhood where my wife, my children, and my friends and neighbors live. This is a lie." Daley reprised all the endorsements he had gathered for the primary, again getting a robust benediction from Stevenson. (No longer the shy bridegroom of 1952, Stevenson really wanted another crack at the Democratic presidential nomination in 1956.)

But, as has always been the case in Chicago elections, there was a certain zaniness to this one. It wasn't the "bullets and ballots" exercise of the 1920s, when Capone's cohorts machine-gunned voting precincts, but it was odd. Daley's running mate for city clerk, Alderman Benjamin Becker (40th Ward), resigned from the ticket March 8 after the Chicago Bar Association began investigating charges that he had split fees with a zoning lawyer, charges that undoubtedly shocked his fellow city council members. Daley defended Becker vehemently until the day he dropped him.

Daley decided he needed all the vote-getting help he could get. This was no time for friends or favors. He looked over the February 22 primary results and discovered that Morris B. Sachs, who ran a string of neighborhood clothing stores and had been Kennelly's candidate for city treasurer, had run 75,000 votes better than Kennelly. Daley asked Sachs to join the Democratic ticket in the clerk's slot. But Sachs had a better idea. "I found after the primary I had 25,000 campaign buttons left with the slogan 'Elect Morris B. Sachs City Treasurer' and nothing else. So when Dick Daley asked

me to run I told him I knew nothing about clerking, but I
did know something about saving money." Daley asked his
ticket mate for treasurer, John Marcin, to move into the city
clerk slot and offered the city treasurer vacancy to Sachs.
Sachs took it and Marcin went on to run side by side with
Daley for the next twenty years—even though he lived in
Wisconsin for nearly all those years, a fact not discovered
until the 1970s when he finally stepped out of politics.

With his ticket restructured, Daley now tried to get his
defeated comrades on board. Tom Nash, who had supported
Kennelly in the primary, finally came around. Daley breathed
easier. Nash's 19th Ward had drubbed him 16,000 to 6,000
in the primary. He sent emissaries to woo Adamowski and
Kennelly. Adamowski was adamant. "I said I would not support the Morrison Hotel organization. I guess that's just
about the same as saying I will not back Daley. But if he
wants to talk, I'll sit down and talk." Kennelly almost
endorsed Merriam the night of the primary, but held off and
then decided against it when Merriam's campaign rhetoric
became critical of the police and other city departments,
remarks that Kennelly felt reflected poorly on his reign. But
Frank Keenan had no illusions about getting back in Daley's
favor. He supported Merriam enthusiastically and as county
assessor was a key fund-raiser. There was one small opening. A week after the primary, Keenan told newsmen, "We
might be able to work together" if Daley agreed to dump
Dawson. Keenan said, "We campaigned sincerely against the
bosses, and couldn't go along with them now." There is no
record of Daley's reply, but Dawson was still bossing the
black wards at his death fifteen years later. Merriam, though
a turncoat Democrat, also got help from Republican Governor William Stratton, who viewed the possible capture of City
Hall by a Republican as a plus for his flagging re-election
effort in 1956.

So Daley was not being unduly cautious as he approached April 5 with far less confidence that one would expect of the standard-bearer of an organization that had won City Hall six straight times. The general election turnout would be higher. He could count on picking up some of the Adamowski vote. But the North Side was dangerous, as his primary results showed. On February 22, the man who would become his political alter ego, Tom Keane, had carried him 3 to 1 in the 31st Ward, Botchy Connors had gotten him a 4–1 majority in the 42nd, and the clownish but effective Paddy Bauler had squeezed out a margin in the 43rd Ward. Daley had narrowly won the 30th Ward and Gill's 46th. But Adamowski and Kennelly had won all the rest of the North Side. Charlie Webber's 45th Ward was a sure loser. Parky Cullerton had lost the 38th in the primary. Rostenkowski might pull through the 32nd. Daley would again have to lean on the West Side and black wards.

Daley and Merriam met in four debates during the campaign. Merriam's theme was obvious: "The syndicate is not supporting Bob Merriam for mayor. It is going all out to beat me. And that is significant." Daley: "Is the Republican candidate without a party? Does he have less of a machine than the Democrats? Without the GOP he would be helpless. With that party, Chicago would be helpless."

Merriam charged the Democrats had "between 75,000 and 100,000 ghost voters on their registration lists." Daley rebutted to a clergymen audience: "The great hoax the Republican candidate has been attempting to sell the people of Chicago is that I am the tool of a corrupt machine. I challenge him to tell you what acts against the public interest I have committed at the dictation of or under the control of any political machine. Where are the facts?"

Meanwhile, politicians were making tough choices. Some of Keenan's top aides defected. David Hartigan, Keenan's choice for alderman in the 49th against George Lane (who was backing Daley), switched to Daley a week before the election. Simon Murray was a Republican committeeman of the 22nd Ward, one of the West Side bloc of GOP pols who routinely took orders from their Democratic counterparts to share in some of the patronage crumbs they couldn't get from their own party. He distributed literature throughout the ward urging voters "to do everything possible to assist to make the vote for Democrat Daley for mayor as close to being unanimous as possible."

In one of the final rallies, Daley spoke to the sheetmetal workers' union, to which his father, Michael, had belonged for fifty years. The elder Daley also spoke. "Give Dick a vote. We've never had a member or member's son elected to such a high office." If Daley was often accused of provincialism, it clearly was genetic. Merriam, whose father was a renowned sociologist at the University of Chicago and had been a losing mayoral candidate in 1911, picked up the endorsements of all the newspapers except *Chicago's American*. But the dailies' treatment of Daley was more institutional than personal. They regretted the return of City Hall to the organization, but they hadn't found anything personally offensive about Daley beyond his membership in the Democratic Party.

And they took heart when he announced immediately after the primary: "Upon my election I will resign as Democratic chairman to devote my full time and attention to the duties of the mayor's office." In an effort to hold him to that pledge, or at least to publicly remind him, the *Tribune*'s election-day story read: "Richard J. Daley, Democratic county chairman, was elected mayor yesterday in a moderate turnout of 1,338,554 Chicagoans. He will quit his party leadership and also as city clerk."

Daley did quit as city clerk. Ignoring the *Tribune*'s flat prediction, he served ten more terms as party chairman.

Daley's triumph over Merriam was easier than it looked, but it had the same construction as the primary win. The final total was 708,222 votes to 581,555. The job paid $25,000 a year.

It was the closest mayoral race in a dozen years but it wasn't that close. Dawson's wards and the river wards, along with Daley's own 11th, accounted for 125,000 of the victory margin. The Morrison Hotel was the site of the same sort of revelry that had taken place six weeks earlier. Arvey, Gill, Horan, and the ticket partners, Marcin and Sachs were there. So were the judges, the Shrivers of the Kennedy clan, and Bailey and Lee and Germano from the unions. Daley promised to make Chicago great and walk humbly with his God. Paddy Bauler said, "Chicago ain't ready for reform." He also said, "Daley's the dog with the big nuts now."

If Bauler knew it, so did the rest. Richard J. Daley—52, DeLaSalle class of 1919, DePaul Law class of 1934, Democratic Party, registered at birth, former errand clerk, representative, state senator, deputy controller, revenue director, county clerk, committeeman, and party chairman—was now the mayor of all Chicago. All the streets and all the alleys and all the parks and all the playgrounds. All the sewers and all the beaches. All the trains and all the buses. They would be lighted and cleaned and expanded. And he had all the people. The police, the firefighters, the sanitation workers and sewer workers, the park workers and bus drivers, the plumbers and electricians and bricklayers, the lawyers and accountants, the clerks and judges, the bailiffs and jailers. And the council and the committeemen and the precinct captains. Whether he was in residence at City Hall as "the man on five" or holding court on the third floor of the Morrison Hotel, he was in charge of everything and all of them.

"Just a kid from the stockyards," he had said.

CHAPTER 6

"My Kind of Town, Chicago Is"

WHEN RICHARD DALEY HUNG UP THE TELEPHONE AT 3 A.M. ON November 9, 1961, he probably knew he was the first person to call Jack Kennedy "Mr. President." Kennedy never forgot it. After Daley proudly broke the news to Kennedy that he would carry Illinois, the mayor/chairman remained secluded in his third-floor Morrison Hotel office for the rest of the long morning. He did not appear in public until his victory was certain and total. He waited, in fact, until after noon, when he received another call from Kennedy—who had waited until Nixon's concession before making his official calls of gratitude. At 1:15 P.M. Daley came out of his office and was swarmed by reporters. "I am very happy over the election. It appears as though Senator Kennedy will win Illinois. This is a tremendous win for a great candidate," he proclaimed. Daley had spent those long morning hours constantly scanning the vote totals, alternately fretting over new downstate numbers and calculating with joy that they could not overtake his massive Chicago total for Kennedy.

But he was also fretting and, ultimately, chortling over Bennie Adamowski. As long as the 1960 election is discussed nationally, it will be part of the legend that Dick Daley elected John Kennedy by either stealing votes or delivering a miraculous effort—or both. In Chicago, the real question was whether the huge margins in the organization wards were driven by Daley's desire to elect John Kennedy or his obsession with defeating Ben Adamowski's bid for another frightening term as state's attorney. The two goals were far from mutually exclusive. Daley wanted every controllable vote turned out for the election. He wanted every possible Democrat at the polls on the assumption that even though all them might not be blindly loyal to the straight ticket, a big majority would be for Kennedy—and more of them than not would be for his state's attorney candidate, Daniel Ward, the law school professor he had plucked in another of his patented slatemaking efforts to portray the organization as enlightened and full of integrity.

There was a pecking order in the pattern of the organization's vote hustling, in each of the fifty wards, in each of the three thousand-plus precincts. For starters, the thirty thousand patronage employes and their families could be expected to vote the straight ticket and get many of their friends and bar mates to do the same. In the black wards, there was an unspoken demand that was buttressed by Kennedy's late decision to succor Martin Luther King, Jr. There were the thousands of visits made by the thousands of captains to earn election-day loyalty from the precinct residents. But there were also certain rules. When a voter balked at a straight ticket, a good precinct captain did not press the issue beyond a certain point. The first priority was always to elect the ward committeeman. The captain could not take no for an answer, because the committeeman was his "rabbi," his "chinaman"—the man who had gotten him his job. The second priority in Chicago was to elect whoever the committeeman was supporting for mayor, a job that became very easy during the successive regimes of Richard Daley. Even in presidential election years, the local ticket still commanded more devotion than the national and state candidates. This was proved in 1952, 1968, and 1972, when Daley carried local offices in the face of national and state GOP triumphs.

So a precinct captain faced with a Democrat or independent considering a split ticket had to accept some disappointment. In 1960, a voter who wasn't enamored of Kennedy would be beseeched to vote for Ward. Given the bulk of blacks and Catholics, the precinct captains had a fairly easy time of it, provided they made sure the voters got to the polling booths. The Adamowski difficulty was the Polish bloc. It took a lot of arm twisting, and sometimes it didn't work, to get a vote for Ward in the Polish wards. Adamowski won the 33rd, 35th, 36th, 38th, and 39th by substantial margins, even though Kennedy whipped Nixon in these areas. The 35th, where Daley's city clerk, John Marcin, was committeeman, carried Kennedy by 6,000 votes and lost to Adamowski by 5,000—a swing of 11,000 votes out of 33,000 ballots counted. Even the lace-curtain Irish 19th Ward, which always favored Republicans (Truman lost by a 2–1 margin to Dewey and Eisenhower humiliated Stevenson in 1956 with a 41,000 to 19,000 plurality) went to Kennedy by 1,500 votes. It also went against Daley's state's attorney choice by 6,000 votes.

In the hard-core Democratic wards, Kennedy outpolled Ward. In the five black wards, predictably, he gathered 15,000 more votes than Ward. But in the river wards, many of them approaching majority black populations, the two Democrats ran even. That suggests that whatever chicanery was going on involved straight-ticket ballots. These were the wards where Republicans scoured for vote fraud and where the subsequent GOP vote challenge focused. These were the wards where ghost voters, people registered but long since dead or

moved away, still cast ballots. These were the wards where
ballot boxes were sometimes whisked out of the polling place
to be counted away from the prying eyes of a Republican
judge, and where the Republican judges were often wolves
in sheep's clothing: Republicans for one day and Democratic
payrollers the remainder of the year.

There is no question that Kennedy and Ward benefited
from the traditional abilities of the Democratic committeemen in these areas to alter the vote count.[1] But there is
also no question that Republicans in the suburbs and in
DuPage County and downstate also benefited from outdated
registration sheets. In fact, the building pace in the suburbs
and collar counties, especially Will and DuPage, was so frantic by the late 1950s and 1960s that the transiency of home
owners resulted in registration sheets that were hopelessly out
of date—and extremely useful to GOP precinct captains on
election day.

In 1996, the Chicago Board of Elections did a thorough
canvass and eliminated 250,000 names from voter rolls,
reducing the number of registered voters in the city to
1,265,259. Although the city's population is five hundred
thousand less than it was in 1960, and many city residents
are immigrants not eligible to vote, it is clear that the
1,950,000 voters registered for the 1960 elections included
many names of the dead and gone.

The miraculous effort turned in by Daley in 1960 was
similar to the Truman vote the organization had milked in
1948 but not as big a Democratic triumph as the one Daley
would give Lyndon Johnson four years later. By then Johnson had passed the 1964 Civil Rights Bill, and Chicago's
black voters responded with a thunderous turnout. The 3rd
Ward (which Kennedy had carried in 1960 by 20,000 to
5,000) went for Johnson over Barry Goldwater by 33,525 to
985. The 17th Ward, now virtually black, had gone for

Kennedy 22,000 to 6,500 but said "thank you, Lyndon" with a 26,450 to 1,078 margin. Kennedy's miracle margin in Chicago was 436,000 votes ahead of Nixon, but Johnson left the city with a 670,000-vote lead over Goldwater. Goldwater, not Daley, got most of the credit for Johnson's enormous pluralities in Chicago and everywhere else in the nation. But Kennedy rarely gets the credit for complementing Daley's great effort in 1960.

Kennedy ran better in the suburbs than any Democrat before him. Although it would be three decades before sociologists began to explain the "edge city," the Kennedy strategy in 1960 focused on America's suburbs. Kennedy recognized that in his critical states from New Jersey to Illinois, the Democratic vote in the big cities would be balanced by the Republicans in small towns and rural areas across Pennsylvania, Ohio, Michigan, and Illinois. His chances of making inroads with farmers were not worth the effort, but the suburbs, which held some of the most hostile Republican enclaves, were getting too big to ignore. The 1960 election, the Kennedys knew, would be the first time that the bedroom communities of America were vital. They were just beginning to grow up.

In 1946, when Kennedy took James Michael Curley's seat in Congress, when Daley lost his only election, a contractor who had learned assembly-line construction in the Seabees came home from World War II with an option on a thousand acres of potato farms in Hempstead, Long Island. William Levitt had a dream. He would be the Henry Ford of the housing industry. The housing shortage after World War II was critical. Nothing much had been built during the Depression and virtually nothing at all during the war. The birthrate was up, the veterans were returning to jobs, and people everywhere needed a place to live. In Chicago, 250 old trolleys were sold to people who moved them to vacant lots and lived in them. In 1946, Bill Levitt began to fill the old potato farm with small, cookie-cutter houses that sold for $7,800, less than three times the annual wage of a factory worker. And the suburban housing boom began.[2] About a hundred thousand houses were built throughout the country in 1944. The number jumped to 1.7 million in 1948, most of them in the suburbs. And in Chicago as well as the rest of the country, the people who were moving to them were middle-class Americans, many of them Protestant, many of them Republican, and all of them white.

Kennedy went after them. Not only in Chicago, but in Detroit, Cleveland, Newark, and Philadelphia. He didn't win many, but he chopped down Nixon's margins. In Evergreen Park on the Southwest Side, Kennedy got 5,000 votes compared to Nixon's 6,700. In 1952, Stevenson, the incumbent governor, had gotten only 2,000 votes to Eisenhower's 4,000. The growth in a single decade was apparent in north suburban Skokie, as was Kennedy's personal appeal. In 1952, Skokie had cast 9,000 votes for Eisenhower and 3,000 for Stevenson. In 1960, Kennedy carried Skokie 16,000 to 14,000—a swing of 8,000 votes to the Democratic side in one suburb fueled by the growth that produced a turnout that went from 12,000 in 1952 to 30,000 eight years later. In west suburban Berwyn, a Republican bellwether, Kennedy lost by 2,500 votes. But Stevenson in 1952 had lost by 7,000. Kennedy made few inroads on the staunchly Republican North Shore, but everywhere in the thirty suburban townships of Cook County, he ran better than Stevenson in his good year. (Comparisons with the 1956 landslide give Kennedy even greater gains but are not a fair statistical example.) All in all, JFK gathered 194,725 votes to 297,774 for Nixon in the Cook suburbs, taking a greater percentage of the now more important, growing suburban vote than Truman in 1948.

In the collar counties, Kennedy helped himself even more. Whatever DuPage County Republicans did to stop Kennedy, it wasn't enough. He got 44,197 votes there compared with 101,115 for Nixon—30 percent in the most Republican county in the nation. Truman had gotten only 24 percent in 1948 and Stevenson only 22 percent in 1952. But as Kennedy recognized, it was the growth. In 1948, Truman got 14,000 votes in DuPage. Four years later, Stevenson got 22,000—half JFK's 1960 totals. The gains of 5 and 8 percent over his predecessors would have been insignificant if the populations were stable, but the great suburban growth multiplied Kenendy's totals in the collar counties and elsewhere in the metropolitan suburbs of the East and Midwest. Undoubtedly, the televised debates helped him. And while the suburbs were heavily Protestant, the white flight from the core cities also brought higher percentages of Catholics into many areas. But Kennedy's gains in the suburban Chicago area were as instrumental in clinging to his narrow victory as Daley's precinct captains were in some of the hard-core Republican city wards.

None of that mattered in the Democratic euphoria in the first twenty-four hours after victory in 1960. Attention focused on Illinois because of the mystery, the tradition, and the closeness of the balloting. But if Daley was credited with "stealing" the election, Lyndon Johnson and Sam Rayburn were shortchanged. In Texas, where Johnson's 1948 victory in the U.S. Senate race was more tainted than anything in Chicago history, Kennedy prevailed by 40,000 votes. Although the Nixon loyalists complained for years that a switch of just 5,000 votes in Illinois would have swung the state to their man, there were several other states where the same wishful thinking could have been applied. In New Jersey, where Newark and Jersey City delivered huge majorities for Kennedy, the final victory margin was only 20,000 votes—a shift of a mere 11,000 could have won that state's 16 electoral votes. Montana, not nearly as significant, fell into the Nixon column by less than 5,000 votes. Hawaii was only 100 votes apart until the recount. Kennedy survived Delaware by 2,500 votes. And California was thought to be Kennedy's until all the absentee ballots gave it to Nixon two weeks after election day.

Kennedy's campaign chief, Larry O'Brien, in looking back, thought if anyone deserved credit for pilfering votes for JFK, it might have been Paul Powell's pals. "There was a degree of hanky-panky in Illinois, but I always felt that what-ever it was—and I had no knowledge of it and if it indeed existed—it appeared to be in the southern part of the state because they were very adept at that sort of thing." He also noted that Illinois wasn't as special as it seemed. "It was just a darn close race [nationally]. You could look across the results and Illinois didn't stick out in any sense. You lost a couple here and there by small margins, you won a couple by small margins—more than a couple, it was a very, very close election."[3]

Few people reflected in later days, when Daley had firmly grasped the role of kingmaker, that Kennedy needn't have won Illinois. He couldn't have lost both Illinois and Texas, but he could have lost one of them. Whether or not Daley privately acknowledged it, he owed something to the Sulli-vans, Cermaks, Nashes, Kellys, and Arveys who had birthed and nurtured the machine legend that now made him the most powerful city leader in America.

And he owed it to the news media. Political reporters are the most reactionary of any journalists. They are prisoners of the past. Since Democrats had won on the strength of big-city machines for most of the century, there was no reason to look elsewhere in 1960 to ascertain the roots of the Kennedy triumph. The reporters focused on the few bosses that were left, and Daley's orchestration and loud predictions had many of them ready to dub him the chief power broker before the votes were counted—provided he won. But most of all, it was Jack Kennedy who anointed Daley. Kennedy realized before his first night's sleep in the White House that if anything beyond his own charm and cunning were needed to keep him there for eight years it would be Daley—who if he wasn't really the kingmaker, was certainly the last man left who could claim the title.

And Daley should have given Pat Nixon some credit for his new image. A few weeks after the furor of vote stealing died away, the sad, somewhat bitter wife of the man America would ultimately elect but never love, told a reporter, "If it weren't for an evil, cigar-smoking man in Chicago, Sidney T. Holzman, my husband would have been president of the United States." Holzman laughed.[4]

Kennedy took his crown on January 20, 1961, and gave the nation a New Frontier of programs and a Camelot of style. That evening, at the main inaugural ball at the Washington Armory, ten thousand guests reveled in the presence of the new American royalty. Kennedy left his box and walked over to the table where Daley, Eleanor, and all their children except Richard (who was in the midst of mid-term exams at Providence University) were sitting. "I just want to visit," Kennedy said. He talked a few moments about the inauguration and what an exciting day it had been for him. Daley told him he thought his speech was wonderful and Kennedy asked what was the best part. "When you said, 'Ask not what your country can do for you. Ask what you can do for your country,' " Daley replied. Then Kennedy glanced at the children and asked about each of them. "Why don't you bring them to the White House tomorrow and have a look around?" the new president said. "There'll be a call at your hotel in the morning."

At 9 A.M. Saturday, the telephone rang in the Daley suite at the Sheraton Park Hotel. A White House aide said the president was expecting him at 10:15 A.M. The Daley family arrived on the dot. As they were entering the Oval Office, they met the only person invited to John Kennedy's White House before them—Harry S Truman. Truman and Daley shook hands and the former President invited the mayor and his family to visit his library in Independence, Missouri.

"After Mr. Truman left," the mayor later told John Madigan of *Chicago's American*, "we sat around and talked with the president. We didn't discuss politics or anything like that—it was just an informal get-together." Kennedy signed notes on White House stationery for each of the children and volunteered to give them a tour. "There's President Andrew Jackson's sword," he pointed out to the Daley boys, Michael, John, and William.

"We didn't mention anything connected with politics," Daley said. "At the ball, though, the President did thank me for the help the Democratic Party in Chicago and Illinois gave him. I feel humble and at the same time proud to be shown such a historic place by a man who will add to its wonderful history."[5]

The nation's media took note of the visit. Of all the Democratic leaders in the nation, only Richard J. Daley had been invited to spend part of Kennedy's first day in the White House with the new president. Camelot's king had chosen the first knight for his Round Table.

But the question still lingers in Chicago political klatches. Was the huge vote orchestrated to enthrone Kennedy or destroy Adamowski? One motive involved glory, ambition, power, and passion. The other was about survival.

Ben Adamowski, too, had a spent a long night and day by 6:30 A.M. on November 9, when he emerged from his

state's attorney's office in the county building, the east side
of City Hall. "I will not concede. I will wait for the official
canvass. The way it looks, they have gained a lot of power
and power is corrupt. They are going to have a bigger rug
for Chicago (to sweep the dirt under)." Adamowski had lost
by about 25,000 votes, but he waited another day before
screaming vote fraud. "This is shocking and disgusting," he
said on November 10, announcing he would demand a
recount. The *Chicago Tribune*, not surprisingly, agreed with
him. ". . . the election of November 8 was characterized by
such gross and palpable fraud as to justify the conclusion that
Nixon was deprived of victory."

Adamowski's recount would cost $5 for each paper-ballot
precinct and $2 for each voting-machine canvass. He wanted
5,200 machines in Chicago and 2,100 in the suburbs counted.
The Democrats played a delaying game as they tediously
went through the canvass, and it was December before all the
paper ballots were counted. Nixon had long ago given up,
although he and his supporters claimed for the rest of his life
that they should have had a recount. Daley for one was more
than willing and loudly proclaimed the Democrats would pay
their share. The *Chicago Tribune* ran small boxes on its front
page urging people send $1 or more to the Nixon Recount
Committee—which was really the Adamowski recount committee. In one of the 906 precincts where paper ballots were
used, Nixon reportedly gained 12 votes. On December 2, the
Tribune breathlessly printed a bulletin reporting that Nixon
had gained 1,214 votes after a canvass of the voting machines.
Republicans predicted the paper-ballot canvass would give
him victory. Adamowski supposedly gained 1,614 votes from
the canvass of the machine tallies. By this point, the question was moot for Nixon. Even the end of the long-drawn-
out canvass could only indicate that Adamowski might have

been able to trim 10,000 to 15,000 votes off Ward's lead, not enough to win. Adamowski fought through the courts until the spring and finally gave up.

A final note on the election totals is that 54,599 of the ballots taken in Chicago were not marked for president. Kennedy and Nixon combined drew 1,664,993 votes, but 1,719,592 ballots were taken. It seems remarkable that such adept vote thieves as the Chicago Democrats could have allowed so many ballots to slip through unmarked, since the vote total for the presidential contest has always drawn several hundred thousand more votes than other elections. One explanation is that although many thousands of Chicago voters may have just voted for president and skipped other offices, at least fifty-four thousand skipped the presidential contest. Their major interest on election day may have been the state's attorney's race.

Adamowski spent most of 1961 trying to avoid an indictment immediately threatened by his successor, Daley's blue-ribbon professor, Dan Ward. Ward discovered shortly after taking office that Adamowski had a secret contingency fund of more than a half-million dollars, which he claimed was used for informants and undercover work. That triggered a series of charges about his office using illegal wiretaps. There was no doubt in the minds of the Democratic committeemen that if Adamowski had had another four years in the prosecutor's office he would have inflicted great damage on the organization, whether his motivation was reform, revenge, or ambition. Bennie had a good helping of all three.

But by the time Daley had his personal tour of the White House, the question of vote fraud was well behind him. That year was the pinnacle of his career. His reputation was national. His governor sat in Springfield. His state's attorney would not seat any unfriendly grand juries. His president sat in the White House. He had been re-elected in 1959 by a huge margin over Timothy Sheehan, a valiant Republican who went on to serve briefly but well in Congress and who, like every other GOP mayoral candidate since the Depression, received neither support nor money from the suburban and state Republicans who believed it was futile to spend resources trying to capture City Hall from the Democrats. The newspapers admitted Daley had surprised them with an administration that had none of the trappings of corruption they had feared, although they fretted that his patronage army remained intact and seemed, if possible, to be growing. There were few clouds on his horizon, and 1961 would be filled with speculation about his further ambitions. His power was absolute.

In the meantime, he was continuing to spend and build and tax. He faced a continual protest by the residents of the Harrison-Halsted neighborhood just southwest of the Loop, where he had decided the University of Illinois branch should be located. On April 18, a dummy with a knife stuck in it was tossed into the street outside his house. Daley erupted. "No one is going to threaten me as mayor of Chicago. If I had been there, I would have taken care of them. I'll take care of my duties properly, and if they come back to 3536 (Lowe Avenue), they will be taken care of properly. I don't fear death, either." It was a rare glimpse of the physical nature of Richard J. Daley and it validated the schoolyard stories that he was "pretty good with his fists."

The university site was a simmering controversy that ultimately wound up in the Supreme Court before the old Italian neighborhood centered on Taylor Street was demolished. Daley hadn't really wanted it there. Among his few failures at getting labor or business to do what he deemed necessary for the Great City was his inability to force the railroads to tear down their various stations and consolidate in one location. Had he succeeded, he would have created space south

of the Loop for the university campus. Failing that, a committee chaired by the president of the University of Illinois
chose the alternate site that Daley had decided upon. "The
decision on the Harrison-Halsted site was made by the
trustees and the president of the university. This has been
misrepresented and twisted as though the city had selected
the site," he admonished. The criticism that Daley trampled
neighborhoods at the expense of the central city or to create
some massive building project followed him to his grave.
There was much truth to it. But it is also true that had he
not made some of his decisions, such as the Harrison-Halsted
site, it might have been years before various community leaders, politicians, and civic spokespeople would have combined
to reach a solution on a new inner-city university. Daley's
haste, his initial campaign promise to get things done in a
hurry, often backfired because of his exclusionary methods.
But thanks to him, the University of Illinois at Chicago Circle began classes in 1964. Without Daley's determination,
many minority students and students who could not afford
to go away to school would have had their academic careers
delayed by years.

He spent a lot of time in 1961 appointing committees. In
May, he named David M. Kennedy, chair of Continental Illinois Bank (later appointed secretary of the treasury by
Richard Nixon) to head a new economic committee to stimulate growth of industry and financial business in Chicago.
In August, the Public Buildings Commission, which Daley
headed and had pushed to create as a state senator,
announced a new building bonanza for the city. Daley had
persuaded six banks to lend the city $12 million to finance
the acquisition of the block immediately north of the City
Hall-County Building. There he would build the city's tallest
building, the Civic Center, which would house county offices
and courts and rise 630 feet into the sky. The key banks that

would each lend $4.4 million to Chicago at very favorable rates included, of course, Continental Illinois.

Daley was also holding the usual festivals. A yacht club show on the lakefront was transformed into something called Venetian Night, with entertainment and fireworks. Everyone was invited, from people who owned a yacht to those who once a summer rented a paddleboat. Astronaut Alan Shepard had hardly landed from America's first space voyage before he was handed a telegram from Daley: "Our city would be highly honored if, at the earliest possible date, you and your family will come to us as our guests that we may give visible evidence of the gratitude which is ours for what you have given us." Daley heard that the Mona Lisa was going to be on exhibit in Washington, D.C., and wrote French minister of culture André Malraux that it should also be exhibited in Chicago. Daley probably didn't know any more than the gang at Schaller's Pump why the Mona Lisa was special. But he knew that it was special, and that meant it should be on display in Chicago. It would be the same in future years with the Picasso on the plaza, the Chagall at the bank, and the various Calders around the Federal Building. If they were special, they belonged in Chicago. Daley wanted everyone to see his robust city, his clean streets and lighted alleys and beautiful lakefront parks. And he wanted Chicagoans to see everything.

But 1961, more than anything, was the year of John Kennedy. Daley always seemed to be in Washington that year. He testified before a Senate housing committee in April for Kennedy's bill to provide $3.2 billion over ten years for urban housing. "We will achieve in ten years the Chicago goal of eliminating slum and blight housing from our city." At the same time he boasted of the central business area boom that was erecting twenty-six new buildings valued at $247 million. The remarkable thing about his testimony was that Daley

actually admitted Chicago had slums. His modus operandi
was usually to deny that anything remotely unappealing
existed in Chicago. "Ghettos? There are no ghettos in
Chicago. . . . Syndicate, what crime syndicate? We don't have
those in Chicago. Show me them. Where are they? . . . Bad
schools? Our schools are the finest in the nation."

Daley also testified in May before Bill Dawson's House
governmental affairs committee on Kennedy's proposal for
a new cabinet post for urban affairs. He was immediately
asked whether he was available to fill the new cabinet post.
Daley had no desire to sit in a Washington office shuffling
paper. Besides, the cabinet members earned $25,000 a year
and his job now paid $35,000 plus a no-questions-asked
$65,000 contingency fund for the mayor's office. "The pres-
ident knows my feelings about that and has for some time,"
Daley said.

In early July, Daley went after some defense dollars. He
went to Washington and asked Kennedy to spread some of
the Pentagon contracts around. "Chicago has long been a
great electronic center and has great scientific talent in our
great universities." Kennedy promised to help. In late July,
at the U.S. Conference of Mayors gathering in Washington,
Daley asked for an easing of tax rules on municipal bonds.

On each of these trips he managed a quick visit to the
White House to see his favorite president. Meanwhile,
Kennedy was the main speaker at the Cook County Democratic fund-raising dinner in April. He praised Daley and,
knowing his man, heaped lavish praise on Chicago.

In May, Daley hosted the grand duchess of Luxembourg,
who was touring the United States. A few days earlier she had
been a White House guest and Kennedy invited some friends
to meet her: Mayor Robert Wagner of New York; Peter
Crotty, the Democratic boss of Buffalo; and Daley. But Daley
was invited to sleep over. Only a dozen or so people were

invited to stay in the White House each year. On April 30, after the state dinner for the grand duchess, Daley and his wife moved from the Statler Hilton to the White House. Dick slept in the Lincoln Room and Sis slept across the hall in the Queen's Room. The next morning they had breakfast with the president and Jackie.

Just a kid from the stockyards.

In September, Kennedy began filling federal judicial spots around the country. After eight years of a Republican White House, the Democrats were getting some plums. Daley's problem was that independent Paul Douglas was the senior senator and had his own choices. Daley put an old friend, Roger Kiley, on the U.S. Court of Appeals and gave a U.S. District Court spot to Richard Austin, chief of the criminal courts. Douglas appointed James Parsons to be the first black judge ever to receive a permanent appointment to the federal courts, along with Hubert Will, a liberal attorney and staunch supporter of Adlai Stevenson. These would not have been Daley choices.

The fifth opening was left dangling and Jake Arvey became the point man for the nomination of Abraham Marovitz, his protege from the 24th Ward. Daley insisted throughout the discussions that he had nothing to do with the selections. He insisted he did not confer with Douglas or talk to Kennedy. Marovitz, his old pal from Springfield legislative days, had served in the Marine Corps and carried on a continual correspondence with Daley, who used his influence to make sure Marovitz got his state senate seat back after the war. Marovitz gave Daley the oath of office six times, starting with his first inauguration in 1955. But Richard Daley knew nothing about Jake Arvey's efforts to put Abe Marovitz on the U.S. District Court, where he still serves thirty-four years later. Picking judges was just one of the perks of being mayor. He liked to pick everything, although sometimes there were too many people who had to be told no.

When Newt Minow finished his term in Washington with the FCC, he returned to his Chicago law practice and Daley invited him to lunch. Always on the lookout for someone with a clean image who had demonstrated Democratic loyalties, Daley asked, "Do you want to be governor or U.S. Senator?" Minow said he wasn't interested in running for office. "I would really like though to be a delegate to the convention in 1964," he said. "Oh, no, not that," Daley replied. "Everyone wants to be a delegate." Six months before the 1964 convention, a friend telephoned Minow to say he'd seen in the newspaper that Minow had been selected as an alternate for the Atlantic City conclave. "I never mentioned it to him again, but he never forgot anything," Minow recalled.

As 1961 came to an end, Daley unveiled the largest city budget in history: $567 million, five times his first budget. The independents screamed that the document was filled with "enormous wads of fat" and could have been cut by $40 million. They urged people to fill City Hall for the public hearing in protest. A number of neighborhood groups made plans to do that. Daley railed against the minority aldermen's report, calling it "a vicious smear on the character of thousands of men and women employed by the city government. It [contains] unsubstantiated conclusions, quarter-truths, and distortions." Of the planned protest, he demanded, "Why weren't they in Springfield when we had a dynamic program before the legislature? Certainly everyone is opposed to taxes, but what do these people propose?"

Daley had been trying without success to get the legislature to increase the sales tax by a half-cent for the city of Chicago. Without that needed revenue, property taxes kept increasing. One of his first maneuvers as mayor in 1955 had been to get his longtime friend and law partner, William J.

Lynch, then state senate minority leader, to engineer a deal that gave Chicago home rule powers to increase property taxes and remove the ceiling on the rates municipalities could levy. That move had enabled him to keep raising taxes to get the revenues he needed for all his building and housekeeping chores. Chicagoans were pleased that the streets were staying clean, the police were usually there when you needed them, and the city was well lighted. But there was a limit on how much they would keep paying. Nonetheless, the budget passed and Daley got ready for the New Year and one of his favorite pastimes—slatemaking.

Richard J. Daley didn't always back losers, but he could do it in a pinch. The only mystery is whether he did it on purpose. It was that way almost from the beginning. In his very first election, Daley had to kick his running mate off the ticket because of a scandal. His first choice for governor was dumped after a scandal. His next choice was probably the only Democrat in the state who couldn't have won. He discarded incumbents who could win again in favor of candidates who would never be heard from again. He mixed up ethnicity and blue-ribbon eccentricity to the point that when he finally slated reformers, they were beaten by traditionalists. And when he backed party hacks, they were beaten by reformers. Not always, of course, and rarely in elections that Daley had to win.

Nothing that Richard Daley did attracted as much attention, analysis, and conspiratorial conjecture as the slating of candidates. If by the 1960s the presidential selection process had been somewhat opened to the masses, the matter of selecting local and state candidates in Chicago was still a matter of arcane intrigue. It was the slatemaking ritual as much as anything that led to comparisons between Richard Daley's City Hall and the Kremlin. With reporters jammed against closed doors at the Morrison or the Sherman House or the

LaSalle Hotel, the public caught only scant phrases or whispers of what the politburo was deciding in the inner sanctum.

The press knew many of the rules and took great pains to explain them. The first was balance. There had to be geographic, ethnic, and religious balance. The most important jobs were reserved for the Irish. From the birth of the machine in 1930 to Daley's death in 1976, all the people endorsed by the party for mayor and county assessor were Irish. The city clerk was always Polish, the recorder of deeds could be German or Scandinavian, the city treasurer might be Polish or Jewish. Jews could have a spot on either the city or the county ticket. Italians were usually rewarded with a disproportionate share of the judicial openings. In the early years, blacks got handouts. But in the 1970s they began to appear on city and state tickets.

One of the imperatives of picking the state ticket (until the times and Daley changed it) was that downstate had to have equal representation. This made sense when the population was evenly split between Chicago and the other 101 counties, but as the population shifted, the downstate Democrats realized they were on the short end of an argument. The remaining vestige of this "balance" was in the case of the U.S. Senate. If Chicago held one Senate seat, then the opportunity for the other should be given to a downstater. Republicans, too, followed this axiom.

Those were the rules, and the media prattled on about them. But no one ever really understood Daley's rules. Aside from the now-heroic proportions of the 1960 elections and his own amazing streak of six mayoral victories, the Democratic organization under Daley had, at best, a mediocre batting average.

Aside from 1960, he won the governor's office only once, and that was in the Democratic landslide of 1964. Aside from

1960, he didn't win a U.S. Senate race until he persuaded Adlai Stevenson III to run for the vacancy caused by Everett Dirksen's death. He lost the vital state's attorney post in 1956, the sheriff's office in 1962, the county board presidency in 1966, the sheriff's office again in 1966 and 1970, and the state's attorney again in 1972 and 1976. Granted, he controlled the state's attorney post and the county board for most of his reign, but since Republicans were so scarce in Chicago by the 1960s and since the Republican leadership rarely invested either talent or money in Cook County affairs, many of these triumphs came by default.

In all of the Democratic losses for major offices, Daley's decisions about the candidates raise interesting questions. In almost every case, there were others available who surely would have done better, who were better known, were better financed, had better backgrounds, would have campaigned more effectively. Daley had to consider reasons other than victory—unless his remarkable political instincts, which worked so well in dominating local rivals and exploiting every success of Chicago to his own advantage, somehow disappeared when he sat down alone to choose candidates.

One obvious reason is that there were some jobs Daley didn't want to give to other Democrats. The first of them was the governor's office. Daley had seen how the power of the party dissipated in 1948 when Stevenson was governor, Kennelly was mayor, and Arvey was chairman. They shared patronage, and even more important, the public perception of who led the Democrats. While Daley was consolidating his strength in the 1950s and early 1960s, he did not need nor want a Democratic governor rivaling him for party power. Republicans did just the opposite. While they have controlled the governor's mansion for forty-four of the last fifty-six years, they have shown absolutely no interest in mounting a real challenge in the Chicago mayoral election. They have been equally uninterested in the Cook County presidency, for the same reason.

Daley also managed his resources wisely. He always knew what the chances were of winning a particular office. When he decided he couldn't win, he sometimes used the endorsement as a hollow reward but surrounded it with so much bluster and apparent support that neither the honoree nor his political supporters or ethnic backers perceived that they all had been had. Even when the candidates did suspect they were being used, Daley could puff up their ambitions and convince them that the party needed them.

He also believed people owed the party and somebody had to be on the ballot. His choice of Cecil Partee to run against incumbent Attorney General William Scott in 1976 filled the ticket's need for a black candidate, although it was a suicide mission. Running Roman Pucinski, a congressman, against Senator Charles Percy in 1972 had been prompted by the expectation that Senator Edmund Muskie of Maine would be the party's presidential candidate and Pucinski would benefit from a huge Polish turnout for Muskie. Even for Daley, the best-laid plans sometimes went astray. These were times when deserving fellows had to be sacrificed for the good of the party and for Daley.

There were times when undeserving fellows had to be rewarded for the same reasons. Daley had seen how Arvey had decided Paul Douglas's election to the U.S. Senate would be perceived by the ward leaders as a blessing that sent him nine hundred miles away from City Hall. The only real value a U.S. Senator had was the selection of federal judges and his proximity to the president. By 1960, Daley had learned how obstinate Douglas could be about federal appointments. His own proximity to John Kennedy and later Lyndon Johnson further diminished the value of a Senate spot.

Sometimes Daley won by losing. In 1968, Richard Ogilvie's victory in the gubernatorial election required his resignation as county board president—and the spot was promptly filled by a Daley loyalist.

And sometimes Daley was just wrong. He was, despite what so many Chicagoans thought, not politically infallible.

Daley's early slatemaking sessions drew mixed reviews. In his first year as party chairman, he was cautious, with Kennelly still as mayor and the Nash-Duffy combine still ambitious. There wasn't much to decide. Paul Douglas was up for re-election and there were no state races of any consequence. The party needed someone to reclaim the sheriff's office, which Arvey had bungled in 1950. So Daley found Joseph Lohman in the halls of academia, where he would often find absolution for his machine. Frank Keenan, the 49th Ward alderman and potential enemy, had the votes to be slated for assessor. And Daley winced as the South Side Irish pushed the nomination of Dan Ryan for county board president. Daley, of course, was slated again for county clerk. Since Republicans usually get bored in off years it was a Democratic landslide. The chairman's first election was a big success, although he wasn't very happy with Keenan's or Ryan's victory.

The second Eisenhower landslide would have made 1956 difficult for any Democratic slatemaker, but Daley made it impossible—perhaps in more ways than one. Republican Governor William Stratton was bidding for a second term. Just as the Democratic convention was beginning in Chicago, the newspapers were full of reports that Orville Hodge, the Republican state auditor and one of the most popular politicians in the state, had helped himself to about $2 million of the people's money. One reason for Hodge's popularity was that he never saw a tab he didn't pick up. Hodge's parties at his Springfield lakefront home were popular with politicians

and newsmen. On his frequent forays to Chicago, he was a
Rush Street habitue in the days and nights when Rush Street
epitomized the "toddling town." From Fritzel's in the Loop
to the Empire Room at the Palmer House to the Walnut
Room in the Bismarck, Orville Hodge was a party animal.

Stratton's own party was depressed about his chances,
even when Daley ignored such well-known vote getters as former secretary of state Eddie Barrett and such big names as
Sargent Shriver, head of the school board, and Stephen
Mitchell, the Democratic National Chairman who had run
Stevenson's first campaign. Daley chose to put up against
Stratton Herbert Paschen, the first-term county treasurer
from Winnetka, who was completely unknown throughout
the state and not much better known in Cook County. This
might have been an instance when Daley just turned out to
be wrong. He had tried unsuccessfully to find a blue-ribbon
candidate. Earlier in the year, he and Stevenson tried to persuade highly respected state Supreme Court Justice Walter V.
Schaefer to take the governor's nomination. Schaefer said no.
To "balance" the ticket, Daley gave the downstaters State
Representative Richard Stengel of Rock Island as the candidate against Senator Everett Dirksen.

He rejected former Senator Scott Lucas, who had arrived
at the Morrison Hotel with overwhelming downstate support. Daley ran a vanguard of labor leaders before the
slatemakers opposing Lucas, who noted wryly that he had
won all labor endorsements when he was defeated for re-
election in 1950. Lucas left the slatemaking session and
declared, "This is my swan song." He added he would
"always be curious about the real reason that Daley opposed"
his bid for a last chance. Paul Powell claimed that rejecting
Lucas would cost the ticket 100,000 votes downstate. He was
right.

Daley also ran the three Cook County incumbents for
state's attorney, clerk, and recorder of deeds. Even with vir-

tual unknowns such as Stengel and Paschen at the top of the
ticket, it didn't look too bad. And when the Hodge scandal
broke, it looked even better.

Then, in the midst of the 1956 Democratic convention,
the "flowerpot" scandal broke in Paschen's office. The country treasurer had a fund to which office workers "contributed" to buy flowers for sick and the dead, but Paschen
had used it for a trip to Europe and other personal matters.
Daley stonewalled any suggestion that Paschen would be
dumped during the convention. He was too busy trying to
snare the vice presidential nomination for Kennedy. He
brushed aside reporters with the challenge, "What are the
facts?" A week later he dumped Paschen.

Now Mitchell, a constant critic of the machine and its
implicitly corrupt slatemaking motives, tried again to be
endorsed for governor. There was a suggestion to switch
Chicago lawyer James O'Keefe from the attorney general
spot into the gubernatorial vacancy. At least, some argued,
O'Keefe had been campaigning around the state for six
months and had gotten some name recognition. Sheriff
Joseph Lohman, who had earned a high reputation in his
brief period in office, was also available. But they weren't in
the claque that hung around the Morrison Hotel on election
nights. Richard Austin was.

Austin, a respected judge who headed criminal courts,
was as anonymous as anyone Daley could have chosen. With
six weeks left in the election campaign, Austin hardly had
time to get signs printed or buttons made. Eisenhower carried the state by 800,000 votes and wiped out the Democrats
everywhere. Only Eddie Barrett survived re-election to
county clerk. The Republicans won all the state offices, state's
attorney, and recorder of deeds. Austin, however, ran only
36,000 votes behind Stratton, a margin that raised suspicions
that Daley and Stratton had made a deal, as the downstaters
had charged during the late weeks of the campaign.

The rumors were so public that Daley went to a party rally October 9 in Springfield. "I defy anyone to point to any betrayal in the history of the Cook County Democratic organization," he shouted. "And if you look on the shield of the Daley clan in Ireland you will find the words 'loyalty' and 'faithfulness.'" He pounded the table in the ballroom of the St. Nicholas Hotel and glasses shattered on the floor.

Nevertheless, the Austin vote totals suggest that if all the members of the Democratic organization were loyal, some of them had not been very enthusiastic. In the four black Dawson wards and the river wards, where Daley had run up a plurality of nearly 125,000 votes in his mayoral victory in April 1955, Austin got a plurality of only 95,000 votes—despite the fact that 25,000 more votes were cast in those wards in the 1956 general election. Similar shortfalls occurred in other wards. It is wise to remember that the election of the governor had nothing to do with their jobs, while Daley's election did. Still, the numbers suggest that Austin was right to be bitter about what had befallen him. Although he was rewarded later with one of those spots on the federal bench that Daley dispensed through his good friend Jack Kennedy, Austin remained hostile to the Democratic Party forever.

In 1958, the Republicans were really in trouble, with Eisenhower winding up his presidency and the voters sending one last message to the Republican Party. Daley won everything, although there wasn't much to deal with. Joseph Lohman, having polished the image of the sheriff's office, was handed the state treasurer's spot. The entire county ticket won, with Frank Sain replacing Lohman in the sheriff's office for the party. The victory Daley most relished in 1958 was in the primary. Incumbent assessor Frank Keenan, having been dumped as expected for his support of Kennelly, lost to Daley's man, P. J. Cullerton, who won in the fall.

In 1960, Daley was not interested in sub-rosa intrigue. He wanted to win everything because he wanted to elect a president and get rid of Adamowski. County Judge Otto Kerner was capable and posed no threat. Dan Ward had impeccable credentials, and Paul Douglas was going to lead the ticket. There wasn't much tinkering for Daley.

But 1962 was going to be a problem. The story of how and why Sidney Yates wound up running against Everett Dirksen is a truly twisted tale with many players. Dirksen had become Senate minority leader, a quiet supporter of the New Frontier and a crony of Lyndon Johnson. Yates was a seven-term congressman. In 1961 there was no indication that Yates wanted to run against Dirksen or that anyone wanted him. Paul Powell, now the speaker of the Illinois House, announced in 1961 that he was interested in taking on fellow downstater Dirksen. State Representative Paul Simon, a boyish, bright liberal with a bow tie, was already jousting at windmills and was precociously ready to do battle with Dirksen. And Adlai Stevenson was the ambassador to the United Nations, where he was a constant annoyance to the Kennedy inner circle, often charting a course of diplomacy for America that seemed to diverge from Secretary of State Dean Rusk's. Besides, Kennedy was never quite comfortable with Stevenson after the latter's refusal to recognize the inevitable during the 1960 convention.

Then there was Arnold Maremont. As Mike Royko described him in *Boss*, Maremont was a wealthy liberal who had raised money for the party, campaigned for a $150-million bond issue to revitalize mental health facilities in the state, and dreamed of going to the U.S. Senate. He went to Daley, who told him he wasn't sure if downstate county chairmen would support a Jew. He suggested that Maremont tour the state and gave him the blessing that everyone from presidential hopeful to aldermanic wannabe got: "I'm sure you'd make a fine candidate. Go out and line up your support, then come back to see me." Maremont thought he was on his way to the Potomac, but for the time being he hustled through southern and central and western Illinois, telling everyone he saw he was a Jew and wanted to be U.S. Senator. No one punched him in the face, so he called Daley often to tell him a Jew would be no problem on the ticket.

Meanwhile, the whole question of what Adlai Stevenson should do with his future (a question that had troubled Stevenson all his privileged and gifted life) was looming. On December 1, 1961, Alderman Thomas Keane announced, "We want Stevenson to run." Newt Minow reported to Kennedy confidant Arthur Schlesinger that Daley wanted Stevenson to run.

The next day, Stevenson went to see Kennedy and raised the possibility that he might run against Dirksen in 1962. Kennedy later told an aide, "I told Adlai that he would be even more frustrated as a junior senator that he is in the UN. . . . I told him we needed him in the UN and that I counted on him to stay on. . . . I don't understand that man and I never have understood him."[6]

On December 2, Walter Trohan of the *Chicago Tribune* wrote, "While [politicians] recognized it is good strategy to use the White House as a sounding board for any candidacy for office, they wondered if Stevenson is being eased out of his top diplomatic post by some adroit maneuvering between Daley and the President. Observers do not believe he [Daley] would propose a senate seat to the UN ambassador unless he had consulted with the White House."

Stevenson wrote to a friend, "I have decided to withstand the blandishments of Dick Daley, Jack Arvey, et al. and decided to stick with this ship . . . ."

Kennedy seemed not to know anything about a scheme to get Stevenson out of the UN post. If he did, he failed to give Stevenson the final shove. In fact, he gave Stevenson permission to issue a statement saying the president needed him too badly at the UN for him to consider the senate race. Did

Daley really want Stevenson, or had someone put him up to it? There were reports that Joe Kennedy had telephoned Daley and said he wanted Stevenson out. Since the patriarch of the Kennedy family often acted in what he thought was the best interest of his son, that is possible. How badly did Daley want Stevenson? Well, it may have been a way to absolve some of the guilt he felt for not being able to throw the drowning Stevenson even a token life preserver in Los Angeles. But the fact that Tom Keane, of all people, was sent out to declare, "We want Stevenson," suggests the offer was sincere. At any rate, some of Stevenson's friends were relieved when he declined, for they thought Dirksen would whip him in an election.

The moment Paul Powell heard about Daley's interest in Stevenson, his senatorial ambitions abated. "If Daley wants Stevenson, that's all there is to it. I wouldn't go unless Daley was for me. Daley didn't want him for president. I can't figure it out." Neither could anyone else. Powell had been heartily endorsed by Daley in May when he threw his hat into the ring, but the canny downstater knew those public utterances meant nothing. Paul Simon also said he was out of it if Stevenson was in, and was dismissed forthwith. With no star candidate available, Daley began leaking word about Sid Yates. Royko speculated that Maremont's meandering through Illinois gave Daley the idea that a Jew would be a good candidate. Besides, Yates wasn't the right kind of guy to head the Illinois congressional delegation. Danny Rostenkowski was much more suited to the job.

With Stevenson out of the picture, the question remained: How badly did either the White House or Daley want to defeat Dirksen? Shortly before Kennedy was scheduled to make a campaign visit for Yates in October 1962, he called Ken O'Donnell to join him and the vice president in the Oval Office. O'Donnell said later, "The vice president delivered an impassioned speech on what a disaster it would be for the administration if Dirksen was defeated in Illinois and we had to deal with Tom Kuchel of California, who would become Senate minority leader." O'Donnell told the president it would be quite a coup to knock off Dirksen. "Johnson glared at me. Kennedy laughed and said, 'This is one time when Lyndon is right and you're wrong, but I've got a commitment to go to Chicago and help Yates.' "[7]

That commitment came right in the middle of the Cuban missile crisis. It illuminated just where Richard Daley stood in the world political order.

Kennedy advisors were arguing over the possibility of invading Cuba, launching an air strike against missile sites, or declaring an embargo—all of which risked Soviet retaliation and a possible nuclear war. Kennedy was scheduled to speak at the Democratic dinner on October 19 at McCormick Place. In the midst of gathering with his top aides, he asked O'Donnell, "Did you call off the trip to Chicago yet?" O'Donnell replied, "I don't want to be the one who has to tell Dick Daley you're not going there."

Kennedy didn't want to do it, either. So he went. Rostenkowski insisted later that Daley was sincere in supporting Yates, regardless of what Kennedy and Johnson may have felt. He recalled that Kennedy returned to Washington the next morning because of the missile crisis. "Before Kennedy left, Daley told him, 'Whatever you do, don't you involve Everett Dirksen in this thing.' But Dirksen was cagey. He called a National Guard jet (in Peoria) and flies to O'Hare to get on Kennedy's plane and he makes a speech. 'As far as my reelection is concerned, the campaign is over. My president beckons me in Washington. I am returning to serve.' I looked over at Sid Yates and said, 'Adios, Sid.' Well, Daley is just furious, furious. He called either Kenny O'Donnell, or Kennedy, I think Kennedy, and the president said, 'I had nothing to do with it.' But Daley was mad."[8]

In January 1962, Daley gathered the slatemaking committee at the Morrison. Over the years, the committee had
kept growing. Daley's response to criticism of small, secret
groups of slatemakers choosing candidates was to have big,
secret groups of slatemakers. From a dozen committee members in 1952, he had enlarged it so that forty-eight of the
eighty county committeemen were on the slatemaking panel.
Since they waited for him to tell them who was going to be
picked, he might as well have had the full committee meet.
In fact, he did that in 1968.

When they opened the doors to the Democratic office on
January 9, 1962, Sid Yates was headed for battle with Everett
Dirksen. By the fall, the party faithful began to acknowledge
they had another loser. In fairness, 1962 was the Republicans'
turn to make some gains in an off-year election with a Democrat in the White House. In October, radio station WIND
reported that Daley had written off Yates and was instruct-
ing the committeemen to concentrate on the local ticket,
which included Assessor Cullerton. Daley was incensed.
"The story was a contemptible lie. It's politics. I called the
radio station and told them!"

The *Tribune* reported that in some wards the Democrats
were explaining to normally straight-ticket voters how they
could split their ballots for Dirksen. Yates lost by 140,000
votes and Daley's latest sheriff's choice, Roswell Spencer,
blew the office to an eager young Republican prosecutor,
Richard B. Ogilvie. Daley went hitless in 1962.

And he was running short of cash. The Republican
majority in the legislature had refused for two straight years
to give Daley the half-cent sales tax increase he wanted for
municipalities. GOP leaders boxed him in in 1961 by offering
to provide an increased sales tax for Chicago only, but Daley
was forced to reject that proposal because city residents
might wonder why they were being taxed more heavily than
all their suburban neighbors. He again raised the issue of a

state income tax, not by saying he was for it, but by reminding the news media that he had tried to get one approved in
1939. The legislature's action left him nowhere to go to pay
for all the new projects and city employee pay increases he
was granting to placate his good friends in the labor unions.
Daley put another bond issue referendum for $66 million on
the 1962 ballot. It included $22 million earmarked for low-
income housing. The referendum was swamped. Real estate
taxes had to rise again.

There were even rumors that Daley was being squeezed
in his party. Seymour Simon, a former alderman who had
been appointed to the county board, was being pushed to
succeed John Duffy as president of the board. Duffy, Daley's
old enemy, had died in July 1962, and the newspapers
reported Simon was Tom Keane's favorite for the patronage-
glutted office. Daley was supposedly for Cullerton. But, the
newspapers speculated, that would leave Keane free to push
his brother, George, a member of the Board of Tax Appeals,
into the assessor's office. It seemed Keane was bound to win
one way or the other and raise his bargaining power with the
chairman considerably. The only problem was none of it was
true. Keane, Simon said, had forthrightly told him that his
choice for board president was State Senator Don O'Brien.
After Simon got the plum, O'Brien got—what else—a judgeship. Simon also said he thought Daley had him appointed
to curry favor with Jewish voters in anticipation of the 1963
mayoral election. Daley was aware that many Jews, especially
along the lakefront, were liberal and vulnerable to the growing noises that the bulk of the big spending was going to
finance Daley's dreams for the central city, noises that had
been responsible for bond-issue defeat.

The biggest noise was from Ben Adamowski. Still pout-
ing over his 1960 defeat, Adamowski announced in September he would run for mayor as a Republican. In most places

other than Chicago, the forum for his declaration would have been odd. Ever since Dan Ward had defeated Adamowski in 1960, the state's attorney had been investigating the $490,000 contingency fund Adamowski had used. In response to a request for a conference with an assistant state's attorney, Adamowski mailed an eleven-page reply insisting that the investigation was a "political witch hunt" and that it would interfere with his plans to run for mayor.

Daley was Daley. "It's everybody's privilege to run for office. He was a candidate before."

The Republicans were wary of accepting Adamowski again, but they believed the threat that he would run in the primary with or without their support, so they gave it grudgingly. He declared, "Beating Daley is no problem—the problem is getting the votes counted."

The Republicans had just gone through another disappointing election. Despite Dirksen's victory and Ogilvie's capture of the sheriff's office, the Democrats retained all the other local posts in the face of what had been heralded as a "tax revolt." The *Tribune* blamed the Democratic resurgence on President Kennedy's October 22 speech demanding that Soviet Premier Nikita Khrushchev remove his missiles from Cuba.

But Daley was running again and running scared. Adamowski was getting no more financial or organizational support from Republican leaders than Tim Sheehan had gotten four years earlier. The black vote was solidly for Daley and it was growing. There was not the slightest hint of any unrest in the organization. But Chicago still had almost as many Polish-Americans as African-Americans, and Adamowski had an ethnic base larger than any other candidate ever would have against Daley.

But the black vote exceeded all hopes on April 2, 1963. Daley won comfortably. It would have been rated overwhelming except that public expectations for Daley were now rivaling his own. The final score was 679,497 to 540,816. The Dawson wards cranked out a 70,000-vote majority. The river wards, starting to dip in population and grow in blackness, added another 57,000, and Daley's 11th tacked on another 11,000. Combined, the ten wards equaled his victory margin of 138,000. He got more black than white votes. Adamowski carried nineteen wards, all of them heavily Polish or Eastern European except the 19th, which remained an Irish thorn in Daley's side.

Arvey's old 24th was under even more scrutiny than usual. The black population of the ward had grown to the point where Irwin Horowitz, who had succeeded Arthur Elrod as committeeman, felt compelled to install a black man, Benjamin Lewis, as the alderman. Lewis was reportedly on the payroll of the crime syndicate, which since the Capone era had bought or mortgaged most of the river ward politicians. Either Lewis was planning to vote Republican or he displeased the mobsters. He was found a few days before the election sitting in his office, handcuffed to a chair and filled with bullets. The 24th Ward residents were not too shocked to make it to the polls. There were 968 votes for Adamowski and 17,429 for Daley.

Mrs. Daley told reporters on election night she was willing to have her husband serve the people four more years.

There were other things to praise in Chicago. Loyola University won the NCAA basketball championship, which pleased Daley. The Republicans passed a bill capping the city's property tax rate (which had nearly doubled in Daley's first two terms), and that didn't please him. His friend Governor Otto Kerner vetoed the tax ceiling bill. The Daleys took a trip to Hawaii. Dick was named one of the ten best-dressed men in America by his tailor. The Miami Fishing Association gave him a citation for his "outstanding catch" of a 9-pound, 10-ounce mackerel in February. He played a little golf in Palm Springs with Parky Cullerton and law partner Bill Lynch. He had already opened the new South Side expressway (called the Dan Ryan after his former nemesis). He ordered a study of Soldier Field to see if it could be converted for baseball and football. In the fall of 1963, Daley spent a little more time than usual at the Morrison Hotel because, like Thanksgiving, the autumn ritual of slatemaking was at hand. He was having lunch in his office with several committeemen when his secretary, Mary Mullen, opened the door. She was crying. John F. Kennedy had been killed.

CHAPTER 7

"Hello Lyndon, Well Hello Lyndon"

DICK DALEY BURST INTO TEARS AT THE NEWS OF KENNEDY'S assassination. It was not the last time he would cry for the Kennedy family. But within days of the burial he had to transfer his loyalty and his needs to a new president, a new Democrat in the White House who would offer him the most incredible relationship the Oval Office ever nurtured with a big-city political ruler.

On November 24, two days after he was sworn in aboard Air Force One in Dallas, Lyndon Johnson telephoned Daley from the White House. It was the first of hundreds of telephone calls, letters, and visits between the garrulous Texan and the precipitate Daley.[1] Johnson, having suffered three years of exclusion by the Kennedy inner circle and his own demons of an impoverished childhood and lackluster education, would run his presidency as though he were still trying to be elected head of the student body at San Marcos Teachers College. He spread an incredible number of personal memos filled with the most lavish praise for almost anyone who seemed capable of helping him run the country. But Dick Daley became special. Perhaps Johnson felt he could

somehow equal the spell his dead predecessor had cast over
the political landscape by cultivating the friendship of the
Chicago mayor whom Kennedy had proclaimed the savior of
the 1960 election.

"Johnson was in awe of Dick Daley," said Larry O'Brien,
who had been a close Kennedy aide, a confidant of Johnson,
Postmaster General, and then National Democratic Party
chairman. "Jack Kennedy could understand Dick Daley.
They had a relationship. It was a natural evolvement [sic] in
the political context. Daley could deliver. Daley expected in
return to be duly recognized. But with Lyndon Johnson, a
telephone call from Daley was about as important a phone
call as he could receive."[2]

Johnson wanted to cultivate Daley for his political power,
which Johnson would need in 1964 and beyond. The new
president knew that as the Democratic Party leader, he would
receive that support without question from a dedicated pro-
fessional such as Daley. But he also needed Daley's help to
get the Illinois congressional delegation on board for the
sweeping legislation that Johnson was planning to propose.

"Daley was critical to the success of the Great Society,"
said Joseph Califano, domestic advisor in the Johnson White
House. "A call to Daley was all that was necessary to deliver
the 14 votes of the Illinois delegation."[3] Johnson wanted
more. He wanted to share with Daley the confidences of a
fellow politician, the problems of a president. He wanted
Daley to regard him with the same affection Kennedy seemed
to draw from so many hardened professionals.

Of course, Johnson wanted this from almost everyone.
But by 1964 there weren't many Democrats left who had the
raw political power that Daley still held in both numbers and
reputation. The New York Democrats were splintered into
factions. Dave Lawrence was turning over Pennsylvania to
Joe Barr in Pittsburgh and Bill Green in Philadelphia. Pat
Brown couldn't hold anything together in California. Daley's

normal peers, the governors of states like New York, Pennsylvania, California, Ohio, and New Jersey, were Republicans.

Johnson had labor and he had Texas, but when he looked around the country, he saw Daley as the symbol of the kind of political power he had practiced, understood, and admired. Daley was Irish, like the Kennedys. But he had not gone to Harvard. He was not rich and cultured in the playful way the Kennedys made their affluence charming. Daley was like Johnson. He had started at the bottom and worked hard for everything. Johnson also had his own myth of the northern big cities and the men who ran them. In Texas, winning elections was easy after the first one. There were no Republicans in the Texas where Lyndon Johnson connived his way into Congress and then the U.S. Senate. But people like Daley had to first eliminate all the Democrats clawing at them, then do battle with Republicans and win more than they lost to survive.

Lyndon Johnson made his first presidential appearance before a joint session of Congress on November 27. Dick Daley was invited to sit with Lady Bird for the speech. He and Eleanor had paid their respects to the new president in the White House on the day of Kennedy's funeral. Daley said the sadness of the occasion precluded any political talk.

But the two men would get down to business shortly. On December 3, House Speaker John McCormack telephoned Daley.

McCormack: Dick, John McCormack.

Daley: How are you, John?

McCormack: Dick, on this cotton bill, this is really a bill to help the American cotton industry, it's essentially a business bill—

Daley: I'm opposed to those business bills—we get too many of them, we ought to start getting some Democratic bills.

McCormack: Well, this is a Democratic bill 'cause it's four or five hundred thousand employees—

Daley: Those fellas would be all right if they support any part of our civil rights program or the tax bill, but they won't vote for anything and then not have a commitment back from them. We been doing too much of that. We lost the depressed area [bill] by one or two, which is something to help the northern cities. I don't think we as Democrats can support anything unless there's some kind of an agreement. If there is, that's all right. If there isn't—

McCormack: Well, I'm satisfied we can get the area development bill through in January—

Daley: I don't know about that. But I know and so do you if they can defeat that, let them defeat it, but if we have no agreement on civil rights or on the tax bill or on any of these other Democratic measures that Kennedy or Johnson—Mr. Speaker—then we're making a mistake.

McCormack: Here's the problem, Dick. You don't want to start President Johnson's administration out with a defeat—

Daley: I hope he's not for this bill as the first bill in his administration. This isn't a bill for all the American people. It's for one section of the country.

McCormack: No, it's the east, south, and west, this is a bill which affects everybody. There's four or five hundred thousand employees and most of them are Democrats—

Daley: John, we wouldn't be for it unless you can say there's an agreement on one of these other programs from the gentlemen from the south. Our fellows—

McCormack: No, I couldn't say that—

Daley: Our fellows will not vote for it.

McCormack: Dick, I think you're making a mistake.

Daley: We might be. We all make mistakes. But I think it's about time we find out where we stand on the Kennedy-Johnson programs. If this is a part of the president's program and he tells me that, that's a different thing—

McCormack: Well—

Daley: —I hope he wouldn't start out with a bill like this as a part of his program. I hope we would get something that means something to all the people of America.

McCormack: It's a part of the program. The late president brought it up at two or three of the leaders' meetings prior to his assassination. That was on his agenda, the cotton bill—

Daley: I'd like to see it in its entirety and the only thing— I don't know how you operate down there but surely if you're operating—and this bill is to help certain interests—and it is—then there must be some road back from those same people that are interested in it and we all know who's interested in it, and if there isn't, then there's no purpose in voting on it and voting for it.

McCormack: You've got the bill committed and it's coming up and if it's defeated it'd be a hell of a shattering blow—

Daley: Well, that's all right.

McCormack: I know, but you don't want to take—

Daley: Surely be a more shattering blow if we pass it and then along comes a part of the program on civil rights or something—

McCormack: On civil rights we've got to employ the discharge petition method—

Daley: You can employ more than that. What the hell—

McCormack: How? How? Tell me, Dick, how?

Daley: On this very bill if they're interested in it, and we all know the interest of them, certainly there must be some of them on the Rules Committee that you can discharge the bill and get it out on the floor. This is the most dramatic thing to do for our party and for Lyndon Johnson and for Kennedy. Do it before you vote on this bill.

McCormack: Well, you've got five Democratic votes on the Rules Committee and you've got to have three Republicans and they won't give their votes at the present time. Not until January.

Daley: Well, if we get the five Democrats we'll be all right, won't we?

McCormack: We've got to have eight votes.

Daley: I'm sure you can get the eight votes.

McCormack: It isn't just as easy as that—

Daley: I think, John, sometimes you're better off to try and lose than not to try because then—

McCormack: We're trying the discharge petition. I've come out in favor of it, which is unusual for a Speaker to do. Now, Dick, I can assure you, it'd be a mistake—if—if we get the votes now—

Daley: We all make mistakes. If it's a mistake, let it be a mistake. I'm not concerned about—we make a lot of mistakes. I think it's about time we stand up as Democrats and try to do something. I think this prolonged session down there is a disgrace to everyone, including the Congress—

McCormack: There's no control over that—

Daley: There should be some way—

McCormack: It's very easy to sit back and say that. If you were down here, you'd realize the difficulties—

Daley: I'm out here not sitting back, I'm working every day in the interest—

McCormack: Oh, I know that—

Daley: —of the Democratic party—

McCormack: I know that—

Daley: —and a lot of other people—

McCormack: I know that but—

Daley: —people, right and left, but on this one, John, I think our fellows'll just pass it.

McCormack: See, what I was talking about was the rules and so forth, the parliamentary situation—

Daley: I know that, they've been arguing that for years. But parliamentary or any other way, there's ways and means of taking care of it, parliamentary, if there's a determined effort to do it. And whether we win or not in the Rules Committee, the thing [the civil rights bill] should have been out and tested a long time ago.

McCormack: There's certain factors in connection with that too. Now Dick, I wish you'd get a hold of the members and go along on this bill.

Daley: I'll think it over.

McCormack: Listen, you know there's nobody—you know there's nobody—hell, who the hell did more for your water diversion than John McCormack and who went through—I stood right outside the door there as they were coming in, the members, lining them up, and you're my friends no matter what you do and I'll continue that way, do everything I possibly can, and I always have and I always will.

Daley: Fine, John.

McCormack: Now, wait a minute.

Daley: We'll think it over.

McCormack: Wait a minute, here's the president. Wait a minute, Dick.

Johnson: Dick?

Daley: Yes?

Johnson: Lyndon Johnson.

Daley: Mr. President, how are you?

Johnson: Fine, Dick. We just finished a leadership meeting. This cotton bill, I don't know anything about it, I haven't seen it, but—

Daley: I just told McCormack if it's your bill, that's one thing, but—

Johnson: No, here's the situation—

Daley: I don't like the idea of us having no commitments on some of this other legislation—

Johnson: Here's the situation—

Daley: —you were a leader in the Senate and—

Johnson: Here's the situation, Dick. I don't think it'll do a hell of a lot of harm or good one way or the other if it passes. If it don't, it'll do a hell of a lot of harm. Now, let me tell you what the picture is. This bill affects a half million workers and primarily the textile manufacturers. They call it a cotton bill, but it tries to give our domestic textile people a fair shake against the Japanese, who get our cotton so much cheaper. They have the votes to pass it. President Kennedy talked to them several times and they announced they were going to bring it up, take it up, before his death, they got it all set—

Daley: All I want to know, Mr. President, is are you for it?

Johnson: Yessir.

Daley: Okay.

Johnson: Thank you, Dick. God bless you.

This six-minute conversation explains everything about politics in America. It is a most remarkable conversation on several levels, all of them pointing to the power and knowledge that Johnson and Daley and people like them wielded so effectively. It is also ironic that before the scattering of urban unrest that sputtered in 1964 in Harlem, Philadelphia, and other East Coast cities, before the blazing of Watts in 1965 and the burning of Detroit in 1967, before Martin Luther King's death and the resulting fires on the West Side of Chicago, Daley was facing down the Speaker of the United States, demanding a civil rights bill.

The conversation began in the Oval Office and Lyndon Johnson could have made short work of lining up Daley. Even in his first days as president, he knew the loyalty he could command from the mayor of Chicago. He also knew that he didn't want to start his administration by owing a big chip to the mayor of Chicago, so he ordered McCormack to get Daley on board.

McCormack, a member of Congress since 1928 and speaker since 1962, was trying to prove to his president that he could effectively round up votes for a bill the president wanted. McCormack's problem was that on the other end of the line, Daley understood all this, too. McCormack's cajoling, his reminder of the debt Daley owed him on the diversion of Lake Michigan water (which the city ultimately sold at handsome profits to nearby suburbs), and his plea for empathy with all the parliamentary shackles binding him did no good.

Daley's rejoinders on procedure show he clearly understood how Congress worked. All those years in the legislature had not been wasted. He knew exactly who wanted the cotton bill and knew they were the same members who had prevented Kennedy from bringing a civil rights bill to the floor for three years. His cavalier rebuttal to the possible embarrassment of the president on his first bill was painful for McCormack but clearly calculated to put the person who wanted the legislation passed in the position of having to ask for it. When a worn-out McCormack finally handed the telephone to Johnson, Daley wasted no time in making it clear what should be done and that his support was solely based on loyalty to his president.

"Daley was smart enough to hold back until he talked to the top dog, and then when he would want something from the top dog he got it," explained Dan Rostenkowski, who had become leader of the Illinois delegation and was privy to the Johnson-Daley relationship.[4]

In a thank-you note to Daley dated December 13, 1963, LBJ wrote that he was "grateful for the good judgment that was demonstrated by all concerned."

Daley's first lengthy visit to Lyndon Johnson's White House was on July 10, 1964, for a two-hour lunch. He told reporters they discussed "politics." That was during the period in which Johnson was most troubled by the dilemma of Robert F. Kennedy, who was being boosted for the vice presidential nomination at the Democratic convention in August. Johnson and Kennedy disliked each other, but the new president couldn't figure out how to dump the attorney general without destroying his support from such Kennedy loyalists as Daley.

Daley had dinner with Kennedy in Chicago on July 20 and the next day telephoned Johnson. He also had meetings with Hubert Humphrey and Eugene McCarthy, the two Minnesota senators hoping to be tapped for vice president. He telephoned Johnson with further reports on July 25 and July 29. McCarthy became another among the legions who thought the simple phrase "you'd make a fine candidate" was an endorsement. He told reporters Daley indicated he was "partial to me." Daley said he had said no such thing.

Undoubtedly the subject of the vice presidency came up during the lunch with Johnson and again on August 5, 1964, when Daley was in Washington on one of his many visits to testify in support of Johnson's Great Society programs. He arrived with aides Earl Bush and Ray Simon and was accompanied by Rostenkowski. Johnson told an aide, "Tell Mrs. Johnson that Mayor Daley and two or three of his assistants are here and they'll need separate rooms. I'd like for them to have dinner with me at 8 or 8:30 P.M. and I'd want them to stay all night if that's all right."

"The president wanted me to stay that night," Rostenkowski recalled, "but I said I had to go home and he told me to return the next morning. When I got there I was sent upstairs to the private quarters. There was the president in his bed clothes sitting in bed with a bunch of papers, and Daley, starched collar and tie, listening as Johnson was showing him three TV sets—one for each network. That was something in 1964. You didn't see that. We stayed about fifteen minutes and Johnson—still in his pajamas—had his arm about Daley and said he'll join us downstairs."[5]

But being invited into the President's bedroom hadn't erased all of Daley's fondness for the memory of JFK. "I remember when we first got to his room, Daley said, 'How about a beer?' I called the steward, who said they had no beer. But they had Chivas Regal, which Daley liked. I can remember Daley sitting on this high bed with legs dangling, muttering, 'When Jack Kennedy was here, they had beer.' He was trying to say everything was better with Kennedy," Rostenkowski recalled.

"I know Daley always had this Irish-Catholic thing with Jack Kennedy, but I don't think he ever had the relationship with Kennedy that he had with Johnson. And I don't think Daley realized how special it was. I think he took it for granted that everyone could get through to the president or get invited to the White House every time he came to town," Rostenkowski said. "I know Kennedy invited Daley to the White House on the day of his inauguration, but I don't know how many times he went there after that. I know he spent several nights at the White House with Johnson."

Daley had most of his children with him on a May 9, 1967, overnight visit during which Johnson spent time walking in the Rose Garden with young Richard. But Daley made more than twenty trips to the White House for dinner, lunch, or breakfast during the Johnson years.[6] His treatment was very special.

There is no record of what Daley advised Johnson about his vice presidential dilemma, but a few days after the luncheon visit, Johnson issued a statement excluding his entire cabinet from consideration. It was a charade that all of Washington understood. Robert Kennedy remarked, "I took a lot of good fellows with me."

A few weeks after Daley's bedroom chat, the Democrats convened in Atlantic City for the 1964 convention, which would routinely anoint Johnson and, most speculated, confirm his choice of Hubert Humphrey as his running mate. But Johnson's streak of surliness and his indulgence in the rawness of his power kept Humphrey twisting for several days. Even as reporters were saying that the Minnesotan had been invited to accompany the president to the convention on Air Force One, Johnson hurriedly added Senators Edmund Muskie of Maine and Thomas Dodd of Connecticut to the special flight, extending Humphrey's anguish. No one, not even Daley, who had several telephone conversations with Johnson from Atlantic City, knew the final choice.

Daley had been asked to make one of the seconding speeches for Johnson. So even though the 1964 convention was perhaps the dullest since 1936, it had a little something special for him. Party kingpins weren't needed much at conventions where a sitting president was unopposed for nomination, but it was still important to pay them homage. It was also a rare occasion for one of Daley's top lieutenants to provide a lesson in one-upmanship.

"On the second night of the convention," Rostenkowski recalled, "I got a message to go and see Walter Jenkins, who was the president's closest advisor. I had to go through security to some office underneath the platform, and when I got there Jenkins told me the president wanted me to make a seconding speech for his vice presidential nominee and that he was on the telephone. I told Johnson I'd be delighted and he hung up. Then I left the room and went past all the security again and I realized he hadn't told me who the hell he picked. I had to get back through the security and ask Jenkins. 'Didn't he tell you?' I said no and Jenkins didn't want to tell me and I said, 'Look, I've got to write a speech.' So he told me it was Humphrey. I went back to the delegation and sat down next to Daley and said, 'I'm making a seconding speech for the vice president.' He said that was a nice honor for a young man and he asked what I was going to say. I said, oh, the usual thing, great guy and all that. I knew he didn't know who it was, and I wasn't going to tell him unless he asked me. So I stood up and said, 'Well, I better start working on my speech,' and I started walking away. 'Come back here,' he growled. 'Who is it?' he asked. So I told him and left."[7]

About the only excitement at the convention that year was the debate over seating the Mississippi delegation which was being challenged by the Mississippi Freedom delegation, which took its name from the Freedom Riders then working to desegregate the South and register Negroes to vote. Daley played a small role in arguing that the regular delegation should be seated. He orchestrated the unanimous vote of the Illinois caucus vote by getting Alderman Ralph Metcalfe, a black man and Dawson's protege, to make the argument. While the civil rights group had the sympathy of northern-

ers repulsed by recent racial violence in the South, it had
been self-appointed and had no real basis for demanding credentials. The only argument was whether to kick out the regulars. Illinois supported a compromise, and Daley later
received thanks from the White House.

He also used a new phrase, one that was becoming familiar in America, in his nominating speech for Johnson. "We
have heard much about the backlash. Let us expose the word
for what it means. The choice in this election is not whether
we shall go to the right or to the left but rather shall we go
forward or backward. . . . Forward—urbanization can be the
rich end-product of a democratic civilization, nourished by
diversification and opportunity. The backlash is conformity
and blight that can pit one class against another, and one
group against another. . . . The civil rights bill seeks to estab-
lish equality of citizenship for all Americans. The backlash
is a denial of the birthright of American citizenship, a denial
of human dignity."

It was a political speech, surely intended to contrast with
the perceived elitism of the Barry Goldwater ticket nominated by the Republicans three weeks earlier. But it also res-
onated, for those who listened, with the theme that was
already dominating the nation. That theme was present in the
convention hall in the form of the Mississippi protest group.
It was on the minds of Americans who had watched with
shame the excavation of three young bodies near Philadelphia, Mississippi, where they had been murdered June 21 for
registering voters. Television gave extensive coverage to the
slayings. It mentioned in passing the same week that a new
general, William Westmoreland, had been given command of
American troops in Vietnam. Race, not war, was on American minds in 1964.

But the Daley family and the president were disappointed
that Daley's speech was not carried by network television.

The president wrote: "Dear Dick, There were too many happy experiences for me from Atlantic City to single out anything as unhappy. But I am still sorry that the networks failed to carry your seconding speech—I wanted so much to listen. This does not detract from my great and lasting appreciation of your role. I am and shall always be proud—and I want you to know I am grateful."

Robert Kennedy attended an Illinois delegation luncheon the morning following Daley's speech and said, "I don't know of any closer friend of my brother than Mayor Daley." But Lyndon Johnson was his president now, and Daley never wavered in loyalty to the office. That evening Kennedy led a nostalgic, sad tribute to his slain brother, quoting from *Romeo and Juliet* and receiving a tremendous ovation. Daley was asked if he thought the convention would rather have had Kennedy than Humphrey. "I thought the ovation was directed toward the late president." Asked about RFK's chances of winning a Senate seat in New York, Daley was kinder. "I know nothing about New York. However, inasmuch as his name is Kennedy, I'm sure he'll do quite well."

Daley also thought, as usual, that he would do well. He predicted Johnson would carry Illinois by 250,000 votes. He was reminded he had predicted a 500,000-vote triumph for Kennedy that turned out to be about 492,000 votes shy of his forecast. This time, it turned out, he was too cautious. Lyndon Johnson carried Illinois by nearly 900,000 votes, eclipsing the great Roosevelt margins of 1936. Daley and the Democrats won every office on the ballot, including secretary of state, where Paul Powell finally got a chance to run statewide and won easily.

And the black vote continued to grow in Chicago. With the passage in July of the 1964 Civil Rights Bill, Johnson's pluralities in Chicago's black wards were astronomical. They were swelled by a new state law allowing speedy registration of recent residents. In signing the law, Kerner estimated that 200,000 Negroes in Chicago would benefit from the law. He didn't have to say that Daley would benefit. That continuing influx of migrants from Mississippi had pushed the black population of the city past one million. More than half of them voted, and Johnson got more than 90 percent of their vote. Daley gave Johnson a plurality of 675,000, more than half of it from black voters. In the 20th Ward, one of the original three black enclaves, Johnson got 35,000 votes to 800 for Goldwater. No one cried vote fraud. It didn't hurt Daley's ego a bit that Johnson came for the traditional torchlight parade and declared, "Mayor Daley is the greatest politician in the country."

Daley spent a great deal of time in Washington in 1964. While other cities were going through the early pain of the civil rights movement, Chicago was relatively tranquil. The black community had formed various groups to protest school policies, in particular the administration of schools superintendent Benjamin Willis, but Daley granted audiences and kept a public arm's length from the Board of Education, which bore the brunt of the hostility. But a new politics was emerging, a personal and threatening kind of politics. The Coordinating Council of Community Organizations (CCCO), an umbrella group of various neighborhood organizations led by Al Raby, had sponsored school boycotts to urge the ouster of Willis and speedy integration of the public schools. The Congress of Racial Equality (CORE) had a Chicago chapter that was picketing City Hall because of its inactivity on slum housing. One protestor politely left a package at Daley's reception desk. It was a plastic bag that contained a dead rat.

Daley had given his views of backlash in his Democratic convention speech, and in his mind he was right. The Chicago white community had made very little response to the black protest efforts because as yet they posed no threat.

They were being dealt with appropriately by City Hall. The protesters were politely urged to go away. The political and sociological forecasts of backlash never appeared in 1964 because of Goldwater's extremist campaign. In what must be perceived by modern standards as a highly noble gesture, Goldwater had requested a meeting with Johnson where both men pledged to keep the simmering racial issue out of the 1964 campaign. Johnson, running way ahead in every poll, had no reason to use it. Goldwater may have been tempted, but in losing the biggest landslide in presidential history he retained his integrity. He never appealed to the blue-collar white community that only a few months later would provide the kind of backlash that Daley said wasn't there.

Meanwhile, Daley was testifying for the poverty program, the housing program, the transportation program, the bills that would become the Model Cities program and the Head Start program, and the many urban renewal programs that would come out of the new cabinet agency and the huge education dollars that were waiting in the Department of Health, Education and Welfare (HEW). It was perceived by the White House that Daley really didn't care much for what went on in Congress, but the president repeatedly asked for his testimony and expertise and after a while it dawned on Johnson's aides that Daley did care.

"When Mayor Daley came and testified on the poverty bill . . . he indicated it would work a little differently in Chicago. But everything was different in Chicago. The plus was that Mayor Daley testified. He was not in the habit of coming to Washington and testifying. He really wasn't that interested in Congress," Larry O'Brien said.[8]

O'Brien and others misunderstood. Daley was very interested in getting federal dollars for Chicago. He asked for $140 million in poverty funds, $60 million in HEW money for schools, and untold millions for urban renewal. And, as

O'Brien noted, it would be handled differently in Chicago. The poverty programs were designed to involve community leadership, but Daley decided he would pick the leaders. The man who he picked to head the poverty program, Dr. Deton Brooks, produced an excellent record. But Daley could never convince the black community of his sincerity because he would never share control of the federal dollars. That was inevitable. There was no way Daley could relinquish that kind of power. Black leaders viewed his refusal to share power as either more of the old paternalistic plantation mentality or an intellectual racism that held that blacks had no experience with such complicated matters as federal funding and city administration. It was a little of both, but it wasn't entirely racial. Daley always believed he could administer whatever was needed for the city better than anyone else, whether they were black, white, red, or brown.

More avowed opponents charged that Daley was simply using federal monies to expand his patronage in new areas of high-priced positions and six-figure contracts. Daley admitted the latter. "What's wrong with a Democratic committeeman sending a capable man or woman when the test is on the person's qualifications and not who sends him?" He shared power only when it was essential or beneficial, not as a matter of etiquette.

In late 1964, Daley became the father of the bride when his daughter Mary Carol married Dr. Richard Vanecko. Daley discussed his new son-in-law's qualifications: "I'm told he's a fine doctor and a fine surgeon. From his conversation and the issues he's interested in, I'm sure he's a Democrat."

On December 7, the Daleys visited the White House for a state reception in honor of British prime minister Harold Wilson. They received Christmas greetings from the White House and an invitation to sit with the Johnson family at the inaugural ball. On Pennsylvania Avenue and Lowe Avenue, it was a fine beginning for 1965.

Daley was corresponding regularly with his new best friend, Lyndon Johnson. There were lots of letters recommending people for jobs and ambassadorships and commissions—which seemed only fair, since in one of their first correspondences Johnson, then Senate majority leader, had written to Daley in 1957 seeking a spot on the Sanitary District for a young engineer he knew.[9] Many of their 1965 meetings dealt with the growing civil rights problem. Johnson appeared in Chicago for various political events and Daley visited the White House for private talks.

On February 22, Daley cut the ribbons at the University of Illinois–Chicago Circle campus, finally ending the long siege of protests (though the scissors did not cut out the bitterness, which the Taylor Street neighborhood would harbor for years). But 1965 would be the first of the "long, hot summers" of the Sixties. In July, Watts burned down. There were thirty-four deaths, nine hundred injuries, and $40 million in damages. In New York, Malcolm X was murdered. Groups such as the Student Nonviolent Coordinating Committee (SNCC), the Deacons for Defense, and the Black Panthers were beginning to ignore the nonviolent preachings of Martin Luther King and his Southern Christian Leadership Conference (SCLC). They were chanting, "Burn, baby, burn." Negroes were demanding to be called black, and whites found out they were now being called "honkies."

In Chicago, the demands of African-Americans for a piece of the action grew uglier. Pickets marched constantly in front of Daley's house. Comedian Dick Gregory was there so frequently he was almost a houseguest—except when he was being arrested. Demands for Willis's ouster grew angrier. Even outsiders, for the first time, took a critical look at the way Dick Daley was running Chicago. Representative Adam Clayton Powell of New York said, "Mayor Daley has managed to completely evade the intent of Congress, ignore the poor, and set up little political fiefdoms run by machine bosses. . . . There is little minimum feasible participation of the poor and maximum participation of the politicians." Whitney Young, Jr., of the National Urban League warned that Daley was cultivating "fertile soil for a man of Reverend Martin Luther King's talents."

On June 20, a massive rally was held at City Hall demanding Willis's job. Police arrested 228 people, including, Raby, James Farmer of CORE, Syd Finley of the Chicago chapter of the National Association for the Advancement of Colored People (NAACP), and Gregory. The march organizers refused to post bail. Many of those arrested told police their names were Mayor Daley or Ben Willis. After Gregory finally signed his $100 bond, he promised that on Monday he would ask every sympathetic person to "turn on their faucets and leave them on, because it's going to be a long, hot summer and we're going to make it even hotter."

Ironically, it was a trio of firefighters who made things very hot for Daley that season. On the night of August 12, a black woman, twenty-three-year-old Dessie Mae Williams, was standing on the corner of Pulaski and Wilcox streets on the West Side when a hook-and-ladder unit struck a parking sign that fell and crushed her head. Three nights of rioting, rock throwing, and some looting followed. Eighty people were injured and 169 arrested. In terms of what had occurred in Watts a few weeks earlier, it was a minor flare-up, but Daley put the National Guard on alert. After the West Side quieted down, he met with members of twenty community organizations and decided the issue was not civil rights. "It was a question of lawlessness and hooliganism."

Daley, although publicly confident and defiant, was privately shaken by the pickets, the protests, and the West Side violence. On August 11, Larry O'Brien had written a memo to the president:

"Congressman Rostenkowski is most concerned about Mayor Daley's current problems and their effect on the mayor personally. Danny would like to have a few minutes of your time to discuss this with you—his thoughts are that the Mayor could be invited to the signing of the Urban Department bill and perhaps you could have an assignment for him to take him out of the country for a week or two. In any event it would be a good touch at this point to have Dan drop by in view of the problems the members of the delegation have had with some recent legislation—caused to a great extent by the Chicago civil rights situation."

Daley did go to the White House on September 13 for the Department of Housing and Urban Development (HUD) bill signing. By that time the situation had eased. Raby and other black leaders decided the city was on edge and called off any further school protest marches. Some of the energy of the protests was dying out, and besides, there were new plans to deal with Richard Daley. On October 3, Martin Luther King, Jr., announced that in 1966 he and the civil rights movement would live in Chicago.

Nothing better illustrated Daley's influence in the White House than the events of early October involving the Elementary and Secondary Education Act, which Congress had passed in September with a $1 billion appropriation for low-income areas. The bill was Johnson's payoff to the 5,000 southern and border state school districts he wanted in compliance with the Civil Rights Act ordering desegregation. Joseph Califano and Commissioner of Education Francis Keppel were ordered to bring those districts into compliance. Califano wrote, "Johnson's objective was to desegregate, not cut off funds. He talked to me several times each day about ideas to spur compliance and gave me the names of politicians, educators, labor and business leaders across the south to call."[10] Keppel said, "[Johnson] damn near drove me crazy."[11] Particularly disturbing to Johnson were the thirty-nine Texas districts that had not desegregated. He twisted arms and called on old friends, and by Labor Day he had succeeded in bringing the recalcitrant south to the table of civil rights with $1 billion waiting in gratitude.

"In late September," Califano said, "as we were patting ourselves on the back, the first confrontation under the 1964 Civil Rights Act came unexpectedly from a city in the North."[12]

Chicago had qualified for a $32-million grant. Keppel and HEW Secretary John Gardner understood Johnson's goal to be desegregation and were committed to it. Al Raby of the CCCO had filed a complaint with HEW suggesting that Chicago schools superintendent Willis was planning to use some of the $32 million in high-income neighborhood schools. On October 1, Keppel wrote to Illinois School Superintendent Ray Page and to Willis, notifying both that the federal disbursement would be deferred until an investigation showed that Chicago had complied with the civil rights order desegregating schools. Keppel notified Douglas Cater, the White House aide for HEW, but no one had notified Lyndon Johnson—or Richard Daley.

On October 3, Johnson went to New York to meet with Pope Paul VI, making his first American visit. When Johnson arrived at UN Ambassador Arthur Goldberg's suite in the Waldorf Towers, he found Daley waiting. According to Irving Bernstein, "Daley battered Johnson with outrage and though a devout Catholic, kept the pope waiting ten minutes. The president offered no defense whatever. He said that he would look into the matter immediately."[13]

Califano recalled that Johnson then went to meet with the pope, who was accompanied by his longtime aide, Monsignor Paul Marcinkus of Chicago. The pope praised the president's efforts in support of education for poor children. Johnson was pleased but then blurted, "That's the work I want to do, your Holiness . . . but they're trying to stop me. One of my own cabinet members wants to shut off funds for poor children in one our largest cities, Chicago, run by a fine Catholic mayor. Your Monsignor comes from Chicago; he'll tell you what a fine mayor Richard Daley is."[14]

Cater had prepared a memo for Johnson: "You have instructed HEW to keep Mayor Daley fully informed in advance on any future action they take. You are determined that Daley not be caught by surprise. . . . Sarge Shriver reports that Daley has never liked Willis. It's ironic [Daley] is being saddled with this problem. The Chicago school board is totally independent of the mayor. [Shriver] points out that Superintendent Willis is an able but intransigent man. He has never worked positively on the segregation problem."[15]

Whether Cater was simply telling the president what he now wanted to hear, or whether Shriver was inflating the power of the school board (which he had headed in the 1950s), it is doubtful that Johnson was so naive as to believe anything in Chicago acted "independently" of the mayor. Johnson didn't need the memo anyway. Chicago got its money immediately, and several heads rolled in Washington. Johnson was furious that his subordinates had dared to offend Daley. No matter that his civil rights legislation was the first priority of his administration and would be one of his proudest legacies, no matter that he had badgered HEW, his staff, and Democrats all over the South. Richard Daley came first.

Daley spent much of the next two years trolling Congress for poverty and housing funds, appearing before many committees to testify about the needs of the cities. But he really didn't need much congressional help.

Rostenkowski noted, "He never had to ask me. He had a direct line to the White House, to Marv Watson, Valenti, O'Brien. He got what he wanted." Watson and Jack Valenti, Johnson's top domestic advisers, along with O'Brien had become the key conduits between the president and Daley.

In 1966, his use of $25 million in antipoverty funds came under fire again. Representative Charles Goodell, a Republican from New York, said, "I am against feeding the political machine in Chicago with poverty money." But Barnard Boutin, deputy director of the Office of Economic Opportunity, praised Daley. "We could argue about methods, but the fact is Mayor Daley is really running an outstanding program. It is the best in the country."

Daley stopped in at the White House in March 1966 on his way to telling Congress that Chicago needed a big piece of the $2.3-billion urban renewal program proposed by Johnson. Daley said it wasn't enough. Seeking to have Chicago chosen as a demonstration city for the program, Daley was asked how much the city alone would need. "I would be talking in terms of a billion and a half to two billion dollars," he told a subcommittee of the House Banking Committee.

Fernand St Germain, a Rhode Island Democrat, exclaimed, "You've done so much, you're already a demonstration city, a model for the whole country."

"Modesty prevents me from answering," shrugged Daley, who already sensed that Congress felt Chicago had no need of additional federal dollars. He quickly added, "There remains much to be done in ridding our communities of blight."

In April, the General Services Administration announced it would delay indefinitely a $45-million construction plan for a new forty-five-story federal building, citing the president's request to cut spending wherever possible.

Daley said, "We want that building." He had lunch with Johnson, and the funds were disbursed. The building stands today on the block bounded by Dearborn, Adams, Clark, and Jackson streets.

In December 1966, Califano called Daley. Then he informed the president about the progress of Daley's various requests.

To: President

From: Joe Califano

I read this to Daley.

Set out below are the HUD projects for Chicago about
to be approved or under review.

1. Approved but not announced
   - $1.3 million neighborhood facilities grant
2. Can be approved in next several weeks
   - $45,000 open-space grant
   - $500,000 urban beautification grant
   - $550,000 for two mass transit grants
   - $3.75 million grant to Loyola University for
     college housing
3. Negotiations under way with the city
   - $10–$15 million in urban renewal. Projects
     stressing rehab and low-income housing.
4. Requests received—will be reviewed promptly
   - $380,000 for two open-space projects
   - $45 million for two urban mass transit grants
   - $115,000 for two water sewer projects.[16]

O'Brien explained Daley's success simply. "Daley was a
Buddha. You could sit and talk with Daley and his voice level
wouldn't alter. The communication would be somewhat limited because he would speak in brief sentences. He could
express his position in about three sentences, no more than
necessary. He was truly a boss, and you'd better believe it."[17]

Califano's telephone call was a $65-million Christmas
present. Besides that, Daley got a card and White House pictures. Johnson was widely known for being churlish and even
cruel to associates and subordinates. But he also loved to send
things. He was constantly sending the Daley family pictures.
On July 19, 1966, he wrote:

Dear Dick,

Photographs have a way of preserving cheerful valuable moments. I hope you will feel that this little album
does just that. It is sent with my enduring affection and
respect.

In October, he asked a secretary to send another batch
of pictures to Daley. She sent him back a memo listing the
nine dates on which she had sent Daley pictures. Johnson
scrawled "okay" on her memo. The one word seems somehow to convey his disappointment that more pictures were
not needed.

Daley was just as solicitous as the White House file shows.
On October 9, 1965 after having gall-bladder surgery,
Johnson wrote:

Dear Dick:

Your telegram and your message to the people of
Chicago touched me deeply. I have come through a brief
time when I had nowhere else to go but to my knees to
pray to God. The knowledge that strong and loyal friends
like you were also offering your prayers has helped sustain me and restore me. Lady Bird and I are grateful to
you. Whenever you are needed you are always here.
Thank you, my good friend.

On October 23, 1965, he wrote:

Dear Dick:

You have been so kind all through the days I have
been in the hospital. Jack Valenti has told me of your daily
calls and I could not let another hour go by without telling
you how much I appreciate your enduring loyalty and
your warm friendship.[18]

On December 21, 1965:

Dear Dick and Mrs. Daley,

At this Christmastime, Lady Bird and I wanted you to know we were thinking of you. We hope that you will like the two-volume set of the *Public Papers of the Presidents*. May God bless you and your family.

Lyndon Johnson.[19]

CHAPTER 8

"We Shall Overcome"

IF THE EVENTS OF 1968 HAD OCCURRED IN ANY DECADE OTHER than the Sixties, 1966 would be indelible in the minds of Chicagoans. It wasn't exactly tranquil anywhere else in the country, either. In 1966, there were mass murders that chilled cities and tornadoes that eliminated them. There were heart transplants that fascinated a wealthy nation already wondering how to live long enough to enjoy its prosperity. There was still civil war in a dozen new African countries and a civil war in Southeast Asia, although the White House wasn't calling it that.

Young Americans were questioning the war, the draft, love, marriage, children. New singles housing complexes began to appear. Singles bars replaced the "Happy Hour" cocktail parlors on Michigan Avenue. In February, the Senate approved $4.8 billion to fight the Vietnam War. In March, the Defense Department announced there were 235,000 U.S. forces in Vietnam. In April, the cover of *Time* magazine asked, "Is God Dead?" On July 1, 1966 the first eligible recipients of Medicare checked into hospitals. Cook County Hospital reported bed occupancy was below normal. Medicare, it appeared, would not have much of an impact. The U.S. military increased its bombings of North Vietnam, calling the carpet barrages of the huge B-52s "rolling thunder." In November, the Roman Catholic Church abolished its mandatory rule against eating meat on Fridays (affirming, some thought, the *Time* cover).

James Meredith, who had broken the racial barrier at the University of Mississippi, led a march from Memphis to Jackson to prove that Negroes were no longer afraid to demand their rights in the South. On June 6 he was struck to the ground by a blast of birdshot, and black leaders from everywhere descended on Mississippi to take up his crusade. But they were no longer in agreement. Martin Luther King's nonviolent posture still had the support of the traditional Negro groups; the NAACP and the Urban League. But a new brand of black activist was preaching a different gospel. Willie Ricks, a member of SNCC (called "Snick"), spoke in Yazoo City, Mississippi, on a hot June night. The twenty-three-year-old Ricks, sometimes called "Reverend" for his rhetoric, excoriated the evils whites had perpetrated on Negroes. Several times he shouted, "Black Power!" A few days later in Greenwood, Mississippi, halfway point of the Meredith march, SNCC leader Stokely Carmichael was arrested for erecting tents for the marchers without city permission. After seven hours in jail, he emerged, stood on the back of a flatbed truck, and shouted, "We want black power. We want black power. . . . It's time we stand up and take over. . . . From now on, when they ask you what you want, you know what to tell them. What do you want?"[1]

"Black Power!" the crowd yelled, and their voices were heard in every American city where Negroes lived in inadequate housing and attended inferior schools and were employed at the lowest end of the job market. A short time earlier many blacks, Black Muslims in particular, had been preaching, "Black is beautiful," a phrase from Harlem Renaissance poet Langston Hughes. White America was a little jumpy about that. But black power unsettled even black America. NAACP leader Roy Wilkins said black power "is the father of hate and the mother of violence."

King called it an appeal to racial pride but continued plans for nonviolent demonstrations in support of open housing and integrated schools. King had won the civil rights war in Montgomery and Selma. In 1966, he picked a northern battlefield: Chicago.

The anti-Willis protestors and the advance guard of King's SCLC had been active through the spring. Marchers with signs in Chicago's Loop, never seen before, had suddenly become commonplace. King had been in and out of Chicago for months, attacking Daley's poverty program, schools, and housing programs. In January he rented with great fanfare a $90-a-month apartment in Lawndale (though he stayed in a Michigan Avenue hotel). By July of 1966, he was ready for a full-scale nonviolent war. King staged a rally July 10 at Soldier Field. He hoped for 100,000 supporters; not quite half that many showed up, but it was impressive. Daley was not happy when King said, "This day we must decide to fill up the jails of Chicago, if necessary, in order to end the slums." They marched from the lakefront stadium to City Hall, where King and Raby taped a list of demands to the main door. They were surrounded by a crowd carrying signs that read, "End Modern Slavery—Destroy Daley Machine." As they marched they sang movement songs and chanted "Daley must go!"

Many young priests and nuns were in their midst, and Chicagoans expressed shock and disappointment that Catholic clergy would be involved in street demonstrations. But John Cardinal Cody, who had been appointed archbishop the previous year, had a record of vigorous liberalism and civil rights advocacy. In his previous assignment in New Orleans, he had actually excommunicated public officials who refused to segregate schools.

Daley had been oddly restrained in his comments on King's constant criticisms. King had begun to ruffle Daley as early as May 1963, when he told a Freedom Festival Rally at McCormick Place—with Daley on the speakers' platform—"Chicago is just as much a segregated city as Birmingham, Alabama." On July 1, 1963, Daley spoke to the NAACP annual convention and got that usually placid group angry by declaring, "Chicago has no ghettos. There are Negroes living in some bad housing, but we are trying to correct this as quickly as we can." He blamed the housing dilemma on the failure of voters in 1962 to approve his $66-million bond issue, which included $22 million for housing renewal.

Three days later, on the Fourth of July, Daley marched with the NAACP for an hour through the Loop to Grant Park, where he was asked to make some welcoming remarks to a crowd of twenty thousand. They booed him off the stage. Never had Richard Daley been subjected to that kind of embarrassment in the city he had ruled for eight years. Yes, there had been boos from the group protesting his University of Illinois site selection, and there were boos from independents and Republicans at some campaign events. But here were twenty thousand Negroes denouncing a man who believed he was their best hope for a better way of life. Only a month earlier he had won an election by getting more black votes than white votes. He had thought Negroes understood what he was doing for them.

Daley was awed by King, but he understood that the man had a following, he had support. As Daley always cautioned political hopefuls from Jack Kennedy to the latest aldermanic dreamer, "Go out and get your support, then come back and see me." Daley had watched as thousands followed King to the Pettus Bridge in Selma. Still proclaiming the wonders of improved housing and jobs for blacks during his tenure, Daley agreed to a City Hall meeting with King and his entourage in July 1966. Daley was extinguishing the fire with unusual courtesy.

The meeting, however, was not unlike an interview the author had with Daley that same summer. After each question, Daley would turn to press secretary Earl Bush and say, "Didn't we talk about that in Washington, Earl?" Bush would sort through a huge stack of paper and produce a copy of something written by an aide. The next question would produce, "I think we addressed that in the speech to the builders." And Bush would quickly finger through the pile. In an hour, Daley never directly answered one question. The reporter left with a huge mound of speeches but no story.

It was the same with King. "We are addressing that. Why don't you help us with that? We'd be glad to look at that," Daley kept saying. At one point, King wondered if Daley realized how many people in Chicago went to bed hungry. Never breaking stride, Daley turned to an aide and ordered, "Get their names." It's no wonder that after the meeting King expressed his dissatisfaction to reporters and promised that many more marches would take place. Daley had on his stone face. "We asked them, 'What would you do that we haven't done?' They had no answers. I asked for their help and their suggestions and they frankly said the answers were difficult."

Privately, Daley was livid about King's invasion of Chicago. He believed it had been politically inspired by East Coast liberals and people like Governor Nelson Rockefeller of New York who contributed money to the SCLC, perhaps to keep King out of New York. Other civil rights leaders also thought it was a mistake. King picked Chicago because all it

took to change things, he thought, was to change Daley.
Nowhere else in America could one man create change effi-
ciently and immediately. King believed, as Lyndon Johnson
did, that Dick Daley was not a kingmaker but a king. But
King misunderstood the complexity of the racism, the anger
he would attract, not from the establishment (which was
more irritated than threatened), but from the white community, which had none of the sometimes kindly paternalism
southerners exhibited toward Negroes. In the South, they
didn't want blacks drinking from the same fountain. In
Chicago, they didn't want them breathing on the same block.
King didn't know this. Daley did. And Daley also knew that
while he could control the black political establishment, he
couldn't control the many young blacks who were listening
to the cries of "Black Power." He knew this even before
Stokely Carmichael began his gospel.

King, Raby, and others went off to plot strategy. It was
too hot for anyone to worry about marchers. It was so hot
that in many parts of the city the kids had turned on fire
hydrants and were splashing in the water. Lake Michigan
beaches were closed because of a pollution warning. On
Tuesday, July 12, at the corner of Throop and Roosevelt (the
gateway to what once had been the Jewish neighborhood
where Jack Arvey's parents settled in 1895), some black children had turned on a hydrant. A fireman ordered it turned
off. A crowd gathered, complaining that hydrants in white
neighborhoods weren't being turned off. The police explained
that because of the heat, the city's water pressure was low.
The police left. The kids turned the hydrants back on. The
police turned them off. The kids turned them on. The police
turned them off and arrested one youth. Someone threw a
rock. Someone picked up a bottle. In a three-flat building
someone fired a gun.

Police reinforcements arrived, and the familiar summer
street scene of the mid-Sixties played out on Chicago's West

Side. Lines of helmeted policemen trailed by television crews with flashing lights; porches and windows filled with jeering blacks; an occasional rock or bottle smashing near a policeman. Then a phalanx of police charging toward a house, an alleyway, or an intersection, dragging one or two or three young blacks toward a patrol wagon and then a period of quiet. It always got quiet right before dark. Then it would start, Molotov cocktails and rocks, and when the police went in one direction, the looters went in another.

On Thursday Daley angrily blamed the rioting on "outsiders" and said he had tape recordings to prove that aides to King fomented the unrest. It got worse that night as the looting and window smashing moved west along Madison Street to Lawndale and Garfield Park. Daley finally caved in and asked Governor Kerner to call out the National Guard. He hated to do it because he thought it would show that Chicago was like other riot-stricken cities and could not control things on its own. Guardsmen were platooned on almost every business intersection of the West Side by Friday afternoon.

Califano sent a memo to Johnson, who had been talking to Daley by telephone. "The situation in Chicago continues to deteriorate. Senator Douglas has been in touch with Mayor Daley and Senator Douglas just called up and asked that we put together a package to speed up Federal grants in public housing and on-the-job training programs that are now pending. . . . Before I call Daley or do anything on the Douglas proposal, I wanted to make sure you were in agreement. . . . At the same time I think we should stay out of the situation in terms of sending a Presidential representative, or your involvement in it. But Daley is very discrete [sic], and we face none of the problems we faced with [Mayor Sam] Yorty and [Governor Pat] Brown in Los Angeles."

Lyndon Johnson had viewed the Watts rioting as a disaster for his Great Society programs and had severely scolded

Califano for authorizing federal troops to go to Los Angeles in 1965. Johnson wanted to distance his government from the racial unrest and felt betrayed by blacks, whose lives he was trying to improve. He told Califano, "Negroes will end up pissing in the aisles of the Senate," and making fools of themselves the way they had after the Civil War. "Just as the government is moving to help them, the Negroes will take unwise actions out of frustration, impatience, and anger."[2]

He was right. When Johnson tried to pass legislation ending discrimination in the rental or sale of housing in the fall of 1966, in the aftermath of rioting in more than forty cities that year, even his good friend Everett Dirksen, mindful of the Chicago violence and its backlash, did not lift a finger to find a Republican vote. The bill died in the Senate.

Hearing the reports from Chicago, Johnson must have remembered one of his bedroom sessions with Daley the previous year. Lady Bird Johnson had written in her diary of ". . . Lyndon propped up in bed, the Mayor in the rocking chair, all of us with coffee—and the Mayor telling us how he hoped to handle the problem of a race riot in Chicago. He said he would not permit his policemen to wear steel helmets. They would simply wear caps—he hoped each one would look like the friend down the block instead of a soldier—The crisis is imminent now because everybody is on edge, waiting to see when race riots will break out in Chicago. All of this was described in a soft, mild, smooth, most determined voice. I would not want to put myself in opposition to that man. I admire him tremendously."[3]

On Friday night, July 15, the rioting subsided. There were still injuries and arrests but the anger had worn out. Two Negroes had been killed, sixty people and several police officers injured, and three hundred arrested. The 3,100 National Guard troops remained on duty for five more days. Daley met with King on Friday and said it would serve no purpose to back up his charges that King aides started the riots. "What we are trying to do is to bring all forces together in our city in hopes of getting some cooperation, not controversy."

Daley and King agreed to put sprayers on all hydrants and Daley promised to build ten more swimming pools in the Negro neighborhoods. One cynical civil rights worker told Mike Royko, "I think they're hoping we grow gills and swim away." Daley may have hoped that, but the end of the rioting did not mean the end of marching and violence that summer. As if he didn't have enough problems, a homicidal maniac was running loose somewhere in Chicago.

On Wednesday night, July 13, a pregnant fourteen-year-old Negro girl became the first person killed in the rioting. Early the next morning, a pockmarked merchant sailor named Richard Speck forced his way into a two-story townhouse dormitory on the Southeast Side. Over a period of five hours, he stabbed and strangled eight student nurses. One of the dormitory occupants hid under a bed and survived. The largest manhunt in Chicago history took place for the next three days after fingerprints lifted from a door identified Speck as the killer. Even Chicagoans and suburbanites who lived miles from the West Side violence were double-locking their doors.

On Saturday night, a doctor at Cook County Hospital was cleaning up an attempted suicide victim who had been brought in from one of the Madison Street skid row flophouses. His arms were covered with blood from the slashes he had made on his wrists. When the doctor wiped away the blood he saw a tattoo, "Born to Raise Hell," and called the police. Speck was convicted and sentenced to death in 1967 by Judge Herbert C. Paschen, the man whom Daley had bounced from the 1956 ticket after the flower fund scandal.[4]

Ray Simon, Daley's top aide, told reporters the week's events had shaken the mayor. "He is enormously moved by some things. . . . The murder of the nurses is another great tragedy, and he felt it very strongly."

The open housing marches began at the end of July. On a beautiful Sunday, the Reverend Jesse Jackson, a young King aide, led two thousand people through Gage Park, a South Side enclave of second- and third-generation Lithuanians, Poles, Croatians, Ukrainians, and Irish. Police guarded the marchers as they picketed a real estate agency. Jackson told a reporter, "All white people wonder why Negroes always drive fancy Cadillacs. These people have money and GMAC is all too happy to take it. Now we will see if these real estate agents want to take it."

Whites sat on porch railings and in their tidy front yards on lawn chairs, swigging beer and tossing empty cans and bricks at the crowd. There were many arrests. For the first time, the freedom of the Sixties combined with the anger of racism on the lips of many girls and young women, who freely shouted, "F*** you!" at the Negro marchers. Thirteen cars belonging to the marchers were set afire; twenty-five people were injured. At one intersection a mob of whites smashed the windows of a car driven by a black woman, who screamed uncontrollably. Police pulled the crowd away from the vehicle and took her to an ambulance. On July 31, the group marched on the Northwest Side in the Cragin neighborhood. Even more police lined their route and the brick tossing was limited.

The following day, the nation's attention went elsewhere. In Austin, Texas, a twenty-four-year-old architectural engineering student shot his wife and his mother to death, then climbed to the top of a tower on the University of Texas campus and shot forty-seven other people, thirteen of them fatally. Charles Whitman was finally killed by police. That was on Monday.

On Friday night, while the world-champion Green Bay Packers were demolishing the College All-Stars in what

Chicago called its midsummer classic, Martin Luther King was marching again in Gage Park. He was struck in the head by a rock. "I have never seen such hate, not in Mississippi or Alabama, as I see here in Chicago," he said. King was beginning to realize how different Chicago was from the South.

The bottle tossers and rock throwers cared more about their small Georgians and bungalows than anything else in life. They were the descendants of oppressed people and they zealously trusted that their legacy to their children would be their homes, with the pine-paneled basements and prefabricated one-car garages. The intrusion of blacks into their neighborhoods would decimate the value of these prized houses. No liberal priest or menacing policeman scared them as much as the thought that one of their neighbors would sell out to a Negro.

King and Daley met again on August 17 at the St. James Episcopal rectory on the near North Side. Nothing was resolved. But Daley was getting feedback. His police were scuffling with and whacking decent white voters on the head—and it was being shown on television. Daley hadn't minded so much when his police were roughly arresting Negro rock throwers on Madison Street a few weeks earlier. He was genuinely concerned for his city and equally concerned about his image. This was not the kind of political fight he instinctively knew how to win. He was used to dealing with politicians, not movements. You couldn't put black power on the ballot and defeat it the way you defeated Republicans. You couldn't offer King or Raby a seat on the federal bench to shut up. If Negroes didn't appreciate that he, Dick Daley, and his friend, Lyndon Johnson, had just passed the most sweeping civil rights package in American history, what could he do about it?

He went to court. Daley got an injunction stopping the marches. On August 20, Daley made a rare live television appearance. Solemnly he spoke for ten minutes explaining the new court order to regulate the marches. He spoke sincerely of the right of civil rights leaders to demonstrate. More importantly, he told his white constituents that he was trying to do everything he could to stop them.

King assailed the injunction as "unjust, illegal, and unconstitutional. The mayor seems more concerned about stopping our marches than in bringing justice to Chicago. . . . We are prepared to put thousands into the street if need be. The city hasn't seen the number of people we can put there." He suggested if the police couldn't prevent violence, Daley should again call out the National Guard. King then scheduled a march for August 28 in suburban Cicero, a blue-collar enclave notorious for housing Al Capone's headquarters in the 1920s and burning out the home of a Negro who moved there in the 1950s.

King was not winning his battle, but he was taking plenty of prisoners. Chicago was on edge. Even harmless picketers who had been circling the new Civic Center Plaza for weeks now seemed ominous. Blacks strolling along State Street seemed threatening and Daley seemed nervous. He and King continued talking and on August 26 reached an agreement with community leaders on an open housing plan. King agreed to halt his marches. "The total eradication of housing discrimination has been made possible," King said. "Never before has such a far-reaching move been made." Daley, smiling as he usually did the day after an election, called it a "great day." Daley agreed to propose a city open housing ordinance. King called off the Cicero march, cut his losses, and left town. Daley sincerely wished him a good trip. Not all blacks were as satisfied: Robert Lucas, Chicago head of CORE, scheduled another march in Cicero. "All these people want is publicity," Daley cried.

Daley didn't have to deal with the Cicero march. On

Sunday, September 4, three hundred marchers walked into Cicero ringed by police and National Guardsmen. They were attacked by a huge mob, struck with stones and bottles, and eventually stalled in an underpass "like cattle in a canyon," as an Associated Press report put it. The AP also tallied up the summer's toll: seven dead, five hundred injured, three thousand arrested in forty-three cities where rioting occurred. Chicago was exhausted with all the riots, the marching, and the murders. It was, some said, a summer that would never end.

And still there was more. On September 18, the day before autumn officially ended the summer of 1966, an intruder with a glass cutter quietly broke into the lakefront mansion of Republican senatorial aspirant Charles Percy, who lived a few miles north of Chicago in Kenilworth, America's richest community. The intruder made his way to an upstairs bedroom and stabbed and bludgeoned 21-year-old Valerie Percy to death. The murder of Percy's daughter caused a moratorium in his campaign against Senator Douglas and may have won him a sympathy vote.

But after the summer of 1966, Lyndon Johnson, Dick Daley, and the Democrats needed sympathy. The November elections were a GOP rout. Only two years after political reporters wondered in the aftermath of the Goldwater debacle whether the GOP could continue to exist, the Republicans, abetted by two years of urban violence and a spreading disunity over the war, virtually wiped out the Democrats. Douglas, the three-term liberal conscience of the Senate, was gone. "I'm caught between a 'white backlash' and a 'Negro backlash,'" he lamented. Sheriff Richard B. Ogilvie moved up the ladder to president of the Cook County Board, giving the Republicans a precious patronage haul of twelve thousand jobs. Joseph Woods, a brother of Richard Nixon's secretary who sometimes wore Nixon's hand-me-down suits, won the sheriff's office with its three thousand jobs. The critical positions of assessor and county clerk were retained. Adlai Stevenson III, already distrusted by many of the same committeemen who didn't trust his father, captured the state treasurer's position, thrusting him forward as a senatorial or gubernatorial nominee in 1968.

Daley was deflated but not defeated. King had returned to Chicago the week before the November 8 election and Daley suspected the civil rights leader had done it to extract some political vengeance. "I don't think there's any doubt about it," he told reporters. "His appearance here is what is happening politically. What has happened last summer, if we read the press, might have some effect on the voting public. I hope it doesn't. I hope that the forces of hatred that are unleashed in our community and throughout the country would be some way put into proper focus." He didn't explain how, but everyone understood what he meant. He accepted the election calmly. He had been around long enough to know you couldn't win them all.

There were a few bright spots in 1966. His friend Lyndon Johnson had put his older friend, Bill Lynch, on the U.S. District Court. In May, Daley had cut the ribbons on the new Civic Center Building, now the city's tallest structure. He reiterated his plan for a new sports stadium to replace or sit next to Soldier Field and predicted it would open in 1969.

In the midst of his dealings with the obsessive marching, Daley sent off birthday greetings to his president, and Johnson replied: "Dear Dick, Your birthday wishes hearten me. I am deeply grateful to you, your fine family, and the good people of Chicago for your kindness."

Later that fall, Johnson was back in the hospital for removal of a throat polyp and repair of a hernia. Obviously everyone in Chicago said prayers, or at least, he assumed so. He wrote on November 17:

I suspect I must have all Chicago to thank for such a simple operation and swift recovery. I am feeling fit and looking forward to some Texas sunshine. All the family are grateful for your friendship and prayers.

> Lyndon Johnson.

On the final working day of the year, December 30, Richard Daley walked from his private office and told City Hall reporters that he was running for a fourth term as mayor. It was hardly a story.

The Republicans' quadrennial sacrificial lamb was John Waner, another successful businessman who had been Charles Percy's campaign manager the previous year and who would get no money, no attention, and not many votes. Daley was a constant, but the faces around him were beginning to change. Benjamin Willis had finally departed, to be replaced by James Redmond. O. W. Wilson, the reformer who had resurrected the police department's image after the Summerdale scandal of 1960, shuffled off to retirement in 1967, and Daley reverted to tradition by naming James Conlisk, a cop from a long line of cops, as the new superintendent. Conlisk didn't figure to be as innovative or scholarly as Wilson, but he would be loyal.

In January, 1967, McCormick Place, the showcase exhibition hall on the lakefront, burned in a spectacular fire that raised many questions about how such a new structure could be so devastated. No one answered the questions, and the rebuilding started with the same protests from the same groups who originally fought both Daley and the *Tribune* for desecrating the lakefront. The new hall opened in 1969, looking just as intrusive and incongruous as the original box structure.

Things were still going well in Washington. Califano was looking out for Daley. He sent the president a memo on February 16, 1967: "Today I was able to shake loose the largest urban renewal project [$6.9 million] that was in HUD. Daley will announce it tonight and HUD will announce it tomorrow. [HUD Secretary Robert] Weaver has informed me that he believes he can release the other four urban renewal projects, totaling roughly $8.1 million, sometime tomorrow. I will call Daley when I hear from Weaver."

Throughout Johnson's presidency, Daley received priority treatment. While other state or city leaders trusted their congressmen to deliver, Daley didn't have to. "He never needed me when it came to money," Rostenkowski said. "He had direct lines all over the White House, to (Marv) Watson, Califano, O'Brien."

At the same, Rostenkowski added, Daley rarely pressured the delegation. "There were only two times when he called me. We had in the poverty program a clause that allowed a governor to veto something if he didn't like it. The guys from New York and California, who at the time had Republican governors, wanted to revoke it. I wouldn't go along. Johnson called me and I told him I wouldn't go along because it would embarrass Governor Kerner. The next call is from Daley. He starts telling me that the president called and then I said we would look terrible if we supported a bill that hurt our own governor. Did he want us to look like we didn't trust Otto Kerner? He paused and said, 'You're right. I never called you.' "[5]

If Daley's patience with King and the civil rights movement was worn through by election day 1966, his decision to end any pretense of accommodation was surely spurred by his 1967 election. After three terms in which city property taxes had risen dramatically, after a summer of dissent and mayhem, in the face of his unwavering loyalty to a president whose war was becoming more unpopular with each evening newscast, Daley scored the biggest mayoral victory in thirty-two years. Maybe all those federal dollars were being appreciated.

He carried all fifty wards, winning for the first time in some old GOP enclaves of the North Side, even thumping Waner in his own ward. White Chicago, which only four years earlier had preferred Ben Adamowski, approved of the way Daley had handled Martin Luther King and the looters and torchers on the West Side. Daley was endorsed by all four newspapers. The *Chicago Tribune* was finally applauding Daley without restraint. Its new devotion stemmed from its agreement with his law-and-order posture. And if the vote totals meant anything other than habit or intimidation, black voters did, too—at least those who voted.

Dick Daley's machine was changing again, and the fascinating question is whether he caused it deliberately. In the 1967 election, voters in what now were twelve predominantly black wards gave Daley a 185,000 plurality out of a total of 250,000 votes. That was even better than the 155,000 margin those wards had given him against Adamowski in 1963. But there was a critical difference. In 1963, the black vote had made Daley a winner. In 1967, with a margin of 792,238 to 272,542, the black vote was not the critical factor. In 1963, his own 11th Ward, Tom Keane's 31st, the 40th and the 50th were the only white enclaves in the top ten vote-producing wards. The rest were black. In 1967, only the 3rd and 20th wards remained black ballot powerhouses. Now the once suspicious 19th Ward, the 18th, the 13th—those Southwest Siders who previously saw Daley as too progressive—emerged as new loyalists. So did Parky Cullerton's 38th and the nearby 36th on the Northwest Side, areas where King had marched the previous summer. And the total black vote slipped a touch. The margins were still impressive, but it was clear that in the biggest landslide of his career Daley had either plotted or stumbled on a new coalition.

One thing he could not have known in early 1967 was that the Great Society, which he loyally supported, would change the politics of the nation as drastically as the New Deal had. With the passage of Medicare and Medicaid and the new Aid to Dependent Children legislation, poor blacks in the inner cities, like poor whites a few generations earlier, began to rely more on the federal government and less on the local political organization. Daley had been blending compliant blacks into his Democratic party for the previous decade and had even co-opted the reformers who surprised the machine once in a while. But the patronage powers that were the enforcement mechanism of the organization would be less effective when municipal jobs, except those for white-collar and trade workers, were worth little more than welfare payments.

Blacks, of course, never found any reason to flock to the Republican column, nationally or in Chicago, but their interest level in elections would continue to decline in the city for the remainder of Daley's years. It would not awaken until the 1980s, when with the splintering of the party it became apparent blacks might actually win control of City Hall. Perhaps Daley foresaw this, as he certainly foresaw and fought against the courts stripping his patronage powers.

Ideologically, Daley and most Chicago Democrats were far more conservative than the stereotype of the big-city Democratic machines. He did agree with Johnson that government should help the needy. The problem for Daley after the summer of 1966 was that it was hard to look at people who burned cities as needy. He was also a victim of his times in that he could not understand why blacks seemed to prefer lower standards of living and failed to follow in the footsteps of all the previous ethnic groups that had climbed up the socioeconomic ladder. That was the ambivalence of northern racism. On the one hand, whites wanted to believe that given the opportunity blacks could assimilate into society as upstanding, taxpaying, ballot-casting Americans. But on the other hand, there was a consensus that was sadly reflected in all the stereotypes of singing, dancing, and eating watermelon.

Of all the big-city organizations, Daley's was one of the first to incorporate blacks, and when he thought the timing was right, slate them for offices they could win (and sometimes those they couldn't). But the sociology of the underclass was not what preoccupied Daley. What worried him most was another summer of burning and looting. Throughout the autumn of 1966 and during his campaign in the early months of 1967, over and over again, Daley preached, "As long as I am mayor of Chicago there will be law and order." There was no doubt that he was talking about Negro riots. This was not code; everyone knew what he meant. The question is whether he was more concerned about votes, which he didn't need, or intimidating the marchers and protesters, who he believed had fueled the unrest the previous July.

His victory totals, however, could not pass unnoticed. And coming so soon after the Republican triumphs of 1966, his fourth mayoral triumph was seized on by Democrats throughout the country as a sign of party popularity and a signal that law and order was not only a winning issue but the only issue at the local level. While Daley and his counterparts may have been concerned about their reputations and the physical damage to their cities—not to mention their re-elections—whites throughout America were wondering when Negroes would decide to stop destroying their own communities and bring "black power" to white neighborhoods. Newton Minow, chair of the party's congressional re-election fund-raising dinner in Washington, suggested that to spice things up a Democrat of the year should be named. The

Democrats were so pleased with Daley's victory that it was no surprise who was picked.

"The surprising thing about that dinner," Minow recalled, "was that Daley refused to sit at the main table. He had bought a table before he even knew he was going to be honored, and when I got to the dinner I went down and told him he should be up at the speakers' table."[6]

"I'll just sit here with the family," Daley replied. But he was pleased. Lyndon Johnson, who was almost as delighted with Daley's victory as Daley, would send more congratulatory telegrams after Daley's acceptance speech.

"I believe in civil rights, but with law and order in our streets, and not with disorder," Daley declaimed. Then he addressed the flagging support for the president. "Today we have many faint hearts in our party. We never had faint hearts before. We have always had the courage to stand up and speak out for what is right." The Daley family spent the night at the White House. Before the dinner, the president spent time with several of the Daley children walking through the Rose Garden.

The president had invited John Steinbeck to spend the night, but on May 4 his secretary noted, "Marvin (Watson) said that Mayor Daley was bringing his wife and four sons to Washington next week. Does the President want all six Daleys invited as overnight guests at the White House Tuesday night?"

Johnson wrote on the memo, "Ask them to stay all night Tuesday night—and move the Steinbecks to Wednesday."[7]

A Nobel Prize in literature was a wonderful thing—but it took second place to Dick Daley and Illinois' 26 electoral votes. After the dinner, Johnson and Daley spent more than an hour alone in the White House. They undoubtedly talked politics and the threat of renewed rioting in the summer. Surely Daley lobbied Johnson about bringing the Democratic convention to Chicago in 1968; Daley had been working to get every party convention in Chicago since 1956, the Democrats' last visit. And they talked of the war.

While urban unrest was the major fear, the Vietnam War was coming home. A new breed of protester was seen more frequently on American streets, a young, unshaven male, burning his draft card. There were silent vigils and some not so silent. At Thanksgiving, the protesters marching in front of the White House began to chant for the first time, "Hey, Hey, LBJ, how many kids did you kill today?" It was a slogan that Johnson said haunted him. And in New York, Berkeley, Chicago, and every other metropolis, the young were beginning to chant, "Hell, no, we won't go," "Peace now," and "Ho, Ho, Ho Chi Minh."

In February of 1967, Robert F. Kennedy visited Daley in Chicago. The mayor was asked about speculation that Kennedy might challenge Johnson for the presidency. "He comes from a fine family and there's a place for him," Daley answered. But he was emphatic about his loyalties. "I never equivocate," said Daley, who had always equivocated on such subjects. "I'm for President Johnson in 1968."

During the summer of 1967, Daley met with many community groups and particularly with representatives of the riot-scarred Lawndale neighborhood. He announced that he had gotten $7.3 million in federal grants to fund 5,300 jobs for West Side residents. Robert Weaver, secretary of HEW and the first black person to hold a cabinet position, gave Daley approval to start rehabilitation of one thousand apartments in Lawndale. In August, the City Council passed a new open housing ordinance that met with the approval of Martin Luther King. But all was not quiet. Daley continued his "law and order" chant whenever possible.

On July 12, Newark went up in flames. In a decade the city had gone from 62 percent white to 62 percent black and

Puerto Rican. The rioting now had a familiar pattern. It would start with a police incident, usually the arrest of a black man and charges of brutality, a rock, then a bottle, then some arrests, the sounds of nightsticks thumping bodies, then looting, then fires, and in 1967, gunfire, sniping from rooftops and alleys. Governor Richard J. Hughes of New Jersey called Newark "a city in open rebellion." Almost half the city's twenty-four square miles was in the hands of rioters for five days. The National Guard and state police restored order on July 17. Twenty-seven people were dead and losses were estimated at $10 million.[8] A week later it was Detroit burning. This time forty-three were dead and seven thousand arrested.

Johnson called Daley at the mayor's Michigan retreat to discuss the Newark riot and again after Detroit to see if anything was happening in Chicago. The most militant black leaders were saying Chicago would be next. Daley issued another defiant warning that he would not tolerate in Chicago what was happening elsewhere. "We are prepared to act immediately in any situation where there are acts of violence and anarchy," he declared on July 27, the day they counted all the dead in Detroit. A reporter asked about King's remarks, which had all the elements that had led to riots in other cities. "We don't need him to tell us what to do," Daley said angrily. "He has been asked to join in our constructive programs and he has refused. He only comes here for one purpose—or to any other city he has visited—and this is to cause trouble."

That summer there were riots in 114 cities in 32 states. They left at least eighty-eight people dead and another four thousand injured. The riots were no longer confined to the large urban centers sheltering the most concentrated of the underclass. There were riots in South Bend and Grand Rapids, in Milwaukee and New Haven, almost everywhere blacks lived in America. But not, to any extent, in Chicago. That convinced Lyndon Johnson that the Democratic convention of 1968 should be held in the International Amphitheatre, just down the street from Dick Daley's house.

It has been reported that Daley did not want the convention and its attendant threat of more riots. The antiwar groups were threatening to demonstrate at both parties' conventions, but the main worry was the militant black uprising. In the aftermath of Detroit and the subsequent tragedies of assassinations in 1968, no doubt part of Daley wished the convention had been set somewhere else. But he still reveled in the trust the president had given him and he accepted that charge with a fierce determination to conduct a secure convention and a total intolerance for any potential disruptions. Chicago civic leaders had pushed hard to get both parties in Chicago and although Daley may have begun to have second thoughts, he said nothing about them to Lyndon Johnson.

Colonel Jack Reilly, the ubiquitous director of special events who spent much of the Sixties getting astronauts into Chicago parades as soon as they were hauled back from space, was particularly insistent about the convention. Dan Rostenkowski recalled, "I don't really know whether Daley wanted it. I told him we shouldn't want it and I think it was his guy [Reilly], who somehow had a great relationship with Johnson, who really wanted it." On October 4, Reilly cabled Johnson and Watson: "May we respectfully suggest that the President knows that it is ridiculous to think of Republican Florida putting on the kind of spectacles that only Chicago has the 'know how' and organization to deliver. . . ."⁹ Although Reilly was an obstinate man (he embarrassed Daley by declaring in August that he did not want the Picasso sculpture sitting on the Civic Center Plaza) it is hard to imagine that even he would send such a missive without Daley's knowledge.

Larry O'Brien said, "Chicago was determined a couple of years earlier. Daley wanted the convention and with the good Mayor, none of us, including the President of the United States, fought him when he was adamant about something."[10] Marv Watson had written the president that he favored Chicago. "Security is best in Chicago. . . . I have a lot of faith in the mayor's ability . . . to keep public demonstrations and riots in hand. I'll grant that there are more Negroes in the immediate area [of the Amphitheatre] than in either of the other cities but I think the control factor is far, far superior to Miami and a cut above Houston."[11]

Rostenkowski remembers the moment the decision was announced the night of October 7. "We had gone to St. Louis to see the World Series and then flew on to Washington for a fund-raising dinner at the Statler Hilton. Before the dinner, Johnson comes to our table and gives Daley a big squeeze. Then he bends over and tells Daley something and leaves. I said to Daley, 'What'd he say?' Daley says, 'He gave us the convention.' I said, 'No, no, we'll get killed with all the protests, it'll ruin us.' Daley just looked at me. 'He gave it to us. We'll handle it.' I can't really say if he wanted it or not, but I didn't."

Either way, Daley put on the best possible face the next day. "We will roll out the red rug and green rug for them." And more, much more.

CHAPTER 9

"Let Us Die to Make Men Free"

THE YEAR 1968 COULD HAVE BEEN A GLORIOUS ONE FOR DICK Daley. Throughout each political twist and each new tragedy, opportunities arose and then vanished. What might have been the most stunning display of power by a political leader in America other than the president of the United States dissolved into a tableau of bitterness, anger, hatred, and blame. All of those emotions were shared by an entire nation—though at the end Daley endured more of them than anyone else, deserved or not.

There would be opportunities in 1968 for Daley to defend his president against divisive challengers. The possibility that Daley alone would rise above all other Democratic knights to restore Lyndon Johnson to another term was clearly a possibility. Then Johnson was gone, leaving Daley without the most natural, strongest magnet for his loyalties. But the chances to anoint a new king were innumerable. Every Democrat in the country who wanted to succeed Lyndon Johnson and all of those who had horses in the race came to Chicago to discern what they might about Daley's choices.

It was a year of "what ifs." What if Robert Kennedy had
not challenged Johnson and remained alive to get to the convention? What if Johnson had not decided against seeking
another term? What if Edward M. Kennedy had decided to
take a spot on the ticket? What if Hubert Humphrey had sev-
ered his candidacy from Johnson's Vietnam policy? What if
Dick Daley had let the kids sleep in the park?

Although Daley and Johnson were worried about a sea of
black anger washing the International Amphitheatre in a wave
of Molotov cocktails, 1968 was all about the war.

Daley had been against the war for some time. At first,
it was merely good politics. Prior to the 1966 election, Larry
O'Brien, then postmaster general, went on a scouting trip for
Johnson to assess the mood of the nation. He said, "There
was a conversation I had with Mayor Daley, initiated by him,
where he expressed great concern about Vietnam, where it
seemed to be tending, what it was causing by way of dis-
ruption and public concern. You wouldn't find a greater hawk
than Dick Daley or a more loyal Democrat or loyal Johnson
supporter on the Hill or anywhere else—a man who did not
have to be concerned about his political power being eroded
by Vietnam . . . he said this was a growing disaster and this
was going to be devastating to the Democratic party. I sent
the president a memo, 'If Richard Daley has become that
concerned about Vietnam, you've got to realize that it is not
some passing cloud.' "[1]

Daley had told Johnson earlier that year, "When you've
got a bad hand, you should throw in your cards." Daley
would fall in love with certain phrases and repeat them. This
was one of them. "That's what he said to me," Newt Minow
recalled. "I often heard him say that," Rostenkowski said.
Robert Kennedy reported Daley had told him the same thing.
But to the press, the public, Daley revealed nothing. He had
another pat statement for them. "We have commitments

made by [John Foster] Dulles and presidents Eisenhower and Kennedy. Johnson didn't start it." It was a convoluted form of absolution for Johnson's war policy. If Kennedy was involved, it couldn't be so bad, could it? And if anyone thought it was, well then, it was the fault of the Republican, Eisenhower. But Ike had been a great war hero and you couldn't put too much blame on him. Well, then, blame Ike's secretary of state, John Foster Dulles, one of the eastern establishment.

Daley had been against the war for a long time. "There was always a conflict in his mind," said William Daley, his youngest son. "He always told the story of when John Kennedy came to speak in 1954 at the Democratic dinner the first time he [Daley] was chairman. Kennedy warned that it would be a mistake to try and fight a war ten thousand miles away. He would always mention that, years later. He had all these negative feelings about the war itself, but he would defend Johnson and the authority of the government. He believed in 'My country, right or wrong, my country.' "[2]

Almost every historian or biographer dealing with the campaign of 1968 says Daley turned against the war after the son of a very close friend was killed in 1967, but he had been warning Johnson long before that. "Jay McKeon, who was Mike's best friend, was killed in April 1967," Bill Daley recalled. "He had seen lots of kids in the neighborhood going to Vietnam, getting killed. I remember plenty of other kids . . . one of their mothers came to the door one night crying because her son had been wounded in Vietnam. So he would fight with Johnson in the Oval Office and then go outside and tell the press that Johnson's policy was great. He had to support the President, he viewed it as a challenge to authority."

"And the harder the opponents [of the war] attacked the President, the more my father came to his defense. It was a real knee-jerk reaction for him. He would defend Teddy

Kennedy [after Chappaquiddick]. There was a critical book
on Nixon that came out and he defended him. That was just
the way he was. He didn't believe in attacking authority," Bill
Daley said.

Bobby Kennedy announced on January 30 that he would
not oppose Johnson's renomination under any foreseeable
circumstances. That day was the beginning of the Tet offensive, the Viet Cong assault that threatened to overrun the
U.S. embassy in Saigon and wrecked what little remained of
the administration's credibility on the conduct of the war.
Johnson, anguishing over both his inability to resolve the war
and his countrymen's refusal to acknowledge that he was
trying, claimed to intimates that he was not worried about
challengers because "Dick Daley, the best mayor in the country, was standing by the President. . . . Daley had come by
a while ago [August] and told the President how in 1948,
when Ed Kelly had been boss of the Chicago delegation of
the 1948 Democratic convention, Ed Kelly had decided Truman couldn't win and let the Chicago delegation make up its
own mind. Only two of the Cook County leaders had stuck
by Truman—Dick Daley and Jake Arvey. With people like
Dick Daley on your side you don't worry about people like
Gene McCarthy and Bobby Kennedy."[3] It is impossible to
recall any other point in history when one city mayor was
rated so vital to the political fortunes of a sitting president.

But Daley's loyalty began to be tested when Robert
Kennedy spoke in Chicago on February 8, 1968, when Americans believed—erroneously—that the Tet offensive had been
a major Viet Cong victory. "Half a million American soldiers
with seven hundred thousand Vietnamese allies, with total
command of the air, total command of the sea, backed by
huge resources and the most modern weapons, are unable to
secure even a single city from the attacks of an enemy whose
total strength is about 250,000," Kennedy said. Later that
day, Daley told Kennedy that he believed Johnson "should

cash in his chips" on the war. But Daley did not want the party split. "How about a commission appointed by Johnson to review the entire course of the war—a commission of such national eminence as to give the administration moral authority for a switch in Vietnam policy. Would that please Bobby?" Daley said.

Theodore White asked Kennedy whether he had asked Daley for his support. "No," Kennedy said. "You can't do that to any man, it's not fair. If I announce, then I have the right to ask Daley for support . . . but unless I announce first, I've no right."[4] Kennedy or one of his aides leaked to reporters the remark about Johnson cashing in his chips, but Daley refused to confirm ever having given the president that advice. He also never acknowledged his role in the attempt to set up a Vietnam commission. Daley telephoned Johnson the next day to inform him about the Kennedy discussion, or perhaps to float the commission idea if he hadn't done it previously.

The idea of a commission to deal with a war seemed odd and fascinating to many people, Kennedy and Johnson included. Their biographers and historians of the period seem to find it especially odd that the originator of such an idea was the apparent antithesis of political diplomacy, Richard Daley. Yet Daley probably wondered why Johnson hadn't done it long ago. Appointing commissions and blue-ribbon committees was the way Daley attacked every public crisis. Commissions were body armor, the way school boards absorbed the brunt of anger for segregated classrooms and civic leaders accepted whatever criticism came from the newest Loop high-rise proposal, highway, or college campus.

Bill Daley thought he was trying to give Johnson a way out of a corner. "My dad knew that even if in Johnson's heart he wanted to get out of there he had to have a way, and the commission was an attempt to get him out. All these whiz kids who got him in there, McNamara, Rusk, were all

Kennedy guys. They weren't Lyndon Johnson guys and that rubbed my dad the wrong way. Then they turned on Johnson as some hick from Texas. They were the Harvard elite and my dad knew they were the ones who got him in the mess and that very much rubbed him the wrong way. He wanted to keep Bobby Kennedy out [of the presidential race], and he thought that would get Johnson re-elected and then position Bobby for the future."[5]

Johnson sent his representative and later Defense Secretary Clark Clifford to meet with Kennedy on March 11, 1968. No agreements were reached and the pace of 1968 was too swift for further talks.

The following day, Eugene McCarthy won 42.2 percent of the vote in New Hampshire against 47 percent for the president. Daley appeared nonplussed. "It is obvious his showing, in my opinion, was like all primary elections. You remember the great showing of Senator [Henry] Cabot Lodge four years ago in New Hampshire? What did it mean when it came to the convention? . . . Many people are concerned and disturbed. I don't know if it's a negative vote or an affirmative vote. . . . In 1952 Kefauver won a majority of all the primaries and was not a candidate for president. You have to remember that," Daley said.

Daley was not surprised by McCarthy. He knew the Democratic party was in trouble on the war, and only his stubborn loyalty to Lyndon Johnson and his propensity for concealing his inner feelings from the public prevented him from revealing them. McCarthy was following his conscience but Daley's public allegiance was to the ranking Democrat not the dead of Southeast Asia. There wasn't much Daley could do about McCarthy, although a serious challenge to the president might enhance his role at the convention. Daley would be loyal to the president above all, but he really wasn't looking forward to another routine anointing. In 1964, his powerful presence had hardly been noticed in Atlantic City.

A president who needed someone to ensure his nomination would offer more of an opportunity to cement the reputation of the last kingmaker.

When Robert Kennedy saw the New Hampshire results, he immediately announced he was re-assessing his position and telephoned Daley to tell him he was planning to run. Daley immediately called Johnson but the mayor and the president played telephone tag all day until Daley finally got through to the White House at 11:22 P.M. The two men talked for half an hour.[6] The next day Daley refused to say whether he had heard from Kennedy. Finally he admitted to reporters he had talked to him. "I tried to give him some advice," he said. "Did you turn him down?" he was asked.

"I said I would support the president if he was a candidate for re-election," Daley replied, raising another flurry of questions about the possibility that Johnson might not be the candidate. Daley demurred. Obviously he had been candid with Kennedy but left open a small door. Or, in the late-night conversation with the president, did Daley sense that Johnson might not seek another term? It is possible. Although Johnson said he didn't decide to withdraw from the 1968 election until the exact moment he uttered the words, he was torn for the last year of his presidency between an urgency to end the war and leave office in glory and his deep conviction that only he could continue to lead the country. He undoubtedly had rambled on to Daley about this ambivalence, as he had to others who were close to him.

Reporters, curious about Daley's "if" statement, began to ask others about the president's thinking. Everett Dirksen said that the Kennedy announcement probably made Johnson want another term even more. "I think he's had all he can take from a certain family." Daley said the Kennedy challenge would not split the party, spouted his "Dulles, Eisenhower, Kennedy" mea culpa for Johnson and said, rather eloquently for him, "Everyone is entitled to their positions but we need unity. Dissent is one thing; division is another. . . . Even the Lord had skeptical members of his party. One betrayed him, one doubted him and there were only twelve of them. You have to take human nature for what it is." Kennedy must have wondered if he was the betrayer or the doubter.

Two days later, Kennedy announced he would fight for the nomination. The defections from the Johnson camp to Kennedy came immediately. Larry O'Brien led the list. But Johnson's assessment of Daley was holding. Asked if Kennedy could defeat Johnson for the nomination, Daley said only one word. "No."

The national political scene was frenetic. The White House was trying to hold on to support while a late-breaking Kennedy was furiously trying to attract it. McCarthyites were suddenly split on whom they were angry at: the president who would not stop a war or the latest Kennedy trying to climb over the back of their candidate. Democratic senators were hiding, their friendships for Johnson, Kennedy, McCarthy—all colleagues at one time or another—wrestling with their loyalties to the White House and, even deeper, their convictions about the war. Congressional Democrats were splitting in all directions, and tens of thousands of young people and black people briefly jumped into the political arena.

In Chicago, Daley had to put together a state ticket. It was time for another joust at Dirksen, and Otto Kerner had been talking about seeking a third term. And always at the top of the priority list was the state's attorney's office. It was occupied by an appointee, John Stamos, who had taken the post in 1967 after Daniel Ward was elevated to the Illinois Supreme Court. Daley had no shortage of candidates, but the 1968 slate was one of the most curious and second-guessed of his career. He had approached Adlai Stevenson III about running against Dirksen. But Stevenson really wanted to run for governor. He might have accepted the Senate slating, but he privately warned Daley he was becoming disenchanted with the president's policy on the war.

Then Daley turned to Rostenkowski, who (disputing the conventional wisdom of the time) vowed that Daley had always wanted to beat Dirksen, even in 1962. "In October of 1967 he called me to meet him at the Sherman House. He gives me the 'what are we doing to do about the Senate' business and says we have to get a good candidate. He wasn't too enthusiastic about the others. Then he starts, 'You know, Danny, your father would be so proud . . . U.S. senator, a nice Polish name, what a tremendous honor. . . .' I said Dirksen would be tough to beat and take a lot of money. 'You'll have all the money you'll need.' But he's still tough. 'Not with you running against him, he won't be.' I said I'd think it over but I'd have to ask my wife. Daley says 'sure' so I leave the office and wait about thirty seconds in his reception room before I stick my head back in and shout, 'Laverne says no.' Daley stared at me for a few seconds, then he laughed and said, 'You sonuvabitch.' But he wanted to beat Dirksen."

Daley went after Sargent Shriver, who had wanted to run for governor in 1956 and 1960 when he was just a Kennedy in-law. Shriver had headed the Peace Corps and then taken charge of Johnson's antipoverty program, spreading stacks of money into Chicago and vigorously defending Daley's use of it. Johnson made a pitch for Shriver. Daley pitched Shriver on running against Dirksen. Shriver didn't like that prospect much and said it might look like there were too many Kennedys in the Senate. Shriver also backed away from the governor's race. Daley was running out of star-quality hopefuls to run against Dirksen.

But the governor's office was of far more importance to the party. Daley had been publicly promoting Kerner for a third term, but now there was a vacancy on the U.S. 7th Circuit Court of Appeals. Kerner had always wanted a spot on the Appellate Court, where his late father had served. But he was currently chairing the President's Commission on Civil Disorders and beginning to murmur about higher ambitions and wonder about a spot on the Supreme Court. After seven years of polite obedience, he was making noises like a political force in his own right. He had wanted to dump Secretary of State Paul Powell and also two-term incumbent Attorney General William Clark, who Kerner never forgot had tried for the gubernatorial nomination that Daley gave to Kerner in 1960. Daley suggested strongly that the vacancy on the federal court was just the right place for Kerner to move his newly discovered ego. Kerner got the appellate appointment and resigned in favor of Lieutenant Governor Samuel Shapiro, a longtime legislator from Kankakee who was also a Daley favorite.

Shapiro figured to have a shot at being slated, but there were plenty of bigger names to deal with. Stevenson, who had emerged from the Democratic ruins of 1966 with the state treasurer's post, was the party's top vote getter. Clark had wanted the slating eight years earlier, and two big wins statewide hadn't hurt his chances. Paul Simon was again seeking a crack at Dirksen. Alan Dixon, a state senator from Belleville with enormous popularity and great political skills, could have been slotted in either of the two top positions. Perhaps the most popular choice was State Auditor Michael Howlett, who was the favorite of the news media the minute Kerner took the opening on the federal bench. But Howlett didn't figure. "Daley never did like guys like Howlett or Eddie Barrett, who seemed to be real popular," said Rostenkowski, who chaired the 1968 slatemaking committee.

Stevenson was a key factor until the Friday, February 23, meeting of slatemakers in Springfield. Stevenson said publicly what he had said privately to Daley about opposing the president's Vietnam policies. Then he dared the Democrats to ignore him by saying he would clearly be their strongest candidate for either U.S. senator or governor. Daley might still have tried to push Stevenson into the Senate spot, but it really wasn't worth the argument.

"The thing with the Senate," Rostenkowski said, "is what did you get out of it? Daley wanted to win, sure. Anytime anybody he picked won, it was like power to him. But if a candidate couldn't raise money, didn't have much of a chance, there was no reason to waste a lot of effort and resources. If a guy looked good and could win, then Daley could take a bow, the party could take a bow. If not, there were other offices that were more important."

On February 27, Daley huddled behind closed doors at the Sherman House with his slatemakers. Political writers had all kinds of dream-ticket scenarios. Stevenson for governor, Clark for senator, Stamos for state's attorney. Or maybe Howlett for governor, Stevenson for senator, Stamos for state's attorney. How about Stevenson for senator, Clark for governor, or let Clark run again for attorney general and run Howlett for governor. Maybe Stevenson for governor and Simon for senator. Shapiro, they reasoned, was a nice guy nobody knew. He couldn't lead the ticket.

The first sign of the witches' brew that Daley concocted came in midafternoon. State's Attorney John Stamos, figured to be a shoo-in for slating because of his incumbency and heavy financial campaign promises from the Greek-American community, stormed out of the closed-door session and practically ran over the media mob. "I'm out," he shouted. "Who's in?" someone yelled. "Hanrahan," Stamos replied.

U.S. Attorney Edward V. Hanrahan had a solid record and the one requisite for the chief prosecutor's position that Stamos lacked—he was Irish. A few moments later, one of the party's caricatures slid through the closed doors, sorting reporters out of his way. State Senator Bernie Neistein, the committeeman of the now nearly all-black 29th Ward (despite his residence in a Lake Shore Drive high-rise) was short, bald, rarely without a huge cigar in hand, and a highly accomplished concert violinist. "What's the ticket, Bernie?" a reporter shouted.

"Clark, Shapiro, Simon, Powell, Howlett, and Fannie Jones."

"Who the hell is Fannie Jones?" someone yelled.

"She's our candidate for clerk of the Supreme Court," Neistein retorted. None of the others made history in 1968, but Fannie Jones did. She was the first black person ever slated by the Democratic party for statewide office in Illinois.

Daley had ignored the "glamour" name of Stevenson, the proven vote getter Howlett, and the individual wishes of everybody but Shapiro, who was tickled to death to be slated, and Powell, who was happy to stay put in the secretary of state's office. As it turned out, Stevenson's antiwar posture was moot since Clark almost immediately repudiated Johnson's war policy. Stamos had been offered the chance to run for attorney general but told Daley and the slating committee, "Go to hell!" (He was later made a judge.) Daley called Frank Lorenz, who had briefly been the appointed state treasurer in the early 1960s, and Lorenz raced over to the Sherman House in time to take his place in the attorney general's slot.

Bill Daley said Shapiro always had the inside track for governor. "The Jewish community came to Dad and urged him not to turn his back on Sam Shapiro. There was a question whether a Jew could win statewide and I think he got boxed. He wasn't keen on Adlai for governor, but I think he felt if he dumped Shapiro it would look bad in the Jewish community." The ticket looked especially weak later in the spring, when the Republicans selected the highly capable and highly visible president of the Cook County Board, Richard Ogilvie, as the gubernatorial candidate.

But Daley was undoubtedly distracted by the national happenings. In Los Angeles, late in March, Bobby Kennedy gave an interview to Jimmy Breslin of the *New York Daily News*: "What about Daley?" Breslin asked. "He's been very nice to me personally, and he doesn't like the war," Kennedy said. "You see, there are so many dead starting to come back it bothers him. . . . He has been a politician for a long time. And party allegiance means so much to him. It's a wrenching thing for him. We'll have to win the primaries to show the pols."

"If you get Daley," Breslin asked, "where do you stand?"

"Daley means the ball game," said Kennedy, adding another layer to the myth.

Daley responded the next day with a clearly satisfied laugh. "He means I'm a great White Sox fan."

The White House was getting nervous over Kennedy's courtship of the mayor of Chicago. On March 29, Marvin Watson sent a clipping of the Breslin interview to Daley with a note: "I'm not surprised that others would put out this type of information, for your strength is immeasurable. . . ."[7] The Johnson forces would not be behind anyone when it came to worshipping the Daley legend and presence.

And as further evidence that no one but Johnson knew of his ultimate plan for 1968, on March 29 LBJ got a memo from aide George Christian:

I paid a courtesy call on Mayor Daley in Chicago this afternoon. This is the essence of his attitudes, some of which is no news to you.

1. Concern about the war. He says we just have to develop a better way of explaining what's going on. He feels we are losing the people on this issue.

2. There has been no public statement of consequence on the *Pueblo* for some time. But the people are

still quite concerned as to why we have not obtained the release of the crew.[8]

3. Daley says he understands the Wisconsin organization is developing the state okay but he believes there is no chance whatever of carrying the state because of their Republican crossovers.

4. He sympathizes with the president's burdens of the war and the fiscal situation and says he doesn't know how a human being can put up with so much work.

5. He says we need to get back on the offensive and the key is somehow pulling the people back on Vietnam.[9]

Obviously both Daley and Christian were concerned about McCarthy's chances of winning the Wisconsin primary, where Johnson's name was automatically placed on the ballot. It is clear from the timing and content of their meeting that neither expected anything like what they heard on Sunday, March 31, 1968.

Bill Daley recalled the night. "Jack [Marvin] Watson called right before Johnson was going on television and my dad took the call upstairs, where he had a private line. We were all sitting down in the den where he had his office. He came downstairs and said, 'The president's going to announce he's not running.' "

At exactly 9:01 P.M. EST, as Daley sat in his den on Lowe Avenue watching, Lyndon Johnson stunned the nation:

". . . I shall not seek, and I will not accept, the nomination of my party for another term as your president."

Johnson wrote in his memoirs, *The Vantage Point*, "Now it was history and I could do no more. We walked from the Oval Office back to the Executive Mansion."[10] He was with Lady Bird, his two daughters, and son-in-law, Pat Nugent. The first telephone call he accepted was from Chicago.

"We're going to draft you," Daley began. Johnson told him he would not accept it. Daley said his speech was "the biggest bombshell."[11] Johnson then told Daley that he was going to fly to Chicago in the morning to give a speech to the National Association of Broadcasters. It was the first time Johnson told anyone he had accepted the long-standing offer from the broadcasters. (The White House staff had to scramble the next morning to prepare for the trip.) Daley said he would meet him at the airport. After that, Johnson took calls from his vice president, Hubert Humphrey, and his longtime protégé and friend John Connally. Daley immediately called Rostenkowski and told him to go the airport with him to greet the president.

"I remember riding in the limousine," Rostenkowski said. "There was Frank Stanton, the head of CBS: Tom Foran, who had just been appointed U.S. attorney; the president; Daley; and me. I said to the president, 'You know, today is April Fool's Day. You could say that you were just early with your speech last night.' Nobody said anything."

On the return trip, the bus carrying the press corps that accompanied the president was involved in an accident on the Kennedy Expressway and Johnson's plane sat on the runway for an hour. Daley's sons John and Bill were also aboard the plane and Johnson gave them each a deck of playing cards embossed with the seal of Air Force One. Bill Daley remembers Johnson reminiscing at length about all of his campaigns and successes. Until he had told Daley the previous night he was coming to Chicago, the White House staff had been uncertain of his plans. Bill Daley surmised, "There was this sense that he came out as much to see my dad as anything else. My dad was asking him to reconsider—'Think about this, Lyndon. What will you do?'—and so forth. I remember when we left, my dad went up to him and there was a very genuine warm hug between the two of them. Johnson had been through so much, he was beaten down. There was a real friendship there, you could just see it."

"The next morning," Rostenkowski recalled, "Daley called me and said, 'It's terrible what he did to Hubert.' I said, 'Well, it's Bobby now.' He said, 'Oh no, no it isn't. Humphrey deserves his chance as a reward for his loyalty. He's been loyal to the president and it's his turn now."

Daley was again displaying his code: in politics, loyalty was the highest virtue, at least next to winning. But Humphrey was still collecting himself from the shock of Johnson's withdrawal. McCarthy and Kennedy, by contrast, were in full gear. Both men called Daley. O'Brien, who joined the Kennedy camp in mid-April, said Kennedy told him, "Daley will wait for June. . . . He'd be interested in how Bobby does in the primaries." It was the same old Daley dictum: "Go out and round up your support, then come back and see me."

O'Brien recalled the strategy in the Kennedy camp: "What happened after Jack Kennedy was elected, where the relationship became closer and closer, would indicate that Dick Daley would certainly lean toward Bobby. But you couldn't take that to the bank . . . we were making sure he knew what we were doing. We knew he knew we were conducting a vigorous campaign, that we were anxious to have his support. You don't go beyond that with Dick Daley, and even with that we were using kid gloves."

On April 2, Daley confused reporters when asked what kinds of qualities he would consider supporting in a candidate. "Well, I think the qualities we had in the former president, the qualities we had in Senator Kennedy, and the qualities we had in President Johnson." The Chicago newspapers interpreted that to mean Robert F. Kennedy had the same qualities as John Kennedy and Lyndon Johnson. Daley's press secretary had to explain that the mayor meant John Kennedy both times.

Daley also did not rule out the possibility of a Johnson draft. "That's a decision that will come later on," he said. But he added, mindful of his own conversations, that the president was emphatic. Daley also said he thought there "should be a cessation of politics in order to let the president negotiate a just peace." He was even beginning to use Johnson's Vietnam rhetoric.

The moratorium on campaigning began two nights later, but it wasn't exactly what Daley had in mind. Another of those mutations of history intruded into the already crowded year of 1968. His name was James Earl Ray.

Martin Luther King, Jr., was shot to death while standing on the balcony of the Lorraine Motel in Memphis, Tennessee. Ray's high-powered rifle had virtually ripped away King's throat. He was pronounced dead at 7 P.M. Thursday, April 4.

Daley was at home eating dinner with two of his sons, John and Bill when Jack Reilly called. Daley answered the telephone and then told them, "Martin Luther King's been shot and killed." Bill Daley remembered, "It was real quiet that night, but sitting at that table we all just knew it was going to happen, you knew it. The next day all hell broke loose."

In Washington, Lyndon Johnson canceled his appearance at a Democratic fund-raising dinner and almost immediately went on television to eulogize King and express hope for a nonviolent honoring of his memory. It was futile. Only blocks from the White House the sadness, shock, and rage of black America erupted again. Fires and looting broke out. A white man was dragged from his car and beaten to death. Stokely Carmichael called for war. Lyndon Johnson called out the Army.

Daley conferred with Police Superintendent James Conlisk and Lieutenant Governor Samuel Shapiro. Kerner was
vacationing outside the country. Thursday night in Chicago
was calm. Friday afternoon was not. Blacks began harassing
white students in schools. The schools began to close, dis-
gorging thousands of black youths into the streets on the West
and South sides. At Farragut High School, a memorial service for King had to be hurriedly cancelled and white teachers were ordered to leave as the black students grew
menacing. White shopkeepers closed early on Madison Street
and wheeled iron gates across their storefronts. By 3 P.M.,
huge crowds had filled Garfield Park and bands of youths
began trolling the West Side, throwing rocks and stones.
They broke into storefronts and soon teenagers and smaller
children were pushing grocery store carts filled with boxes,
cans, and food. The police didn't bother to stop them. There
were too many. At 5:40 P.M. the president called Daley.
"There's all kind of hell-raising here in Washington," Johnson said. "How are things there?"

Daley replied that so far there was only window smashing and a few fires. Daley said he had asked Shapiro to call
up six thousand National Guardsmen and they were assem-
bling in the city. "I have called out the Army," Johnson said,
and he offered federal troops. "Anything you need is at your
disposal."[12]

Shortly before midnight, Johnson told advisor Joseph Califano that he "had information that Daley was marked for
assassination and to see the FBI gets this information to
Daley's police people."[13] The fires started in the late afternoon and by nightfall stretched for two miles from Damen
to Homan Avenue. The sniping and shooting began at dark.
Fire departments from several suburbs joined Chicago firefighters, who did not have enough equipment to attack all the
blazes. Many of the fire trucks were being held in reserve in
case the rioting spread to the Loop or Michigan Avenue. Fire

Commissioner John Quinn asked the National Guard to provide fuel trucks for his stations on the West Side; the trucks were going back and forth so often they were out of gas. Thirty-six major fires were reported by 10 P.M. After that, the calls came in faster than the fire alarm bureau could count. Many of the buildings blazed uncontrolled. Firefighters simply stood and watched because they had neither the equipment nor the staff to battle them. After his inspection, Daley said, "Things are under control."

The next day was just as bad. The havoc continued past midnight. On the first night nine people, all black, were killed by gunfire (although one man may also have had his head smashed by an axe). Brigadier General Richard Dunn, commanding the Guard, said the troops' weapons were loaded with live ammunition and that "orders to shoot to kill will depend on the commander on the spot."

On Saturday, Daley called in the Army. General George Mather arrived to take control of five thousand troops from Fort Hood, Texas, as well as the National Guard, which had been federalized. Daley ordered a curfew beginning at 7 P.M. for anyone under twenty-one years old and banned the sale of guns, ammunition, and gasoline in portage containers.

Daley was asked if the curfew implied that all violators were under twenty-one. "It speaks for itself and it was suggested by the commanding general, the police superintendent, and the fire commissioner." Another committee decision, never a Daley decision.

Another reporter asked, "Are we having a problem because looters think they won't be shot?" "Well," Daley replied, "it's a pretty serious thing to talk about shooting looters, but I am hopeful there will be sterner action taken by both the military and the police department in the handling of the situation." The meaning was clear; the wording was guarded.

That night, with the military guarding every intersection

on the West Side, it was relatively quiet. More Molotov cocktails were tossed, more buildings set ablaze, and three more
people, all black, killed.

On Palm Sunday, Daley and Fire Commissioner Quinn
flew over the West Side in a helicopter. Daley was almost as
devastated as the smoldering section of the city he saw
beneath him. "It was a shocking and tragic picture of the city.
I never believed that this would happen here. I hope it will
not happen again," he said.

Daley was later ridiculed for his naiveté. It was impossible, critics said, for him not to be aware of the frustration of
black people living on the West Side in the worst conditions
in the city, ruled by white Democratic leaders, sustained by
federal grants dispensed through Daley's political machine,
and growing increasingly separate from the rest of society.
But surely Daley was making one of those predictable and
expected comments, what he thought was a harmless obser-
vation. He had spent the last three years, ever since Watts,
praying that riots would not happen in Chicago and prepar-
ing in case they did. Perhaps he thought that all his jawbon-
ing about preserving law and order would scare the
firebombers. Perhaps he hoped his police department could
react quickly enough to contain widespread chaos. But he
could not have truly believed that it wouldn't happen. He had
been reluctant in 1966 to call out the National Guard, but
he was not at all reluctant in the wake of King's murder. He
knew what could happen and when it did he could offer only
a veil of sad surprise, not an apology or an explanation.
When the fires died out, 162 buildings had been destroyed,
twelve people killed, and three thousand arrested. Damage
estimates ranged from $12 million to $15 million.

"It was frightening. He was incredibly depressed. How
could he be anything but depressed?" said Bill Daley.
"Things were out of control, he was concerned that he had

lost control, he had to call in federal troops, how else could he feel?"

On Tuesday, April 9, Richard Daley called Marvin Watson to tell him everything was quiet and to thank the president for his help, particularly the federal troops.[14]

On Monday, April 16, he did two predictable things— only one of which had the anticipated outcome. He appointed a committee to investigate the causes of the rioting, headed by Federal Judge Richard Austin, the jettisoned 1956 gubernatorial candidate. Then he made one of his patented angry, defiant, and threatening harangues, which had seemed so popular the previous year. He was particularly incensed that only sixteen of the arrested were charged with arson, which after his helicopter survey seemed to him the worst crime imaginable.

He said he had thought police had orders to shoot arsonists and looters and that when he found out they didn't he immediately told Superintendent Conlisk to issue orders "to shoot to kill any arsonist or anyone with Molotov cocktails in their hand to fire a building because they are potential murderers and to also order police to shoot to maim or cripple anyone looting any stores in the city. Above all, the crime of arson is to me the most hideous and worst crime of any and should be dealt with in this fashion. I was disappointed to learn that every policeman out on the beat was to use his own discretion. This discretion evidently was his. In my opinion he should have instructions to shoot arsonists and shoot looters—to shoot arsonists to kill and shoot looters in order that they be detained. In my opinion there also should have been Mace used on these looters."

Even reporters accustomed to Daley's flares of anger were momentarily surprised. It was one of those odd moments when reporters realize that someone has said something very foolish. A roomful exchanged glances with one another: Had everyone heard the same thing? It was not unusual for reporters to be confused during Daley's disjointed news conferences. There seemed to be an imperceptible pause, a bit of embarrassment, and an expectation that he might quickly recant his statement.

Although Daley was abrupt and even antagonistic toward the news media, he was usually accorded unwarranted courtesy. In the 1950s and 1960s, even his malapropisms were translated into respectable grammar. Only in later years, when the rules of journalism etiquette changed, was Daley subjected to interpretation and, private scrutiny—and at times derision. But for the most part, he enjoyed a friendly press.

Finally, one reporter asked about the young looters, grade-school children. "You wouldn't want to shoot them, but with Mace you could detain youngsters," Daley said.

Was that safe?

"I'm not a chemist, but Mace is safer than having people burn these buildings," he replied.

Someone tried to ask how police could be sure they were shooting only to cripple, but Daley stalked into his office, where in a matter of hours he would be fending off a national barrage of criticism and dismay. Civil rights leaders were the most outspoken. The Reverend Jesse Jackson called Daley's remarks "a fascist response." He said Daley obviously meant police should have more regard for "cans of food" than human life. Adam Clayton Powell said the mayor's statement was the "beginning of officially sanctioned genocide in America." Robert Lucas of CORE, who led the Cicero open housing march, said it gave "racist" power to the police department. Johnson's attorney general, Ramsay Clark, said Daley's statements were a "dangerous escalation" of racial violence. "Police have acted in balance, generally, and because of that we have had fewer deaths . . . less property damage that we had in one riot last year." Senator Charles Percy was one of the few Republicans to weigh in against Daley, saying the statement "might turn out to be the most inflammatory statement made" concerning urban problems. But Percy was accurate in adding, "It has been an unfortunate thing. He doesn't lose his cool very often."

Of course Daley had his defenders, beginning with the *Chicago Tribune*, which wondered what all the ruckus was about. "As the chief executive officer of the city, it is his duty to keep the peace," the *Tribune* editorialized. But it was a lonely voice among the nation's press.

"He was getting all these rumors from police and intelligence that were unbelievable," said Bill Daley. "I remember a rumor that armed black bands were coming down 35th Street to our house. We had an armed camp for two blocks around our house. Rumors were everywhere, people were scared. He decided he had to try and stop this, not let it just continue to happen. He was trying to a put a lid on the fire and put it out by being strong. Then he realized that wasn't working, that he was just pouring more fuel on the fire."

For perhaps the only time in his career, Daley knew he had gone too far. The next day he tried to backtrack and made it worse. His public oratory, always clumsy, became even more fragmented when his face reddened with anger. "They said that I gave orders to shoot down children. I said to the superintendent, if a man has a Molotov cocktail in his hand and throws it into a building with children and women up above, he should be shot right there and if I was there I would shoot him. Everybody knows it was twisted around and they said Daley gave orders to shoot children. That wasn't true."

It was also not true that anyone reported Daley had given orders to shoot children. He had given orders to shoot looters, and many of them were children. Rather than deny what

was impossible to deny, Daley might have taken some of the
harshness out of his statement with an apology and an explanation of his own stress. But thirteen years of almost unin-
terrupted idolatry had wrapped an already huge ego with a
thick coating of invincibility. And to admit that he had
spoken emotionally would be to admit his worst fear, that he
had lost control of the city. Still, he tried to further amplify
and remove the offensive tone of his edict. The next day he
read a statement to the City Council reiterating the need for
severe enforcement by police concerning arson and looting.
Missing from the three-hundred-word document were the
buzzwords, "kill" and "maim."

Daley, whose national reputation was that of political
powerhouse, virtuous administrator, able steward of the
increasingly admirable and efficient lakefront metropolis, a
sphinx on most issues, noncommittal on everything else, in
a moment of bluster had become the kind of intransigent
authoritarian that America was used to seeing on the six
o'clock news from Alabama and Georgia. As things would
play out in 1968, his temper also cost him dearly in the reser-
voir of goodwill he could have used in August.

Curiously, a few of the aldermen who dutifully applauded
Daley's council speech, and unquestionably agreed with his
sentiments, zeroed in on the problem: "Bad timing." There
was no outcry on the first day of the burning—not even from
black activists—when Brigadier General Dunn said street
commanders had the discretion to "shoot to kill." And there
had been universal applause the previous summer when, a
day after they finished counting the forty-three dead in
Detroit, Daley said he was ready to put thousands of guardsmen on the streets within an hour and "There will be no sub-
stitute [blank] cartridges in their guns." It was virtually the
same order, missing only the harshness of "kill."

But there was no national empathy with the rioting of 1967, the torching of Newark and Detroit. In April 1968, even white America felt a sort of collective complicity in the racial history that led to the killing of Martin Luther King. Whites abhorred the violence but understood that blacks, especially ghetto blacks, at least had a right to be angry this time. King's assassination had raised their consciousness about black frustration. Whether out of fear or sympathy, white people instinctively understood that "shoot to kill" orders were no longer the answer. Bad timing.

There were rumors throughout the month that the Democrats would reconsider Chicago as the site of the convention, but there was no way Daley would let that happen.

On March 26, Hubert Humphrey entered the presidential race. "Daley was only grudgingly for me for president," Humphrey would later write, but Daley had been accurate beyond his belief when he told Rostenkowski, "This is a terrible thing for Hubert."

The apostle of the politics of joy was now embarked on one of the saddest odysseys in American politics. "My father thought he was a real decent guy, but he was weak," Bill Daley said. And in the spring and summer of 1968, that's what most Americans thought. Humphrey, though, deserved his chance, and if he had run well in the primaries he would have had the wholehearted support of Daley. But he didn't.

On May 15, Daley celebrated his sixty-sixth birthday. Lyndon Johnson wrote a note thick with melancholy. "Lady Bird and I want you to know that you are much in our thoughts today, even as the long friendship we share is always in our hearts. Your birthday brings you the warmest wishes of all the members of our family. We have observed and learned much from the fine relationship that all of you have with each other. All of ours wish for all yours the fullest measure of every good in the years that lie ahead and please remember we will be talking and acting together from time to time always." It was signed "Lady Bird and Lyndon Johnson."

Also in May, Bobby Kennedy won the Indiana primary, right under Daley's nose. Then he won in Nebraska. A victory in Oregon could have put Humphrey right back on top, but McCarthy came in first, stalling Kennedy but leaving Humphrey listless.

Humphrey had three problems that he never resolved. All of them were Lyndon Johnson. First, Johnson was adamant that Humphrey not renounce his Vietnam policy. He persuaded the vice president that open divisiveness in the administration would doom his peace efforts. Second, there was among southern leaders in particular and party professionals, including Daley, a wistful hope that Johnson would reconsider his withdrawal. Although most of them were prepared to support Humphrey, they never gave him the kind of enthusiasm that inspires confidence in a candidate. Third, Lyndon Johnson clearly was having some fantasies about a convention draft. Joseph Califano wrote that he would have turned it down but wanted it as a validation of his presidency.

It is not certain that Johnson would have turned it down, but in any event he subjected Humphrey to thoroughly degrading and derogatory rhetoric. Johnson had once crassly told reporters, "I've got Hubert's balls in my pocket." He told another newsman, "He cries. He cries." In the summer of 1968 he would privately tell people, and Humphrey himself, that he wasn't capable of being president, that he was too weak, a topic Johnson surely discussed with Daley.

So it was that Hubert Humphrey, the once lonely but eloquent voice of civil rights and humanity, became portrayed as a hawk on the war, a man in favor of killing, while

McCarthy and Kennedy gleaned the rolls of the increasing majority anxious to stop the bloodshed. Most ironic, for Humphrey, was that the role reversal would hold into the fall campaign against Richard Nixon, easily the most hawkish American politician this side of Lyndon Johnson. Yet Johnson still did not want the nomination to go to Kennedy and was trying to keep everyone in line for Hubert. This explains Daley's constant coolness toward the Kennedy candidacy. Daley made calls in April to his fellow mayors in Pittsburgh, St. Louis, Philadelphia, and Detroit, urging them to delay any endorsements. And Humphrey was rewarded for his long political record by the unrestrained loyalty of big labor. AFL-CIO chief George Meany was among the first to proclaim his support, and lesser union leaders everywhere joined the parade. All in all, Humphrey still looked strong for the nomination, and a decent showing in the California primary would push him closer to capturing it. As it turned out, the nomination was going to be his after the California primary, regardless of his showing.

Robert Kennedy stormed back into the Democratic lead on June 5 by winning California. He claimed victory shortly after midnight in the Ambassador Hotel in Los Angeles, shouting out, "On to Chicago, and let's win there."

A moment later, another historical accident appeared. His name was Sirhan Sirhan, a Jordanian native celebrating the first anniversary of the Israeli-Arab war of 1967. Sirhan hated Jews. Kennedy liked them. Sirhan shot Kennedy in the head. Kennedy died 24 hours later—at 1:44 A.M. Pacific daylight time, June 6. The President was awoken fifteen minutes later and informed. Humphrey joined the president for an early breakfast. At 8 P.M. Johnson made his first telephone call outside the White House staff. He called Daley, and the two men talked for nearly an hour. Kennedy's death cast a new pall on a country that suddenly was sharing the same feelings as that of the man who had offended them a few months earlier, Richard Daley.

"What is happening to our society?" Daley agonized. "What is happening when we have all this violence and disturbance? Is this the way you reasonably settle arguments and differences? Certainly when we lose a president and when we gun down a great religious leader, and now a candidate for public office, it must give all of us in America occasion to reflect and stop a moment and ask ourselves, what is happening to society?"

The Daleys flew to New York for the funeral, which was attended by every American of stature from Lyndon Johnson on down. Ten thousand people stood in line outside St. Patrick's Cathedral to attend an all-night vigil. In one corner of the huge church sat Tom Hayden, a leader of Students for a Democratic Society who was organizing the antiwar protest in Chicago. Up front, at the request of the Kennedy family, sat the Daleys. They all had tears in their eyes. They sang the "Battle Hymn of the Republic." It was Saturday, June 8. The Democratic convention was three months away.

CHAPTER 10

"Happy Days Are Here Again"

THE KINGMAKER HAD NO KING. AS THE 1968 DEMOCRATIC National Convention drew near, the only Democrat in America who could have seized the power to choose a king was stalemated. Dick Daley had a president who might win but would not be drafted. He had a vice president who was running but could not win. He had a senator who could win but would not run. And another senator whose crusade to get out of Vietnam matched Daley's personal sentiments but whose disloyalty to his president was inexcusable, even though an Irish Catholic would help the local ticket. The one person who had wanted to run and could win was dead.

Daley had the promise that tens of thousands of scruffy-looking, longhaired men and foulmouthed women without proper undergarments were coming to disrupt his convention and his city, to foul his parks, his avenues, his lake. They wanted to violate his law by staying overnight in the parks, where they would probably smoke dope and fornicate and commit all other sorts of illegal acts. He would not let them do that.

Daley's partnership with labor, which had contributed to his many elections and their many sweetheart contracts, was collapsing. He had the telephone workers on strike, which was angering the television networks. He had the taxi drivers on strike, which was angering the delegates. The black bus drivers were ready to go on strike. He had to wonder if anybody was working in the city that worked.

Daley had built redwood fences all around the vacant lots between Michigan Avenue and the International Amphitheatre so none of the delegates would see anything but tidy homes and clean streets as they drove through his neighborhood. They would also see the five thousand federal troops who surrounded the Amphitheatre and the hundreds of secret service agents and Chicago police who seemed to be checking credentials in the Amphitheatre and every hotel lobby in Chicago. No matter how much criticism Daley had taken for his harsh "shoot to kill" statement, the president had kept the convention in Chicago because he knew Daley would preserve the law. The white ethnic voters who had swung decisively to him in 1967 had applauded his tough stance on arson and looting. He would not make bargains or provide loopholes in the law for the Yippies or hippies (or "flippies," as he called them).

There were several conventions going in Chicago the week of August 24. There was the one that everyone saw on national television that displayed the huge divisions in the Democratic party. They were split over the war and bossism and credentials and unit rule and their choice of candidates. There was the convention within the convention, the old-fashioned power-broker horse-trading where Daley, try as he might, could not put together the kind of deal that Democrats had always worked out, one that would send everybody home happy or bought. There was the convention of the streets, which went on for seven days in many places but which the whole nation thought they saw in an eight-minute film loop that has spun for nearly thirty years. There was still another convention, one that weighed far more importantly on the mind of Richard Daley than his usual obsession with winning elections. That was what he feared would be a convention of black fury in his neighborhoods. The prospect of a weak presidential candidate, an unruly group of delegates, a stripping away of the old political process, and even the grotesque war protestors did not scare him as much as his memories of the previous April.

Lyndon Johnson had been running the convention since spring. He was irrevocably committed to making sure it did not retreat from or embarrass his Vietnam policy. Merriman Smith of UPI wrote a story in May outlining Johnson's direct control and his discussions with Daley. The president was furious and demanded to know within fifteen minutes who was the source of such erroneous information. Tom Johnson, his deputy press secretary, filed a memo saying, "It looks like someone has filled Smitty in pretty well."[1]

In May, John Criswell, the convention director who had taken up residence in Chicago, reported that he had met with Daley, who had accepted Johnson's choice of Senator Daniel Inouye as the keynote speaker. Daley made it clear he wanted a spotlight on Ted Kennedy. He was also taking care of the local ticket. Daley also said he wanted to make Shapiro, his hope for governor, rules committee chairman and to give William Clark, his U.S. Senate choice, an important committee since Dirksen had been selected to chair the Republican convention platform committee.[2] He got both. The planning discussions continued, with the White House concerned about the labor disputes and Daley reassuring everyone that he would take care of them by convention time.

Meanwhile, Richard Nixon was making his comeback. By late July, the polls showed he was running ahead of any pos-

sible Democratic opponent except Johnson. Those polls, of
course, had consumed Johnson all spring. His other goal for
the convention was to make sure neither Bobby Kennedy nor
McCarthy received the nomination. As far as anyone knew,
that animus did not extend to Edward M. Kennedy.

Only hours after Robert F. Kennedy's burial, the media
began speculating about what they perceived as a natural
ascendancy for Ted Kennedy. It may be difficult to understand how completely the Kennedy family dominated, captivated, infatuated, and infuriated America in the 1960s. From
the opening day of the decade, when Jack Kennedy
announced for president, until Ted Kennedy drove off a
bridge at Chappaquiddick Island in 1969, the Kennedys were
the centerpiece of American interest. The Kennedy children,
the Kennedy in-laws, the Kennedy games, the Kennedy weddings, the Kennedy births, the Kennedy deaths, the Kennedy
parties, the Kennedy speeches, the Kennedy victories, the
Kennedy legacy. If the media were presumptive about Ted
Kennedy joining the 1968 presidential contest, they were no
more presumptive than the public. It just seemed that it
should happen. Teddy on the ticket seemed just what the
Democrats needed to overtake Nixon and clinch the election.

A good number of Democrats—Mike DiSalle of Ohio,
Richard Hughes of New Jersey, John McKeithen of
Louisiana, and Daley—had been calling Kennedy about taking the vice presidential nomination. Even Humphrey was
persuaded that the boyish, pleasant Teddy would be a plus
and not upstage him. Humphrey said the youngest Kennedy
would be very welcome on his ticket.

On July 25, Daley dangled a bigger plum, or at least
everyone thought he did. He and party chairman John Bailey and Criswell were reporting to the media on the progress
of work at the Amphitheatre and the state of the labor negotiations. Criswell wrote to the president, "The mayor gave us

quite a pitch about being careful what we said and not to get too deeply into such questions as phones at the hotel. . . . We were finished and a reporter asked him if he agreed with Bailey that Ted Kennedy would be a help to the ticket. He said he agreed and then, almost under his breath, added, 'I hope the convention drafts him.' . . . the mayor's statement came as a shock."[3] Whether Daley was suggesting Kennedy be drafted for the no. 1 or no. 2 spot wasn't clear.

Kennedy had several telephone conversations with Daley. He appeared not to be confused. He issued a statement the next day. "I will not be able to accept the vice presidential nomination."

That didn't deter Daley. In early August, his urgent calls dragged Kennedy off a sailboat near the coast of Maine for a conversation that Kennedy held in "a little pay phone in a booth among the rocks," according to Bill vanden Heuvel, Kennedy's sailing buddy, who had been Robert Kennedy's campaign director. Vanden Heuvel said, "It wasn't the first time Daley called and it certainly wasn't the last; they wanted Ted on the ticket. The implication was that the brokers had decided that Hubert wasn't going to win all by himself, that with Ted either the bottom or the top of the ticket they probably could—they didn't make that awfully clear."[4]

The telephone calls continued, but Kennedy continued to withstand the pressures to run. He was tantalized by the suggestion that he run for president. But he believed that once his hat was in the ring, Daley and others would force him into the vice presidential slot.

In the meantime, Lyndon Johnson was still planning his vindication. He was secretly arranging a summit meeting with Soviet Premier Aleksey Kosygin and hoping with all his fragile heart to force a breakthrough at the Vietnam peace conference before the convention. He would settle for nothing less that the "just peace" he had promised at the cost, so far, of about thirty thousand American lives. On August 1, Johnson and Daley lunched at the White House. Afterward he invited Lady Bird and Lynda Bird to join them.

Lady Bird wrote in her diary: "The Mayor was giving Lyndon a sales talk about coming to Chicago. The Democrats wanted to give him a rousing welcome; they wanted to show their appreciation. Lyndon gave him little encouragement. He stopped just short of a positive, 'No.' . . . There was a tape machine on the table and they had been listening to the tape Chuck [Robb] had sent Lynda from Vietnam. Lyndon played it again, and I listened with a strange mixture of awe and compassion and pride, too. . . . I could see Lynda Bird did not like having us listen to the tape. . . . Lyndon and Mayor Daley talked about the war. It was easy to see that Mayor Daley doubted our presence in Asia. . . . the Mayor simply wants out."[5] On August 10, Senator George McGovern of South Dakota announced for the nomination, saying he would serve as the repository of Robert Kennedy delegates who had not shifted to McCarthy. The week before the convention, Johnson's dreams of a great diplomatic success were shattered. On August 20 the Soviet Union invaded Czechoslovakia, ending any chance of a summit meeting. Daley called it a "dastardly act of suppression" and predicted it might "affect some of the doves flying around," a slap at the McCarthy peace forces.

On Friday, August 23, Daley talked again with Ted Kennedy. Ted sent Stephen Smith, Kennedy brother-in-law and manager of Bobby's campaign, to Chicago that day to meet with Daley at the Standard Club, a Jewish hideaway where Irish politicians were rarely found discussing the future of the nation. The discussion went back and forth about drafting Kennedy for president. A "genuine draft" to Kennedy meant he would not have to lift a finger or utter a word to be nominated. To Daley, this was nonsense. At convention time, the American politician takes on many traits stereotyped as Oriental, particularly face-saving. It becomes important who says exactly what to whom and when. For Daley, it would be impossible to secure any pledges from others unless Kennedy stepped forward. Otherwise the pledge would be solely to Daley, and Kennedy could later not be held accountable. Bobby Kennedy had understood this when he knew better than to ask for Daley's support until he officially became a candidate.

Smith flew back to Hyannis Port with Daley still wondering if he would finally have a candidate to his liking. On Saturday, he called Kennedy and much of the same conversation was repeated; Kennedy was troubled by the idea of being seen as an opportunist riding the misfortunes of his dead brothers, or being trapped by the wily Daley into accepting the second spot on the ticket.

But Daley wasn't alone in this quest. Senator Philip Hart of Michigan was trying to get some kind of commitment that would lock up his state's delegates for Kennedy. Jesse Unruh, the speaker of the California assembly, had 174 delegates, most of whom had been for Bobby and were ready to switch to a new Kennedy. As Daley waited at home on the Saturday before the convention, his youngest son, Bill, a member of the host committee, greeted the California delegation at O'Hare Airport. When Unruh arrived, he said, "Where is your father? I've got to speak to him."

"I had a portable telephone in my briefcase—not a modern cell phone, this was really heavy," Bill Daley said. "I gave Unruh my portable telephone and I gave him our home number. When I got home that night, I was planning to go out. There were lots of parties. My dad said, 'Why don't you stick around?' I asked, 'Why?' He said, 'I think we're going to endorse Teddy Kennedy tomorrow morning.'"

On Sunday, Steve Smith and Kenny O'Donnell were back at the Standard Club. Daley told them he would delay the caucus of the Illinois delegation. Adlai Stevenson III had predicted Illinois would give 113 of its 118 votes to Humphrey. State party chairman Jimmy Ronan had a higher number. The Cook County Democrats had a few defectors; the most serious was senatorial candidate William Clark's announcement for McGovern, confirming Daley's suspicions earlier in the year at slatemaking.

Daley convened the Illinois delegation caucus at 3 P.M. Sunday at the Sherman House. They listened to Humphrey, McCarthy, and McGovern, and then suddenly Tom Keane moved for a recess until Wednesday. Daley gaveled the motion through before Keane sat down. He lamely said that because he and Shapiro were giving welcoming speeches at the convention, it might not look hospitable to endorse a candidate at this time. Humphrey's people were in shock. Was this some new infliction of pain ordered by Lyndon Johnson, or was Daley deserting the vice president?

The decision electrified other delegations. On Monday, Michigan caucused and gave 82 votes to Kennedy. New York's 190 delegates were ready to swing to Kennedy. Smith had been making estimates all weekend. Unruh called Kennedy in Hyannis Port urging him to come to Chicago. Kennedy publicly asked that Mike DiSalle not place his name in nomination. Smith's headquarters at the Standard Club were making running estimates and guessed that Kennedy might have more than half, enough for the nomination if he declared, maybe less. Daley told him if he committed he would have the numbers.

On Sunday night, Daley made a final inspection tour of the convention hall. From the Amphitheatre he telephoned Smith. "Is he in or not?" Daley asked. Smith said Kennedy still would not announce. Daley told Smith, "Jack Kennedy knew how to count and Robert Kennedy knew how to count and your young man had better learn quick."

The public awareness of the maneuvering to nominate Kennedy would not really hit until Tuesday, when it had one last explosion. Eugene McCarthy, knowing he could not beat Humphrey and still smarting from the also-ran status he had acquired immediately after Robert Kennedy entered the campaign, offered Stephen Smith a new deal. McCarthy said, according to Theodore White, that "he would like to see his own name go into nomination; but at some point in the balloting, he would stand on the floor, withdraw his name, and urge his people to support Kennedy. Yet he, McCarthy, would not nominate Edward Kennedy."[6] It was another small scene in the egotistic and Machiavellian drama of political conventions, yielding something but holding back more.

By now delegates were running all over the city with Kennedy buttons. Daley knew that the southern delegations were furious with Humphrey over his refusal to support unit rule and ready to bolt with their six hundred delegates. If California, New York, Michigan, and Illinois went too, Humphrey would be stopped. Of course, the southerners were playing the same game, and it wasn't necessarily Ted Kennedy they had in mind. In Daley's mind, if Ted Kennedy wasn't available, who was?

Governor John Connally of Texas had been knocking down a Kennedy candidacy through the summer. Now he and others thought it was likely a draft for Johnson would develop. The president had gone to his ranch in Texas for convention week and had been in constant touch with Chicago. On Saturday, August 24, while Daley was debating the nuances of "genuine draft" with Ted Kennedy, Johnson's top aide Jim Jones relayed a message from the president's floor man in Chicago, Jake Jacobsen: "Jake says the six hundred southern delegates are holding well. . . . Jake says this convention is going to draft the President if there is the slightest indication the draft will be accepted."[7] On Sunday, Califano wrote that Larry Temple had reported to the president that he had been telephoned by Connally, Jacobsen, and Marvin Watson, all with the same message from Daley: "If

Lyndon Johnson wants this nomination, he has got our delegation."

Hubert Humphrey was trying to keep the party regulars from splitting and somehow satisfy McCarthy and Kennedy peace delegates to gain some semblance of unity for the general election campaign. It was an impossible task. There would be no unity in this party. He was under tremendous pressure from liberals to support the Vietnam peace plank, which called for unilateral withdrawal and an immediate bombing halt. Lyndon Johnson wanted a much stronger plank. Humphrey vacillated until finally the president's plank was upheld. He tried to walk the fence between the "new" and "old" Democrats on the unit rule, which held that a majority vote could bind all delegates of a state, retaining big blocs of power in a few hands. The southern delegations viewed the end of unit rule as an opening for blacks to take over their state parties. Moreover, Connally thought he could wrangle the vice presidential nomination for himself if a handful of his good friends controlled all the southern delegations. The unit rule was abolished, leading Connally to hollowly threaten the possibility that he might walk out on his party. He would do that four years later. Now the "new" delegates were furious with Humphrey over the Vietnam plank and the "old" delegates viewed him as a traitor on unit rule.

The delegates at the 1968 convention were not the same as in the past. For one thing, there were six thousand delegates and alternates, twice as many as had been in Los Angeles eight years earlier. Convinced increasing participation would strengthen the party, John Kennedy before his death had agreed to doubling the size of the delegates.

The war and the McCarthy-Kennedy campaigns had brought many new kinds of Democrats to Chicago. There were college professors and elementary school teachers, clergymen and students, poets and actors. There were even enough blacks so that they didn't stick out like interlopers. There were nearly four hundred black delegates and alternates, almost four times the number who had gathered in 1964 and ten times the number who had been in Los Angeles to nominate John Kennedy. There were celebrities. Shirley MacLaine held court in the California delegation.

Some of the delegates dressed just like the protestors on Michigan Avenue. And most of them were angry. They were angry over the platform battles, they were angry at the electronic checkpoints they had to go through at the Amphitheatre, and they were angry at being crowded. There were too many of them in the aging convention hall. There wasn't room to move around. They didn't like where they were located.

Daley and Johnson between them had decided the rebellious delegations like New York and California should be separated from their customary places near one another and moved to the rear. It was hot and the air conditioning wasn't new. And it soon became apparent that the sessions were going to last a long time. That may not have bothered the dissidents, who were angry anyway. But it bothered the regulars, who were used to winding up a convention evening in Chicago with a good steak and several drinks while a handful of power brokers figured out everything. It was sure to be a long four days and nights.

And that was only the political part of the drama. Outside—on the North Side, in the Loop, along Daley's Magnificent Mile, Michigan Avenue—was the other half of the convention week that no one will forget. Up to two hundred thousand peace pilgrims were predicted to be in Chicago for convention week. That was why Daley ordered up the National Guard and flew in five thousand federal troops to guard the Amphitheatre. How many demonstrators actually showed up is hard to know. Some estimates, ridiculing

Daley's preparations, say only two thousand were in the streets. Others say ten thousand.

They were there for two reasons. One was the war. The second was Richard J. Daley. From the moment Daley said, "Shoot to kill," the David Dellingers, Abbie Hoffmans, and Tom Haydens of the peace movement knew it would be easy to create a confrontation in Chicago.

Dellinger and Rennie Davis led the National Mobilization Committee to End the War in Vietnam (the Mobe), an umbrella group claiming to represent more than one hundred peace groups that had sponsored a huge demonstration at the Pentagon the previous October. In June, Davis announced, "Hundreds and thousands of dissenters will come to Chicago to sleep in the parks and to go into the streets for the cause of peace." The climax would be a confrontation at the International Amphitheatre on August 28, the day on which the Democratic nominee would be picked.

Their literature was volatile. "If at all possible, learn first aid measures in your respective cities before coming to Chicago. . . . Bring a supply of Vaseline to be applied against the skin for protection against Mace. . . . Mobile medical teams in white coats will be stationed at strategic areas."

Demonstrators filtered into Chicago in July carrying their belongings in U.S. Army knapsacks or canvas airline bags. They found rooms in makeshift hostels, church basements, and cheap apartments. The Mobe had filed applications to use Soldier Field and Grant Park for rallies, but no one at the Chicago Park District responded. Daley had his aides discuss marches with Davis and Dellinger, but his heart wasn't in it. Daley had understood who Martin Luther King was. He recognized the man could bring political power to bear on the issues of school segregation and open housing. But he didn't know who or what these self-appointed demonstrators were. He could not treat them as political equals. When the

American Civil Liberties Union (ACLU) filed a suit in federal court demanding the issuance of parade permits, his old law partner, William Lynch, dismissed it.

The Yippies began to move into Lincoln Park on Saturday, August 17. There were no problems. On August 20, newspapers reported that three hundred members of the militant Black Panther Party had arrived for nonviolent demonstrations but that other black leaders were leaving Chicago, fearful the antiwar protests would spill over into their neighborhoods. The Yippies dropped their suit to sleep in the park after Daley made it clear he would not ignore the 11 P.M. closing ordinance for anyone. "They have no right to come into the city and tell us what they are going to do. We don't permit our own people to sleep in the park, so why should we let anyone from outside the city sleep in the park? We don't permit our own people to march at night, so why should we let a lot of people do snake dances at night through the neighborhoods?"

He was asked if snake dancing offended him. "Snake dancers never disturbed me. Irish dancing and jigging never bothered me. Nor did Polish hops disturb me. And fine Negro tap dancers are some of my greatest entertainment."

That was the same day Czechoslovakia was invaded. By Friday, August 23, television commentators were making comparisons between the armed camps of Prague and Chicago.

The police had gone into Lincoln Park each night all week to chase the Yippies, who numbered a few hundred. On Thursday, August 22, a seventeen-year-old refused to leave and drew a gun. He was killed by police. There seemed to be no argument that the action was justifiable. It was the only fatality of the convention siege.

On August 23, the Yippies brought their presidential candidate to town. The 125-pound Hampshire hog, "Pigasus," was dragged to the Civic Center Plaza next to the Picasso statue. He was initially surrounded by a dozen Yippies with beards and beads. In a few moments he was also surrounded by a squad of police, who arrested the pig and seven Yippies, the first of what would be six hundred arrests by the end of the convention.

Sunday was quiet. At the Hilton Hotel across from Grant Park, there were a few pickets: "Peace Now, End the War." But the arriving Texas delegates were far more concerned with the fact that they were 120 rooms short of their request. In Lincoln Park, on the North Side, two thousand demonstrators gathered and burned pictures of Hubert Humphrey in a trash can. At 5 P.M., the demonstrators asked to bring a truck into the park. The police said no. Someone swore at the police. Five people, including Yippie leader Jerry Rubin, were arrested and the crowd began to get angry. Police reinforcements lined the perimeter of the park. "Pig!" "Fascist!" the crowd taunted.

The park filled with tension as twilight turned to darkness. When the curfew approached, most of the demonstrators left without argument. Some continued to taunt and hurl rocks and cans until police waving nightsticks cleared the area. A group of about two hundred demonstrators marched to the Michigan Avenue bridge, where a phalanx of police spanned the street and dispersed them. Six arrests were reported.

That same Sunday night the convention host, Richard Daley, was welcoming dignitaries to his cocktail party, explaining there was no mystery behind his decision to delay the caucus vote, and wondering whether he could convince Kennedy to jump into the fray.

The convention opened on Monday and Daley gave the welcoming address. He gloated, "It was an important sign of faith for this convention to be held here, not in some resort center, but in the very heart of Chicago—in a great neighborhood, a black neighborhood." He tried to be conciliatory toward the antiwar protestors, who he conceded made him uncomfortable. "Some are reasonable and others are angry. They hail from all over the nation . . . to demand, to protest, and to dissent. . . . But did you see them at the other [Republican] convention?" He also derided the Republican campaign as being based totally on law enforcement. "At this convention," he said, "we Democrats will nominate a president, a chief executive, not a chief of police." Apparently he saw no irony in the fact that in the same welcoming address he also said, "As long as I am mayor of this town, there will be law and order in Chicago."

The first night of the convention was a mess. There were seventeen separate credentials challenges against the seating of delegations, most of them based on racial imbalance. As the rival delegations argued, odd compromises occurred. Shortly before Daley's welcoming speech, the regular Georgia delegation agreed to the loyalty oath supporting racial balance "good for tonight only." The regulars were led by segregationist Governor Lester Maddox. State Representative Julian Bond, a black man, headed the challengers. Bond would later be nominated for vice president and collect 48½ votes. The problem was there weren't enough chairs for both groups to be seated until the eventual decision. So the Democratic Convention of 1968 started with a game of musical chairs while the band played the party anthem, "Happy Days Are Here Again." The melody would reverberate thoughout the week at the oddest of times, in the middle of vicious anger. But the Democratic Party had a history of disruptive convention battles, so perhaps the FDR theme song was appropriate if ill-timed.

In Lincoln Park, the Mobe scenario was playing out. On Monday, the crowd was larger and the police, who had merely prodded on Sunday, were less patient. At 11 P.M., they mounted a full running charge into the park, clubs aloft. As the demonstrators were forced out of the park, they began to cluster at the triangular intersection of North Clark and LaSalle streets, clogging traffic for several blocks. About two thousand police officers surrounded them, tried to disperse them, and began clubbing randomly. The victims included twenty reporters, photographers, and camera operators, and the hostility between the police and the media was sealed for the remainder of the week. Young people raced everywhere on the North Side, through the Division Street and Rush Street cabaret area, stopping traffic, shouting obscenities, chanting antiwar protests. The police chased them nearly two miles to the Chicago River. There were 154 arrests. Fifteen people went to hospitals and many more took refuge with friends for medical aid.

On Tuesday, a federal judge ordered the police not to interfere with reporters or photographers. Daley did not enamor himself to the media when he said police interfering with newsmen should be "reprimanded." By then the press, equally angry at the restrictive security arrangements and the ominous police presence in the convention and on the streets, were losing their impartiality.

The same scene repeated itself Tuesday night in Lincoln Park as a group of clergy erected a cross and sang the refrains most popular that year, "We Shall Overcome" and the "Battle Hymn of the Republic." At 11 P.M., an electronic megaphone boomed, "Move out now!" The familiar reply came: "Hell, no, we won't go." Tear-gas canisters exploded. Obscenities, rocks, and bottles were thrown. "Hit me, pig," "Shoot me, pig." The chase was on again. Many demonstrators raced to Grant Park where—another oddity in a week of them— police allowed them to remain. The officers ringed the area as the demonstrators lit tiny fires, fired off an occasional obscenity, and continued their vigil until dawn. Yippie founder Abbie Hoffman was arrested while eating in a restaurant for having the word "F★★★" painted on his forehead.

On Tuesday night, August 27, the fight at the convention began over the Vietnam plank. Hale Boggs of Lousiana, the platform committee chairman, denied President Johnson had any influence over the Vietnam plank. "You would be surprised how little help I got from the administration," he said with utter sincerity. Earlier, Stephen Smith had reported the McCarthy offer to withdraw to Daley, who dismissed it with a barnyard epithet.

This was the night Daley had planned to throw a huge birthday party for the president. Perhaps the party would have created a stampede of delegates, as Ed Kelly's sewer boss had done so many years earlier. But Lyndon Johnson wasn't coming to Chicago. He and Daley talked twice on that Tuesday. One last exhortation? Lyndon Johnson still wanted to go to the convention. But the latest polls showed that he, too, would lose to Nixon. That and the first few days of convention protests, coupled with the vitriolic debate on the Vietnam platform, convinced his advisors that a trip to the convention would only embarrass him. Johnson ordered Connally to rally the southern delegates to Humphrey's cause. He put roses on his dinner table, a birthday wish from Dick and Eleanor Daley.

The debate led by the McCarthy delegates went beyond midnight, and Daley was getting furious. The timetable of the convention was being thrown into chaos. At the rate it was going, the nomination would not occur until Friday. Speaker Carl Albert, the permanent chairman, was getting frazzled. He refused to hear an adjournment motion at 1:12 A.M. Antiwar delegates began to chant, "Let's go home."

Albert recognized Daley, who for the first time showed to the nation that famous scowl that all Chicago knew. "This convention is held for the delegates of the great Democratic Party, not for people in the balconies trying to take over this meeting." Then the dictatorial, imperial Daley appeared. "And if they don't . . . . we'll turn them out. Mr. Chairman, they're guests of the Democratic Party and let them conduct themselves accordingly or we'll clear the gallery." The television cameras were not kind. A moment later, he was shown as he angrily drew a finger across his throat in a "cut it off" sign.

The convention adjourned until noon August 28. The delegates returned to Michigan Avenue, where long lines of police were stationed in front of the hotels. They could see the small fires and various flags in the park. They could hear an occasional obscenity or chant. Since they had arrived on Sunday, the intermittent shouts of "F★★★ LBJ," "Dump the Hump," and "F★★★ the Hump" had serenaded them. In his private suite at the Stock Yard Inn, Daley conferred as he had Sunday and Monday night with Police Superintendent Conlisk and Deputy Superintendent James Rochford. The West Side was quiet.

On Wednesday, Daley routinely chaired the Illinois caucus at 11 A.M. It voted 112 votes for Humphrey, 3 for McGovern, 3 for McCarthy. About seventy-five people carrying McCarthy signs booed Daley as he left the Sherman House.

As the debate on the Vietnam plank filled the Amphitheatre, about eight thousand people filled the Grant Park bandshell area. There were McCarthy supporters wearing shirts and ties, hippies in Levis and sneakers; red flags for revolution, black flags for anarchy, Viet Cong flags. One young man climbed a flagpole to pull down the American flag. Police stopped him. Bottles and rocks flew. Police charged a small group. Dellinger spoke to the crowd and said it was time to march to the Amphitheatre. They moved a block before police stopped them. National Guardsmen blocked the southern and eastern exits to the park. The demonstrators moved north, turned onto Michigan Avenue, and wheeled south toward the Hilton. At the intersection of Balbo and Michigan, the street belonged to the police. They had formed a double line, curb to curb. The lights of the hotels and of television cameras, mounted on trucks and hotel eaves, lit the scene as daylight moved toward dusk.

Inside the convention, the roll call for presidential nominations started. Rostenkowski was handed the gavel to introduce the speakers. A fight broke out in the New York delegation. Rostenkowski called on the sergeant at arms to clear the aisles. Suddenly the blue helmets of Chicago police were scurrying among delegates. They took three New York delegates into custody briefly. CBS newsman Mike Wallace, trying to find out what was happening, was knocked to the floor.

At the Hilton, the swelling crowd faced off against the police. The obscenities continued. Someone threw a beer can. The police charged and the shrill cries of hundreds of young women filled the avenue. Nightsticks thudded on bones. Dozens of people were shoved or dragged into patrol wagons. The television cameras were turned on. The violence spread along the sidewalks and police went into the hotel lobbies, chasing demonstrators, reporters, spectators, anyone who stumbled into their path. It was over in eighteen minutes.

Inside the convention, delegates hearing the reports began jeering Daley. Governor Harold Hughes of Iowa nominated McCarthy as more reports of the Hilton violence filtered through the convention. Mayor Joseph Alioto of San Francisco nominated Humphrey, who was watching from his twenty-fifth-floor room in the Hilton. In the midst of the ceremony about to give him the highest honor a political party can bestow, Hubert Humphrey was forced to watch television replays of the battle taking place beneath him. He was terribly disappointed when the networks replayed the tape of the confrontation during a seconding speech for him by Cleveland Mayor Carl Stokes. Stokes, a black man, reminded America that once Humphrey had stood before a Democratic convention and bravely led the charge for equal rights. But neither Humphrey nor America saw the speech.

At the Amphitheatre, the chair of the Colorado delegation asked if there was any way "Mayor Daley can be compelled to suspend the police-state tactics." Senator Abraham Ribicoff of Connecticut, an old ally of Daley's from the 1960 Kennedy convention, rose to nominate McGovern. Instead, he taunted Daley: "With George McGovern, we wouldn't have gestapo tactics on the streets of Chicago." The entire Illinois delegation rose and booed and jeered, Daley in the middle, laughing in scorn and derision at what he saw as the worst kind of betrayal: one political leader, one Democrat, attacking another in public. As the Illinoisans booed louder, Ribicoff pointed at Daley and said, "How hard it is to accept the truth."

The nation saw the image that many Americans automatically recall at the mention of Richard J. Daley. A low camera angle showed him red-faced, veins in his neck bulging, his lower lip curled down. He was shouting and he was mad. It did not matter whether he uttered profanities, which he always denied. In that brief moment, for those who sympathized with the demonstrators, Daley conveyed both raw power and raw anger. It was not a movie taking place in American living rooms. It was a combination of the sickening sound of nightsticks, alien to almost all of white America, separated by only seconds from the rage emanating from this renowned city leader, that would cast Daley in a role he had never imagined: an icon of the corrupt, closed, selfish boss era, which voters everywhere else in America had long since abolished.

What none of the viewers and few inside the convention knew was that Ribicoff had gone to Daley at the start of the

Illinois caucus and in the presence of his own candidate, McGovern, told Daley, "Humphrey can't win. You should get Kennedy to run." Daley replied, "You're very friendly with Kennedy. You call him." Ribicoff said, "You're the only man who can get Kennedy to run." Daley later said that Ribicoff told him he was going to withdraw from his own Senate race. Daley said he first refused to allow Ribicoff to introduce McGovern to the Illinois caucus but then changed his mind. Ribicoff proceeded to praise Daley as the greatest mayor in the country before introducing McGovern.

Nearly an hour after Daley's anger flashed across America, the nominating speeches concluded and the roll call of states began. When it reached Illinois, an obviously embattled and frustrated Daley began prematurely to reel off the vote for Humphrey. Then he left the Amphitheatre for the night. Humphrey was nominated on the first ballot.

The next day, August 29, Daley informed CBS he was available to be interviewed by Walter Cronkite. He began in the slow, soft speech that was his norm, trying carefully to remember what he rehearsed, obviously intent on displaying none of the anger that had flashed at America the previous night. "Let me first say that you're a constant visitor in the Daley home every evening," he said. Then he outlined his defense. "The television industry didn't have the information I had. There were reports and intelligence on my desk that certain people planned to assassinate the three contenders for the presidency . . . that certain people planned to assassinate many of the leaders, including myself . . . ." He went only so far in accepting any blame for his police. "In the heat of emotion and riot, some policemen may have overacted, but to judge the entire police department by the alleged action of a few would be just as unfair as to judge our entire younger generation by the actions of the mob."

Then in a turnabout, Daley began to interview Cronkite. "Did you know what was said to the police and what they went through? . . . The language that was used . . . you wouldn't repeat it. These are terrorists . . . they're against government, not all of them but the majority, and the leaders—did you see some of them, what they have on their forehead? Well, you couldn't repeat what they have on their forehead."

Cronkite finally seized on a pause. "I want to ask you, who is "they" you—

"Well, you know, Hayden? The head of the Mobilization? Surely, you know Dellinger, who went to Hanoi. . . ."

"Well," Cronkite said, "I don't know that they're Communists."

"Well, neither do I," Daley answered.

Whatever the CBS television audience now thought, the Cook County Democrats made sure the nation would know that in Chicago, in his own Bridgeport, Daley was loved. The convention hall on Thursday night was packed with "We Love Daley" signs. The band even interrupted its commitment to "Happy Days Are Here Again" to blast out "Chicago, Chicago," each time Daley's name was mentioned. The delegates were just worn out when Humphrey delivered a passable but not memorable acceptance speech. He was too battered by events to spend the time he wanted to make it remarkable, which was a great disappointment to his staff. One of the reasons people like Johnson and Daley were not enthralled by Humphrey was that he talked too much. But at his best, he was one of the last great political orators.

Daley went to the podium to congratulate him. Then he returned to his suite at the Stock Yard Inn to check in with the police. "His greatest fear of convention week was that riots were going to happen again," Bill Daley said. "The West Side would go up, the South Side would go up. The truth is they didn't have enough cops to stop it. His concern at the end of each convention night was what the police were telling him was going on on the West and South sides, not on Balbo and Michigan."

A short while later Richard Daley telephoned Humphrey, who had returned to the Hilton. He again congratulated him on winning the nomination and told him what a fine speech he had given. Then he admonished, "Be your own man, Hubert. On the war, too." For Daley, the torch had been passed. Lyndon Johnson would serve five more months as president, but the new standard-bearer of the Democratic Party, for better or worse, was Hubert Humphrey. Daley, ever the pragmatist, knew Humphrey must sever himself from Johnson's Vietnam policy to win the election. Daley, who had for five years resolutely defended a war he found repugnant, was now urging a reversal of that defense. Daley, who had treated Eugene McCarthy's challenge to Johnson as treason, was now urging Humphrey not only to reject an expectation of far greater loyalty than the president could presume of a McCarthy or a Kennedy but also to ignore the gratitude that he felt and Lyndon Johnson demanded.

Humphrey and the Democratic Party left Chicago in seeming ruins. Every poll and every political expert conceded the election. No one seemed to understand that Richard Nixon was basically not an acceptable candidate in America. Any other Republican—Rockefeller, Reagan— would have won in a landslide. Nixon made it in a cloud of dust.

Hubert Humphrey didn't take Daley's advice. Each time he prepared to declare himself opposed to the continuation of war, no matter on what terms, it seemed Lyndon Johnson invisibly grabbed him by the throat. Newton Minow, who served as Humphrey's Illinois campaign chairman, said, "It seems strange to say, but I actually think Humphrey was physically frightened of Johnson."[8] He finally made the break ten days before the election in a Salt Lake City speech. In

the final week, the polls narrowed so rapidly that few believed
them. Minow said, "I'm probably as much at fault as anyone. I didn't think we could win in Illinois. When Humphrey
came to Chicago for the traditional torchlight parade, he
asked me what I thought and I told him honestly that we
didn't have a chance."

Daley was angry at Humphrey for not defending the city
more strongly during the convention, and he was doubly
angry that Humphrey had listened to other advice and never
campaigned in the city until the final weekend. Humphrey
knew he had made a mistake. He said, "We had written off
Illinois too soon and so, apparently, had Mayor Daley and
his lieutenants. . . . Had we been there earlier we would have
won it." He was right. Bill Daley remembered his father was
very angry that Humphrey did not return to Chicago and was
even worried that he would fail at the last minute to appear
for the torchlight parade. "They had Ed Muskie waiting in
Cleveland to fly in at the last minute," Bill said.[9] And
Humphrey was right about the Daley lieutenants, who always
took their cue from the chairman. Daley and everyone else
had given up too early on the Humphrey-Muskie ticket.

There was another sinister element in 1968: George Wallace's race-based campaign. While Nixon and Humphrey
dodged about on the war issue, Wallace issued a political battle cry to the South, which had been traditionally Democratic. He was barking up the same law-and-order tree as
Nixon, so in the end it was difficult to assess whether he
affected either major candidate significantly. But he blurred
the future of electoral politics. His vote total, 13 percent, sig-
naled a warning to both parties that the South, particularly,
was ripe for a new direction. The Republicans ultimately
took advantage of it.

On November 5, 1968, Richard Nixon won the presidency with 31,770,237 votes. Humphrey had 31,270,533. It was

not as close as Kennedy's 1960 margin, but it was one of the tightest victories in history. In Illinois, Nixon got 2,174,774 to Humphrey's 2,039,814. Daley, with cause, blamed Humphrey's decision not to campaign in Chicago for the defeat. But he also knew that he hadn't really delivered. Humphrey went out of Chicago with 800,000 votes. In 1960, Daley had delivered 1,060,000 votes for Kennedy and in 1964 an overwhelming 1,131,000 votes for Johnson. Wallace had siphoned off some of the vote, but the numbers weren't there.

In fairness, Humphrey was not the candidate the Democrats had in the two previous elections. And Daley was subject to the same peaks and valleys of enthusiasm as anyone else. Had he believed a month sooner that Humphrey could win, he might have been able to drive out a larger vote, because it was the size of the vote rather than the margins that cost Humphrey. The dozen predominantly black wards, despite the Martin Luther King riots and the four years of school and housing protests, gave Humphrey a 200,000-vote margin—half the city's Democratic edge. But the total black vote had diminished nearly 100,000 from 1968. They weren't ready to vote Republican, but a lot of them didn't vote. The ethnic wards also slipped and some of the best-producing organizations—the 31st, the 38th, the 40th, the 50th—were unable to keep people out of the Nixon column.

Daley brooded afterward that the Democrats would have won with a different candidate. Did he have anyone specific in mind? "His name is the same as that of a recent president," Daley said. It might also be said that if his gubernatorial candidate had the same name as a recent governor, he might have won everything. If Daley had slated Adlai Stevenson III for governor instead of the lackluster Sam Shapiro, who barely outran Humphrey (an anomaly for Daley's local ticket, which always ran well ahead of the presidential candidate) Stevenson could have beaten Republican Dick Ogilvie to become governor.

Moreover, Stevenson could have swayed enough Democrats to give Humphrey a chance of carrying Illinois. The campaign itself would have had a much more optimistic note. And if the polls had indicated earlier that the Democrats were doing well in Illinois, it could have been contagious, especially in states like Ohio and Missouri where Nixon won narrowly, and nationally as well. The premature but ultimately costly pessimism of Democratic leaders was evidenced by rumors in the Humphrey camp that California Speaker Unruh, always a Kennedy man, had bet $1,000 that Nixon would win California. Even Daley belatedly realized he might be able to deliver a winner. On election night, he called Humphrey to say, "Don't give up. The votes are not all in. You can still carry Illinois."[10]

Daley didn't fare too badly in the election. His hand-picked Irishman, Edward Hanrahan, retained the state's attorney's office for the party, which would turn out to be a mixed blessing. Paul Powell and Mike Howlett held on to the secretary of state and state auditor positions. Ogilvie's ascension opened the way for Daley favorite George Dunne to take over the county board presidency, where he remained for twenty years.

William Clark's candidacy against Everett Dirksen was virtually conceded from the start. Rostenkowski noted, "The U.S. Senate was never very important to the organization. What could a senator do for you? There were no jobs. If a Senate candidate raised money and was running well, then the organization would put in resources." They forgot Clark quickly, which also created an aura of pessimism.

But Daley was not the only politician or the only American who ended 1968 saying "what if?" What if Robert Kennedy had lived? "I'm sure my father would have supported him at the convention," Bill Daley said. "After he won California, he would have shown he was the best candidate."

The peripatetic Larry O'Brien, who worked in 1968 for Johnson, Kennedy and Humphrey, wasn't that positive. "If we [Kennedy] had followed California with . . . . New York, we still would be short. . . . I have to state that if Bobby had been able to go on to Chicago, he would have had an uphill struggle to get nominated. That's contrary to what is said by some revisionists who fondly hoped that Bobby [would be] nominated and that hope has translated in the intervening years into an assurance that it would take place. . . . None of us knew what the ultimate result would have been in Chicago."[11]

What if Kennedy had remained on the sidelines? Gene McCarthy thought he would have lost to Kennedy at the convention anyway. What if Humphrey had renounced Johnson's war policy in mid-September instead of late October? What if Johnson had called a halt to the bombing of North Vietnam on August 31 instead of October 31? Such speculations can be made after any election, but rarely do they deal with events of such magnitude.

In the days following the Democratic convention, Daley had a report, "Strategies of Confrontation," prepared to exonerate his police department. He produced a film, *What Trees Do They Plant?*, to exonerate himself. He wore a perpetual scowl in the fall of 1968, and the mirthful spirit he occasionally displayed with reporters had vanished. Liberals derided his "assassination plot" apologia, and his study and film were immediately suspect.

There is no doubt that Daley tossed out the specter of assassins as a late defensive logic, but few people had been so directly affected by the three major assassinations of the decade and fewer still were constantly the subject of similar threats, including the one Johnson had told him about during the April rioting. Surrounding the Amphitheatre with five thousand soldiers is hardly the way to prevent an assassination, and Daley's heavy-handed assertion of plots was not very convincing. But he was getting fragile. It was an incredibly stressful year. He was sixty-six years old and even if he would never admit it, he was probably scared. With everything else that had befallen him, he didn't need an assassination to take place in Chicago—even an assassination of someone else.

But none of that mattered. Daley was as popular as ever in his own city, in his own state. Tim Sheehan, GOP county chairman, had remarked, "If Daley were running for re-election this year he'd be stronger than ever." Among liberals, no amount of explanation would ever repair the images of anger and rage spliced with nightsticks and blood. Certainly someone else might not have armed Chicago as though the Red Army were camped in Gary. Someone else might have wavered on sleeping in the park. But the handful of provocateurs who mixed with the sincere war protestors would have managed to engage the police anyway.

Daley never apologized, never admitted he might have been wrong. Even in his "shoot to kill" blunder, he recognized he had made a mistake. Even back in the Summerdale scandal, he recognized that he could not defend police burglars. He felt no remorse for keeping his promise to preserve law and order.

The battle of Michigan Avenue may have scarred Chicago's image briefly, but the convention itself had far greater significance to the future of American politics. The transition from post-World War II complacency to rebellion against traditional authority was forged in the debate over the war. Those much younger than Dick Daley, who could not grasp in their souls the faith in authority that was part of his birthright, would be further shattered by Watergate. The

1968 election was a stunning rejection of the deceptions of Lyndon Johnson's administration.

There was no guarantee that Richard Nixon's White House would be any different. But if the new dissident politicians could not directly change the behavior of presidents, they could change the way they were selected. George McGovern accurately predicted the future at the end of the convention, taking one last swipe at Daley: "There is something almost obscene about presidential candidates going to one man about what one hundred delegates are going to do. . . . We ought to scrap the entire convention system and go entirely over to the more democratic system of primary elections in every state."[12]

The revolution that took place in Chicago that last week of August took place on Tuesday night inside the convention hall, not on the streets and in the parks. It took place when the delegates voted to change the credentials and rules that had allowed the power of the party to be clutched by only a few strong hands for a century. The events of that Tuesday night bore fruit in 1972 and changed forever the way Americans choose presidents, and not necessarily for the better. But the panorama of the 1968 convention, of the entire year—the assassinations, their aftermath, the political maneuvering, the cultural upheaval—proved that no big-city leader in modern American history had ever been so nationally prominent, so perceivably powerful, as Daley, who was ultimately both reviled and revered.

CHAPTER 11

"Garry Owen"

IN 1972, RICHARD J. DALEY, THE CONSUMMATE MASTER OF political intrigue, the student of electoral mechanics, the repository of the most reliable bloc of Democratic Party strength in the country, was a prisoner of his past. But he was not alone. In 1972, for the first time, more than half the delegates to the Democratic National Convention were chosen in primary elections, which were held in twenty-two states that year. For the first time, the bulk of the votes needed to choose a presidential nominee were not in the clutches of the handful of party leaders who had provided the direction for the Democrats since their birth under Thomas Jefferson and Aaron Burr and who served as the bridges over which the fruits of government moral and fiscal policy traveled to their constituents.

In 1972, hardly anyone but a few political operatives and especially attentive political reporters understood anything about delegate selection. The operatives were making up the rules as they went along. In some states, candidates for delegate ran on ballots under their own names with no indication whom they would support at the convention. This was

the case in Chicago and other party strongholds, where regulars were virtually assured control of usually low-turnout
primary contests. In other states, presidential candidates were
listed on the ballot and would be awarded certain numbers
of delegates, whom they would name later. In another vari-
ation, candidates for delegate were listed along with the presidential candidate they were bound to support. Although the
new Democratic rules of 1972 changed the qualifications for
admitting delegates at the party's convention, individual state
election laws often conflicted with these rules, creating mass
confusion. Almost no one understood this in 1972.

In subsequent years, the Democrats adjusted their rules
and local parties effected changes in state election regula-
tions. By 1984, the rules had been sufficiently streamlined to
ensure that if public sentiment favored Ronald Reagan and
Walter Mondale, they would win the majority of the delegates
and seal their nominations long before the party conventions. The role of the power brokers was forever ended.
Beyond that, the social and cultural changes of the 1960s in
America would reverberate in the 1970s as a political upheaval. The idea that Richard J. Daley could not elect
whomever he wanted as delegates who would bind their presidential support to his ultimate decision seemed ridiculous to
him, if not unconstitutional.

The dissident Democrats who left Chicago in 1968 were
determined to reform the party of Lyndon Johnson and
Richard Daley. The Democratic election defeat left the party
with Humphrey as a titular leader with no following. He virtually conceded planning for the future to a commission
headed by George McGovern, who, after his tardy entry into
the 1968 race, behaved like a gallant Democrat and supported Humphrey loyally through the fall campaign. The
commission not only established new rules for the selection
of delegates but broke with all forms of historic power by

deciding who they should be—not by name, but by gender, ethnicity, race, and age. When they finally convened at Miami Beach in July 1972, the Democratic Party bore no resemblance to the one Dick Daley had served and dominated for the past four decades.

Of the three thousand delegates, nearly 2,500 were attending their first convention. Fifteen percent were black. More than one-third were women, three times as many as had jammed the Amphitheatre four years earlier. Almost one-fourth were under thirty years of age. One Democrat remarked, "Don't pass up any hitchikers, they might be delegates." In fact, many did hitch rides. Others rode buses or crammed into vans. They brought jars of peanut butter and ate in their cheap rooms or at the headquarters of whatever candidate or cause they were supporting.

The 1972 campaign started with twelve Democratic candidates, but there were at least twice that many causes. The usual parade of candidates to the fifth floor of City Hall was muted by the resonance of 1968 and the unusual field of a dozen wannabe nominees. Many of them weren't sure it was politically safe to be seen bowing to the throne beside Lake Michigan. Others weren't sure they would get past the door. The internal machinations of the party were also disquieting. Democrats representing the old line were aware of the changes but made no effort to join them or seem in any way supportive. The politics of inclusion was clearly in keeping with their populist tradition, but the strength of the old city hall–statehouse–courthouse party was that it could always recover from any sudden fits of morality in exchange for the prospect of victory. And the 1972 Democrats did not seem to be headed for victory.

In the beginning, it didn't look too bad, especially for the northern big-city leaders from the Pennsylvania union belt through the rim of the Great Lakes. The early favorite and

private choice of people like Daley was Muskie, the Lincoln-
esque, thoughtful senator from Maine whose 1970 off-year
election eve speech had earned him plaudits and respect.
Daley appreciated a good speech as well as anyone, but what
he had in mind was Muskie's Polish heritage. With the continued white flight and national trend of upward mobility, it
is hard to say with certainty that in 1972 Chicago still housed
more Poles than any other city except Warsaw. But if they
weren't on Milwaukee Avenue, they were still within reach-
ing distance of the Cook County Democratic Party. Of all
the potential candidates (none of whom seemed in the early
winter of 1972 likely to defeat Richard Nixon), Ed Muskie
had the most appeal for a Cook County ticket.

Humphrey was trying again and paid his respects. But
Daley, still smarting from 1968 and more than ever certain
that Humphrey was not a winner, remained silent. Others like
George McGovern and Mayor John Lindsay of New York,
who had forsaken his Republican ways, were respectful.
George Wallace was sticking pretty much south of the
Mason-Dixon line. Gene McCarthy was somewhere out there
again. The war was still being fought, but the passion he had
brought to the debate in 1968 was gone and so were most of
his followers.

There were no spin doctors in 1972, but there was an
increasing amount of television coverage. Muskie's campaign
fell apart when he made the critical mistake of not lowering
his expectations in the nation's traditionally first primary, in
his neighboring state of New Hampshire. The media had
forecast a 60 percent or even 70 percent victory for the front
runner. Muskie smiled and said he hoped so. Then, under a
vicious personal attack from the archconservative *Manchester* (N.H.) *Union-Leader*, which had made some nasty refer-
ences to his wife, Muskie stood on the back of a truck, in
front of a camera, and wept. His opponents used the inci-

dent to portray him as too weak and emotional to lead the country. He won New Hampshire with 46 percent, but McGovern ran up a surprising 37 percent and Muskie for all purposes was through.

In May, George Wallace was shot in a Maryland shopping mall and paralyzed. So McGovern, whose commission had invented the new rules and then built an apparatus for him to capitalize on them, marched through the remaining primaries with only Humphrey trailing along as an alternative. The richest prize was California, where state laws made the primary a winner-take-all affair. That was not in compliance with the new party rules fashioned by the McGovern commission. But when McGovern defeated Humphrey, he was happy to play by the old rules and claim all 271 delegates, putting him fewer than twenty delegates shy of a first-ballot nomination. No candidate in the history of the party had ever approached a convention so certain of nomination, so free of the need to trade, barter, cajole, or beg from the likes of Richard Daley.

But old habits die hard and the core of the old Democratic Party would not accept the fact that they could do nothing to prevent the nomination from going to McGovern, who already had begun to show signs of conciliating every special-issue group from the farthest-left fringes of the Democratic Party. The AFL-CIO, still led by the autocratic George Meany and in its final throes as one of the most influential factions of the Democratic Party, decided to fight the awarding of all 271 California delegates to McGovern. It argued that based on his 47 percent showing, he should receive only 120 delegates. Labor strategists reasoned that would keep him short enough of a first-ballot victory that a coalition of Humphrey, Muskie, and the southern states might be able to deny him the nomination. Of course, Daley was very interested in this kind of strategy. It was clear to him that a

McGovern candidacy would be disastrous. And, despite all his mistakes, Humphrey had come very close in Illinois in 1968.

But Daley was also in a box regarding his own seat at the convention. After the California challenge, the Credentials Committee would deal with a challenge to Daley's delegation. Although his delegate slate had been elected easily in the March 21, 1972 primary, it was being challenged by an alternate slate concocted by independent Alderman William Singer, who had upset the organization candidate in the 44th Ward, and Jesse Jackson, who had made his mark in Chicago as the head of Operation Breadbasket, the economic arm of Martin Luther King, Jr.'s, Southern Christian Leadership Conference. The Singer-Jackson forces had handpicked delegates in various caucuses held in the spring while organization regulars sat in the church basements jeering. Although the Daley delegates did not reflect the kinds of quota requirements demanded by the new Democratic Party, it was inconceivable to almost everyone that they could be replaced by people who had virtually picked themselves.

"They were out to punish him for 1968. He knew that," said Bill Daley. He knew it but he didn't necessarily believe it. The people had spoken, as Daley loved to declare after elections. His delegates had been duly elected. They were, for the most part, the same people he had been taking to Democratic conventions for years: party officials, committeemen, aldermen, state legislators, labor bosses, and his best friends. They were almost all white, all male, and all old.

"I tried to tell him," Newt Minow recalled, "that there were new rules. He couldn't believe it or he wouldn't accept it. But I don't think he understood that you could actually make rules like that."

"We all tried to tell him," said Rostenkowski. "In our [congressional district] we had a slate of delegates nobody could challenge. We had women, we had a student, we had a Hispanic, we had a perfect slate. I told Daley that he had to have slates that met the quotas. Daley didn't read the rules, didn't listen to them. He just couldn't believe that the Credentials Committee would have the nerve to deny seats to people truly elected by the people. He thought there was no way that anybody can challenge people elected at the ballot box."

Frank Mankiewicz, the only member of McGovern's brain trust who had an appreciation for the old party leaders, and particularly for Daley, tried during the spring to see if a compromise could be reached. Daley was not interested in sharing seats with Bill Singer and Jesse Jackson. He was certain that the Democratic Party would not, could not, hold a convention without Dick Daley.

McGovern's staff, which had been so meticulous about the technical aspects of dominating the primary system, relaxed as the Credentials Committee members were chosen. The anti-McGovern forces quietly secured a great many of the 150 places on the committee. Illinois was allotted five members and Daley picked them. The leader was Alderman Claude W. B. Holman, the bombastic City Council president, former Dawson disciple, and one of the most outspoken and illogical Daley loyalists.

On Wednesday, June 27, the Credentials Committee met in Washington to decide the California question. The ten California members of the committee, who would have sided with McGovern, were not entitled to vote. The McGovern forces were beginning to worry that if they lost California, the nomination might disappear. They offered Daley a deal. If Illinois would support McGovern on the California matter, the McGovern loyalists would support some kind of compromise to ensure Daley was seated. Daley turned it down.

The explanation was that Daley could not afford to make a compromise because that would automatically give Singer and Jackson some stature within the Cook County organization after the convention. That was not true. Daley was always capable of making accommodations when necessary and dealing with miscreants later in his own way. His real dilemma was that he truly believed his delegation had the legal right to their seats. He would prove it in court if necessary. This turned out to be a bad miscalculation.

Daley's second problem was pride. He just didn't believe he would be excluded. No one, not even McGovern with his new political movement and new openness, could imagine entering a presidential election campaign without the most enthusiastic support of Richard J. Daley.

Third, he wanted to play kingmaker. He was risking—although he didn't think it was much of a risk—the humiliation of being barred from the convention rather than cut a deal that would force him to sit there four nights with nothing at all to do or say that figured in choosing the nominee of his party. If he ordered his Credentials Committee members to support McGovern, the California delegates would make his nomination certain and the convention would dawdle, with all of his followers demanding television time to whine about their special causes. Daley never thought for a moment he wouldn't be there. And if he was going to be there he wanted to be what he always had been, the most powerful Democratic city leader in the building. He threw in with the Humphrey forces.

With the Illinois committee members voting against him, McGovern lost his fight to keep all 271 California delegates by a 72 to 66 vote. Had Daley switched, McGovern would have won by 71 to 67. The McGovernites were outraged. Mankiewicz, a former Kennedy campaign aide, argued for common sense. No one would listen. On Friday, June 30, the Credentials Committee voted 71 to 61 to kick Richard Daley and 58 of his friends out of their seats. Mankiewicz mused, with all the clarity of the general who predicted war after hearing of Pearl Harbor, "I think we may have lost Illinois tonight."[1]

Daley sent his lawyers to court, where he lost. He still thought he had an ace in the hole. The Democratic National Chairman was Larry O'Brien, an old friend from both the Kennedy and Johnson years. At the New Orleans conference of mayors only a few days before the scheduled Credentials Committee meeting, O'Brien had asked for an audience with Daley. So had Muskie, McGovern, and Humphrey. Whatever feelings remained from 1968, Daley was clearly the center-piece of the mayors' gathering. Surely O'Brien knew the value of Richard Daley. Another old friend, Joe Califano, who had sent all those memos to Daley about his new urban proj-ects, was the party's counsel. While Daley retreated to his vacation home in Grand Beach, Michigan, most of his dele-gates and his sons were in Miami Beach. Daley was in con-stant contact with his sons, Illinois party chairman John Touhy, and Rostenkowski.

Rostenkowski told him not to expect much help from Larry O'Brien. "At one point, I ran into Jake Arvey, who tells me that he's been trying for two days to get to see O'Brien and keeps being told he's too busy. Now Arvey's one of the guys who helped O'Brien get to be chairman, so we went over to his office and I get the same runaround. I said to the receptionist, 'Is he in there?' and then I just bang the door open. Here's O'Brien and Califano sitting around eating apples. They're doing nothing and they're not going to do anything for us. I never went to the Convention Hall that week."

The one last chance was Ted Kennedy. Kennedy had taken himself completely out of the presidential derby in 1972 and did not plan to attend the convention. But on Mon-day, July 10, the opening night of the convention, the Cali-fornia and Illinois challenges would be voted on by all three thousand delegates. If Massachusetts, a devoutly loyal McGovern delegation,[2] voted for Daley, the Illinois regulars might be seated.

Ted Kennedy did nothing to save his family's old friend. Daley was disappointed, but he understood that Kennedy had remained on the sidelines the entire year and it would have been unseemly and a petty slap at McGovern for him to actively register a protest against the presumptive nominee at the last minute. While Daley was able to forgive Kennedys almost anything, many members of his party neither forgot nor forgave. When Kennedy challenged Jimmy Carter in 1980, many of the Chicago Democrats who had to sit in the lobby of the Diplomat Hotel that long week in 1972 sat on their hands. Kennedy was drubbed.

The Singer-Jackson forces had won control of the Illinois delegation. Like so many revolutionaries and insurgents, having won, they had little idea what to do. The Illinois delegation caucused until the wee hours every morning, in part because McGovern's people could never get the convention sessions concluded until 3 A.M. and in part because no one knew what they were doing. Daley had been running the Illinois caucuses like a Marine Corps drill for so long that no one else had ever bothered to learn the process. Clyde Choate, a Paul Powell disciple from southern Illinois and minority leader of the Illinois House, was elected delegation co-chair. He smiled a lot but had no idea what this strange collection of Chicago delegates was all about.

On the evening of McGovern's nomination, the Illinois caucus spent a great deal of time fretting over the Kentucky Fried Chicken box lunches placed at every delegate's chair. The lunches were garnished with lettuce, and since one of the most compelling issues of the 1972 convention seemed to be support for Cesar Chavez's Farm Workers Union boycott of lettuce, the Singer-Jackson Illinoisans were upset. They haggled endlessly over how to express their indignation.

On Wednesday, July 12, during the roll call to nominate George McGovern, it ironically fell to Illinois to cast the votes that put him over the top. Choate, with dozens of people shouting instructions at him (a breach of etiquette that never occurred during Daley's ten conventions) took the microphone and declared, "Illinois, a state which eats lettuce—grows lettuce—boycotts lettuce—lettuce . . . casts. . . ."

The McGovern tacticians had promised almost everyone in the building that they could make nominating speeches, so the candidate never made the acceptance speech that is supposed to kick-start the election campaign until 2:48 A.M. As Teddy White noted, the only place under the American flag where McGovern spoke in prime time was Guam. Of the seventeen million households that had been watching the convention in prime time, only three million still had their sets on when McGovern reached the podium—and no one knows if anyone was watching them.[3]

Banished at his lakefront room, Daley was despondent. His daughters visited him with his small grandchildren. He took them to a little pond, where he put a worm on a hook and with a bobber floating on the water began to teach them to fish. He wanted to go to Miami, but Touhy and others urged him to stay where he was. A private jet had been sitting at a nearby airstrip in case the challenge was dismissed.

On the Sunday before the convention, Daley had had second thoughts. He called O'Brien. "It was a low-key conversation," O'Brien said, "in which Daley made clear to me that, with great reluctance, in the interest of the party, he would be willing to compromise with the McGovern people and split the delegation. I thought that was a very positive note. . . . He assumed I would move the suggestion forward." O'Brien said he called McGovern, who was very enthusiastic about a way out of the deadlock. "I never heard another word," O'Brien said. "Whether he [McGovern] was serious—he was derailed by his advisors. . . . It was clear a decision had been made by the McGovern people to sink Daley."[4]

Bill Daley said, "The only way he could have been at the convention was to do a deal with McGovern. He honestly believed that the delegates were legally entitled to their seats. Two, he wouldn't do a deal with McGovern. He was hurt by being left out. It bothered him tremendously. But he was resigned to it. Then he had to listen to Walter Cronkite reporting there was a rumor that Mayor Daley was hidden in a Miami Beach hotel suite storming around his room. We all told him not to come. Jack Touhy and Danny [Rostenkowski] believed it would not be safe for him to come. Even if we got seated, it wouldn't be safe."

Daley was not alone in exile. More than 220 of the party's 250 congressmen were not allowed in Miami. Neither were Mayor Joseph Alioto of San Francisco, Mayor Sam Yorty of Los Angeles, Mayor Frank Rizzo of Philadelphia, and Mayor Kevin White of Boston—all of them duly elected by the people in their districts. But no one rejoiced or mourned the absence of these men. Richard J. Daley was the symbol of change. While the McGovernites and the Singers and Jacksons and children delegates pointed to his humiliation as the great new beginning of the Democratic Party, others realized it meant the convention forces of 1972 had created an instrument to remove what they most disliked about the Democratic Party of 1968 but had not contemplated what they would do to replace it. That problem would haunt the oldest political party in America for the remainder of the century.

Whatever reasons George McGovern had for allowing his strategists to deny Daley a seat at the convention, he regretted it almost immediately. He visited Chicago in August beseeching Daley for his help in the election. He need not have begged. "I've always been a Democrat and of course we'll support our candidate," Daley said.

Of course, McGovern probably noted that on the day he won the California primary, Daley endorsed Nixon's Vietnam policy with the words, "I may be old-fashioned, but I'll support the president; he knows more than we do." It was Daley again demonstrating his conviction that loyalty to the ultimate authority was the first commandment of men—or, at least, political men. And if that could extend to a Republican president still waging a war that Daley had privately renounced, it would extend to a Democratic presidential nominee who had made certain that Richard J. Daley was no longer the most powerful big-city political leader in American history.

Daley would work for McGovern. But, for once, he couldn't keep all the troops aboard the train. Vito Marzullo, the West Side patronage prince, openly wore Nixon buttons throughout the campaign. In Washington, George Meany, the AFL-CIO's high priest and the Democratic Party's major fundraiser for fifty years, endorsed Richard Nixon. When McGovern came to see Daley in August, the mayor opened the door. In most other cities, Democrats took vacation days. If the events of 1968 had embarrassed the Democrats and Hubert Humphrey, the election of 1972 mortified them and left McGovern, a bright, decent man, an icon of political ineptitude. The Democratic Party convention of 1972 made sure the party would never return to its old ways. The McGovern campaign made sure it would never return to 1972.

His exclusion from the convention was one of a series of disturbing things that befell Richard Daley in the quadrennium following 1968. Dissension was stirring in the ranks of his local organization; Adlai Stevenson III decided in the fall of 1968 to join the criticism by labeling the Cook County organization a "feudal" system. Another ambitious man, Dan

Walker, chairman of the Chicago Crime Commission, was assigned to do a report on the 1968 convention disorders for the President's Commission on the Causes and Prevention of Violence. When the report was released, it was critical of specific police actions but noted that most police behaved responsibly and there was evidence of provocation. Daley reacted calmly and urged everyone to read the full report. The summary of the report, however, was a personal statement by Walker that characterized the convention as a "police riot." Daley was furious. So was Lyndon Johnson. He sent memos all over the White House asking "who is this guy Walker . . . who appointed him?"[5]

In the spring of 1969, Stevenson made a further break with Daley. He endorsed Singer in his bid for alderman. Liberals and independents were now seeking opportunities to exploit cracks in the once-solid wall of Daley authority.

Daley knew it. He realized he'd better open the door a little before someone knocked it down. On September 7, 1969, Daley drove up to the Libertyville farm where his old friend Adlai Stevenson had lived during those memorable presidential campaign years. Adlai III, the rebellious state treasurer who had become the figurehead of the liberal anti-machine movement, was tossing a rally for members of the McGovern Commission, and the pasture along the Des Plaines River was filled with people like Lieutenant Governor Paul Simon, who had written a magazine piece about the Democratic organization in the same tone as Stevenson's "feudal" characterization. Singer and Jackson were there, as were Seymour Simon, McGovern, Governor Harold Hughes of Iowa (another Daley critic), Senator Fred Harris of Oklahoma, who fancied himself a populist, and several thousand other people.

Daley praised everyone, especially Adlai III, accepted a few boos in good spirits, and was applauded. He told them,

"Some people have tried to create a split in the Democratic Party. I say they haven't succeeded. There is a right to disagree, but in the Democratic Party in 1970 and 1972 there'll be unity. . . . We have room for everyone." In late afternoon, McGovern rose to make an announcement. "Senator Everett Dirksen has died in Washington."

In November, Adlai Stevenson III was slated as the Democratic candidate for U.S. Senator. In the 1970 election, he won big, helping Daley elect as sheriff Richard Elrod, the son of the late 24th Ward committeeman Arthur X. Elrod, and retain all his county offices. Daley had found an obscure educator, Michael Bakalis, to elect to the post of state superintendent of public instruction. Others had wanted the post, which provided a nice little package of patronage. Most party members were baffled by Daley's choice. He told them they needed to find professionals for such jobs. He told the Greek-American community he had made up for dumping Stamos from the state's attorney's job in 1968.

In 1971, Daley ran barely noticed for a fifth term. The Republicans found another turncoat Democrat, Richard Friedman, a studious, polite and well-informed candidate who conducted a civil (some would say silent) campaign. Friedman was executive director of the Better Government Association, which supplied investigators to Chicago newspapers to expose park district workers sleeping on the job and sometimes more serious evidence of the sins of the patronage system. He got 29 percent of the vote. Daley beat him 740,137 to 315,969. The cynics of the 1968 convention were silenced.

In the fall of 1972, it was time for Daley to pick another slate. Richard Ogilvie was regarded as an excellent governor but he had—to Daley's relief—finally passed a state income tax, and that was a chink in his political armor. The tax issue was dangling around Ogilvie's neck and Daley did nothing in the way of a bipartisan statement to remove it. As usual, there was a line waiting to be anointed governor. Daley had had such success with Stevenson in 1970 that he decided another rebel would do fine. He picked Lieutenant Governor Paul Simon over State Auditor Michael Howlett and one of his own rising stars, a young aide named Neil Hartigan. Howlett was given the secretary of state slating to battle Republican Edmund Kuharski for the vacant office. Paul Powell had died during his term and the secretary of state's office had taken on a new political allure when it was discovered that Powell left a shoe box filled with $800,000 in cash in his Springfield hotel room. Hartigan got put on the ladder in the lieutenant governor's spot.

Daley's other dilemma was the state's attorney's office. Hanrahan, his pride and joy of 1968, was no longer acceptable to the black committeemen. They were headed by Alderman Ralph Metcalfe, who had finished second to Jesse Owens in the 1936 Olympic sprint and had worked his way up to be the ranking black organization leader, succeeding Bill Dawson when he died in 1970. Hanrahan's police had staged a predawn raid on a West Side apartment on December 4, 1969, killing two members of the Black Panther party, Fred Hampton and Mark Clark. Hanrahan's office reported the two had died in a gun battle resisting arrest. The *Chicago Tribune* eagerly accepted the details of revolutionaries firing from darkened bedrooms at members of the state's attorney's office, but it turned out the only shooting had been done by the police. Hanrahan was dumped at the slating in favor of Ray Berg, a bright judge.

Daley thought he had done all the right things. He'd ignored the party hacks who despised the Paul Simon kinds of reformers. He ridded the party of Hanrahan in the face of opposition from the ethnic ward leaders, whose constituents heartily approved of his raid whether Hampton and

Clark were resisting or simply sleeping in their beds. If there were those who thought his law-and-order posture of the middle 1960s was a blatant appeal to the white backlash crowd, he was now bowing to the wishes of the black community and the lakefront liberals. Daley had changed with the times and he was going to be 70 years old.

But he couldn't change quickly enough. Dan Walker, the author of the "police riot" remark and Stevenson's senate campaign chairman in 1970, announced he would run for the Democratic gubernatorial nomination without the endorsement of the Cook County Democrats. Walker initiated his campaign by wrapping a red bandana around his neck and walking through most of the state, spending time in each town telling everyone the horrors of Richard J. Daley and his machine. On top of that, Hanrahan couldn't be satisfied with a judgeship like every other loyalist who had been dumped from a ticket. He, too, was mounting a primary challenge.

And there was one more challenge. Within the circle of party regulars were young rebels like Edward R. Vrdolyak and Edward Burke. They were clamoring for a piece of Daley's power. So Daley told Parky Cullerton it was time for a new assessor and slated young Thomas Tully, a Cullerton protégé with excellent credentials. This satisfied almost everyone. It didn't satisfy Vrdolyak, who would be one of the most charismatic and influential members of the Chicago Democratic Party for the next fifteen years until a string of comedies and tragedies turned him into one of the many Chicago politicians done in by bad timing. Vrdolyak announced that he, too, would challenge the slated ticket in the primary.

Simon, with his liberal credentials and organization backing, seemed a cinch. But he was a man of integrity. Before Stevenson ever criticized Daley's operation, Simon, who owned a small newspaper, had written a national magazine piece depicting the evils of the Cook County Democrats. Since the income tax issue figured to be the only one in the campaign, reporters had been asking Simon about it. He visited Daley in the mayor's office and told him he planned to announce that he could possibly support an increase in the income tax rather than a hike in the regressive sales tax.

Daley told him, "Don't do it. You say that and you're done." Simon went to his scheduled news conference and said what he told Daley he intended to say. He was done. Walker, with a lot of help from Republicans who crossed over to the Democratic primary, defeated Simon and was now the Democratic standard-bearer for the fall. Hanrahan defeated Berg. Instead of the dream ticket that would satisfy liberals and reformers, Daley was saddled with an unguided missile planning to build his career by destroying the Cook County Democratic Party and a badly wounded state's attorney who was now the main target of liberals and of a vocal black political leadership. And in July, Daley was booted out of his own party convention.

Whatever else Dan Walker was or would turn out to be, in the fall of 1972 he was the Democratic candidate for governor, and Daley delivered. But Walker's victory came mostly because of the income tax tag he hung first on Simon and then on Ogilvie. Daley couldn't deliver Hanrahan, and Bernard Carey captured the state's attorney's office for the GOP. McGovern, of course, went down in flames, losing Illinois to Nixon by 870,000 votes. Daley did carry him in Chicago by 171,928. Daley's usual bright postelection report to the media was a bit inverted: "We elected Neil Hartigan as lieutenant governor and we've elected Walker as governor." And for those who thought his days as a national figure were past, he reminded, "We delivered Chicago for George McGovern, one of the few big cities which did."

He bit his lip and muttered, "Everybody knows Dan Walker will make a great governor." Then he went home to join the party for his eldest son, Richard M. Daley, who had been elected to his father's old seat in the state senate.

On January 22, 1973, Lyndon Baines Johnson's heart, always weak and irreparably broken by the 1968 referendum on his leadership, gave out. The Daleys went to Texas for the funeral. They had also been there for the dedication of the Lyndon B. Johnson Library in 1971. Daley said of his good friend, "Lyndon Johnson was a man of peace and vision who became a victim of a tragic war. He will always be the great legislator, the great president who believed in the Great Society, the man from the South who led the struggle for civil rights."

In May of 1974, Daley's heart began to play tricks on him. Daley had rarely been ill in all his years as mayor. He had grown in girth and shrunk in stature, as happens to most septuagenarians, but his energy, measured by his rapid stride and busy schedule, seemed to be that of a man who not only was healthy but loved his job. No one ever loved it more. But on May 6, he began to feel faint and had himself driven to his doctor's office on North Michigan Avenue. Dr. Thomas J. Coogan, Jr., listened to his slurred speech, and heard about his dizziness, felt his rapid pulse, checked his high blood pressure, and immediately sent him to Presbyterian-St. Luke's Hospital on the near West Side.

Daley's sudden illness stunned the city. Like all things in the personal life of Richard Daley, it was kept clandestine, which fed the comparisons to the Kremlin. The immediate announcement was that Daley had hypoglycemia, a low-blood-sugar condition, and had been taking medication for it. He remained in the hospital for two weeks, during which it was casually revealed that he had suffered a minor stroke

and would undergo surgery to correct a partially blocked
carotid artery in his neck. His press office made daily
announcements that the mayor was conducting business over
the telephone and planning to settle the Lyric Opera labor
dispute from his bed. On June 3, Daley underwent surgery,
as usual a day earlier than had been announced. After a brief
recovery, he was whisked to his Michigan retreat, where he
remained until September.

The City Hall rumor mill ran rampant. Speculation about
the future of Chicago was a constant topic. It was the summer of Watergate, but in Chicago there was more discussion
of Daley successors than the future of the presidency. There
were rumors that his condition was much worse than
reported; that he could not speak, that he walked with a
limp, that there was some paralysis. Every scrap of information was printed or broadcast with urgency. An associate had
talked to Daley on the telephone and thought he sounded
weak. Another had talked to him and thought he sounded
strong.

It was widely believed that Daley would not run again. It
was speculated that Adlai Stevenson might give up his Senate seat to run. That was the order of importance Chicagoans
placed on political jobs. It was thought that young Neil Hartigan would run. That Mike Howlett would run. That state
chairman John Touhy would run. All of these people did
run—they ran from reporters, who might put their names in
the newspaper, where Daley would see them and wonder if
they were innocent subjects or indeed had ambitiously
planted these theories. Simply talking to a reporter was venal;
plotting the future in public was a mortal sin.

During his convalescence, Daley was overwhelmed with
wishes for a speedy recovery from every political figure in the
country and quite a few around the world. President Nixon
and his new vice president, Gerald Ford, telephoned. So did

a lot of people Daley had never heard of. So did the drawling, soft-spoken governor of Georgia, Jimmy Carter, who was the Democratic campaign committee chairman. Carter had spent the year making the rounds of party leaders and had visited Daley before his stroke. Carter called the Grand Beach home many times that summer, even offering to provide an oceanside villa in Sea Island, Georgia, if the mayor wished to continue his recuperation there. Jimmy Carter, who had plans for his own future, did not believe the reports that Richard Daley was no longer a national powerhouse.

Another caller was Bob Strauss, the magnetic Texan who had become Democratic chairman that year. He had been elected with the help of a coalition of labor leaders and traditional governors put together by Daley to bring some order back to the Democrats. Strauss was most concerned about Daley's health.

The year 1974 was certainly not a good one for Richard Nixon, but it had to be one of the worst in Daley's life, especially since the man didn't have many bad ones to begin with. He was seriously ill. He was getting old. He was losing friends rapidly. A few days before his stroke, his longtime ally Tom Keane was indicted by the U.S. Attorney James R. Thompson. A few days before that, two state employes were accused of providing two of the Daley sons with copies of the state insurance examiners' test.

In the past eighteen months, Democrats had been indicted at a rate astonishing even for Chicago. The most celebrated was former Governor Otto Kerner, who was convicted of taking racetrack stock as a bribe to ensure choice racing dates for Arlington Park. Kerner would go to prison while Daley was recovering from his stroke. County Clerk Eddie Barrett, who had been a Democratic officeholder since 1930 and had fought Daley for the 1952 gubernatorial nomination, was indicted in 1973 of taking kickbacks from a voting-machine company. Daley was especially saddened when his protégé, neighbor, and great friend Matt Danaher, clerk of the Circuit Court, died in a hotel room in December 1974, a month before his trial on income tax evasion. Danaher was one of the most popular Democrats in the city and Daley had cautioned him about his affinity for staying out late with the boys. Eight legislators were indicted in connection with extorting the ready-mix cement business to allow higher truck loads on state highways. Aldermen Paul Wigoda and Frank Kuta were indicted.

For the first time in Daley's career, personal finances tarnished his integrity a bit. One of his sons was employed by an Evanston insurance company that had suddenly received a great deal of city business, enough to compensate individuals in the firm with as much as $100,000. The story was made public and Daley screamed. He said the report would be looked into. For months, when reporters tired of the usual platitudes at his news conferences, the question would surface: "What about the report on the Heil and Heil company's city insurance?" Daley would bristle, mumble, and disappear. Or he would make defiant remarks about his children's endeavors: "What's the world coming to when a father can't help his own children? If there's someone who doesn't like it, they can look at the mistletoe hanging from my coat." There is no evidence to dispute the widely accepted belief that Daley was not preoccupied with wealth. But he wanted to help his children. He was a loving father who, despite the demands of his profession, probably found more time to spend with his family than most men who were not obliged to be at a civic or political dinner or a wake six nights of the week and maintain a ten-hour day in the office.

"He was a softie. He was never cross, never hit us. If we got out of line and my mom would have him say something, he would, but most of the time he'd just give us a look and that was all. But if you wanted something, you could always get it from him," Bill Daley said. "We spent a lot of time with him. He always came home in time to toss a ball around the yard for a while before dinner. Then we'd go with him to funerals and wakes and parades. On Saturdays when he went to the office, when we were younger, he'd take three or four of us, whoever was around, with him and drop us off at the Lake Shore Club, where we'd swim. Then he'd come over at noon and swim with us."

"We had to go to the fishing shows every year. He loved the rodeo, which would come twice a year, in the spring and the fall. We'd go see all the exhibits and watch the rodeo and the livestock show. He loved that stuff," Bill recalled.

Richard Daley returned from his recuperation on September 3, 1974, pronounced himself fit to do everything possible to help the Democratic ticket win the election in November, and dispelled any doubts about who the Democratic candidate for mayor would be in 1975.

In December, he returned to the national political scene. The Democrats had scheduled a midterm mini-convention in Kansas City. Delegates had to be elected by the rules promulgated in 1972, and this time Daley paid attention. There were some fresh faces and black faces and brown faces from Illinois, but none of them belonged to Bill Singer or Jesse Jackson. Daley was back in control. Bob Strauss made sure of that. Daley was one of the speakers. He was received warmly. He said the people were counting on the Democrats to restore confidence and spirit in government. He obliquely dealt with 1968 by saying, "We come here not to look inward or backward, but to look forward to 1976."

The Democrats immediately became twisted in debate over the black caucus insisting on more specific language in delegate selection. They threatened a walkout if their position was not accepted. Labor leaders threatened a walkout if it was. Daley supported the black position and was surrounded by grateful black leaders from around the country. He was the chief tourist attraction of the convention. The men who had tried to carry the party's banner in different directions since 1968—McCarthy, McGovern, Humphrey—were in disrepute. The new political faces—Milton Shapp of Pennsylvania, Jerry Brown of California, John Gilligan of Ohio, Dick Clark of Iowa—were untested. Ted Kennedy was an enigma. They represented different regions and different philosophies. Richard Daley still represented power.

"That was his real comeback," Bill Daley said. "He wasn't sure what would happen but they all came to him." The ones who came to him were already making plans for 1976: Morris "Mo" Udall of Arizona, the most thoughtful and witty liberal in Congress; senators Harris of Oklahoma, Birch Bayh of Indiana, Henry Jackson of Washington, and Lloyd Bentsen of Texas; former Governor Terry Sanford of North Carolina, and his phone pal, Jimmy Carter of Georgia. Many people asked for autographs. The day of the boss was over—but not if you were running for president.

The day Daley returned from Kansas City, he announced for a sixth term as mayor.

It was not as inevitable as it seemed. "He gave it a lot more thought that most people believed," said Bill Daley. "I had the impression he thought about it a lot. My own feelings were mixed. There were some days I would say, 'You don't need this anymore. What more is there for you to do?' Of course my mother and my sisters really were against him running again. I think he saw how the young guys were coming on, how they had gone after Parky Cullerton. I think he wondered how much longer he could keep going. But then I would wonder, what would he do? He wasn't going to go practice law. He never cared about money."

All of Daley's friends were gone, through either the door of Nativity of Our Lord or the gates of some federal penitentiary. His best friend and fishing buddy, Billy Lynch, a lifelong bachelor, was more interested in drinking than fishing; Steve Bailey, Bill McFetridge, and all the others of the inner circle were gone.

"I think he thought a lot about Lyndon Johnson. What happened after he left the White House. He just went back to Texas and died probably of a broken heart. I remember we had Johnson to a big event after he left the White House and he came with his hair all gray and long. He looked like he was ready to die. I think my dad saw that in himself if he didn't run again. He just wouldn't have been able to be an elder statesman, going downtown to lunch with a few guys once in a while," Bill Daley said. "It wouldn't have been him."

What was him, of course, was another triumphant mayoral campaign, but one that gave him misgivings. Singer had announced in 1973 that he would run for mayor in 1975 whether Daley was seeking re-election or not. The deflowered Edward Hanrahan also jumped into the fray. Neither of these challengers had the resources—precinct captains or money—to frighten Daley. What irritated Daley was that Walker kept hinting he might endorse Singer, and the governor did have the resources to make it interesting. However, as deeply as he wanted to enhance his image through Daley's demise, Walker needed to win re-election in 1976 to position himself for national office. He decided to stay neutral. The black community introduced its first mayoral candidate in the person of State Senator Richard Newhouse, an articulate reformer who made the Democratic primary a four-man race. John Hoellen, the 47th Ward alderman and the lonely Republican voice who made Daley alternately grumble and laugh for almost twenty years, was going to be the GOP candidate.

In the February primary, Singer got the same 29 percent that Friedman had gathered four years earlier. Newhouse got

8 percent from the black community. Hanrahan took 5 percent from white backlashers. Daley got 58 percent. It was believed in Daley's reign that his organization had a base of about 300,000 votes it could deliver in any contest. When Daley ran the base jumped to 400,000. In his sixth primary victory, he got 432,224 votes and his three challengers added together got 313,000 votes. Aldermanic races were held concurrent with mayoral primaries. Daley put in a little extra manpower into the 47th Ward and John Hoellen lost his seat in the City Council. He observed, "If I can't be elected alderman of the 47th Ward, it's impossible for me to be elected mayor." He was right.

In April 1975, Daley won his sixth term with 78 percent of the vote—536,413 to 136,874—the highest margin ever. He again won all fifty wards. On election night, even Daley lightly conceded there wasn't much suspense in these affairs anymore. "I think, on nights like this, one says, 'I shall embrace charity, love mercy, and walk humbly with my God.'"

He said nothing about revenge, but if his devout Catholicism prevented it from entering his heart, it was incapable of blocking it from his mind. In the summer of 1975, Daley was determined to defeat Dan Walker's bid for another term as governor. There had been nothing even close to rapprochement between the two men. If there were occasionally signals that such an accommodation might be possible, they were either mixed or missed. Daley's disdain of Walker was noted after the 1972 primary, when the mayor did not invite his party's gubernatorial candidate to a meeting for nearly a month. But he did turn out the vote in November. Daley could not help himself.

The Walker administration was marked by confrontation with Daley programs and Daley legislators in Springfield, not to mention Walker's constant comments about the evils of the Daley system. He later admitted he had decided to play hardball with the Chicago Democrats, but there was little he could have done to placate Daley anyway. "It has been suggested to me that if I had taken the time to spend more time with him, it might have been a little different. I don't believe that. There was such a sharp division between us in our approach to politics and government that I don't think having dinner, lunch, breakfast talks would have made that kind of difference," Walker reflected.[6]

In the fall of 1975, Walker visited Rostenkowski in Washington to suggest a compromise before slatemaking. "I mentioned it to Daley," Rostenkowski said. "He just gives me that look and says, 'Don't even bring that up to me again.'"

In the fall of 1975, the Chicago Democrats had pushed through a school aid bill that would have bailed the Chicago public schools out of their perennial fiscal problems. Walker vetoed the bill and Daley made a rare pilgrimage to Springfield to fight for the override of the veto. Walker won. "Walker upheld the veto, and the minute that happened he [Daley] knew Walker was beatable in a primary. He had made everyone in Chicago mad," said Bill Daley.

Now Daley needed a candidate. Michael J. Howlett was contented and no longer wished to be anything other than the secretary of state. Howlett always knew that he was not a personal favorite of Daley's, but he was a loyal Democrat. He had been mentioned many times as a possible successor to Daley or a possible governor approaching Daley's stature in the party. He was once asked by a reporter how it felt being no. 2 his whole life to Dick Daley. Howlett replied, "Daley is no. 1 and nobody is no. 2. That's his edge." When Howlett began to get word that Daley was eyeing him for a race against the charismatic Walker, he announced he was not interested in running for governor and went on vacation to Florida. But Daley was waiting.

He sent Rostenkowski to tell Howlett the party needed him. Howlett said no. "I called Daley and told him. He said,

'He owes it to the party.' The following week Mike Howlett
is the candidate."

The 1976 primary was the most bitterly fought in years.
But Daley exacted his revenge. Howlett won and would now
face the former Republican prosecutor, James Thompson, in
November. Ironically, Howlett and Thompson had been close
personal friends. Rostenkowski mused on how events in 1976
could have been different. "I always thought that if Howlett
had entered the gubernatorial race earlier in the year,
Thompson might have stayed out."

While Daley was expending all on his energies in the winter of 1976 on toppling Walker, the strange southerner who
had been so solicitous during Daley's 1974 illness was expending all his energies in places like Iowa and New Hampshire.
Jimmy Carter had gotten a jump-start on the 1976 Democratic presidential nomination.

His New Hampshire victory sealed the doom of people
like Birch Bayh, Milton Shapp, and Fred Harris, although
they trudged along. Carter's wins in North Carolina and
Florida spelled the last hurrah for George Wallace; another
southerner was carrying Dixie's banner. In Illinois, Carter got
48 percent to 28 percent for Wallace and 16 percent for Sargent Shriver, the 1972 vice presidential fill-in for the disastrous Thomas Eagleton. Shriver had hoped his old Illinois ties
would keep him alive in the presidential hunt. They didn't.
Then Carter stopped Udall in Wisconsin and only Henry
Jackson, who had won in Massachusetts and New York,
remained.

After each of his victories, Carter telephoned Daley.
"Carter himself talked to Daley," said campaign aide Greg
Schneiders. "The calls would always be the same, never specific, never that an endorsement at some point would be
helpful. It was always, 'I just wanted to talk with you, let you
know how the campaign is going.'" Even in 1976, four years

after Daley's banishment from Miami, Carter believed that no other single Democrat, save Kennedy or perhaps Humphrey, had the power to tip the scales at the proper moment.[7] Occasionally, Carter found time to recall that he had led the Georgia delegation in voting to seat Daley at Miami Beach in 1972. He needn't have bothered. Daley had tattooed the name of every state that was with him and against him deep in his heart.

In 1976, the Illinois primary was a hunting ground for delegates. Everyone understood most of the new rules by now. Daley had decided to keep a bunch of delegates uncommitted by having them pledged to Adlai Stevenson, who had declared he was not joining the gaggle seeking the nomination. The presidential hopefuls were uncertain how to handle this. Should they run delegate slates in Chicago against the Stevenson slates, which were really uncommitted Daley slates? That would provoke the mayor greatly. But what if an opponent chose to do it and actually picked up delegates? There was a risk.

Carter made up his mind early not to challenge the Daley slates. He ran slates in all the congressional districts outside the city. No one else ran slates against Daley either. Carter won fifty-five delegates along with his "beauty contest" victory in Illinois, while Daley retained control of eighty-five he would take to the convention uncommitted.

As usual, the old wing of the Democratic Party didn't like the idea of a former Georgia governor who talked a lot about religion and whose main issue seemed to be "I'll never lie to you." Some latecomers who sensed there could be support for anyone who derailed Carter jumped into the fray. Senator Frank Church of Idaho won four late primaries. Jerry Brown of California won in Maryland, Nevada, and Rhode Island and was certain to win the critical California primary on June 8. New Jersey and Ohio contests were scheduled the same day. But big labor wasn't too impressed by that pair. As in 1972, the old Democratic Party seeking to stop the new Democratic Party turned to Hubert Humphrey. Jackson was ready to drop out and turn his support and delegates over to Humphrey. The whole nation waited for Humphrey to announce he would be a late starter in the New Jersey primary. Humphrey said no, but he promised to be available at the convention if his party needed him.

On June 8, while campaigning in New Jersey, Carter called Daley. He told him he was going to lose in California and New Jersey but would win Ohio. Maybe Carter finally asked for the endorsement. Maybe he didn't. But Daley knew the days when a political leader could wait for the convention to play his hand were over. He went to his morning news conference and told everybody he had just gotten off the phone with Carter.

"He started four months ago and entered into every contest in every state and he won 'em and he lost 'em and, by God, you have to admire a guy like that," Daley said. What about reports that party leaders were plotting to give the nomination to Humphrey? "I think anyone who doesn't stand the test shouldn't be running. . . . Who said that he's the man now who should be knighted on a white horse to walk him into the convention? I don't think anyone should be so honored, no matter who he is. This man [Carter] has fought in every primary, and if he wins Ohio, he'll walk in under his own power." Daley conveniently forgot about the New Jersey and California elections. He also showed that he didn't mind all the religious rhetoric coming from Carter and disclosed that he glimpsed a supermarket tabloid now and then. "The man talks about true values. Why shouldn't we be sold on him? All of us recognize the violent and filthy movies and the newspapers with all the mistresses on the front page stripped down to the waist."

Although it was not a bona fide endorsement, it was the best Daley had ever given, and Carter was thrilled. Most observers believed Carter had virtually clinched the nomination after the Illinois primary, but the process was still too new for anyone to be certain of anything. The word in the national political community was that Dick Daley had said Ohio was the ball game—so Ohio was the ball game. Udall, Wallace, and Church all got it; they told Carter the next day that he had won the nomination. In case anyone missed it, Daley clarified the situation: "Carter's victory in Ohio is the ball game. The man has such a strong amount of support throughout the country . . . . there's no use in hesitating now. I'll cast my vote for him and there will be a Carter victory." He announced that he and Stevenson were releasing their eighty-five delegates to Carter, and he made plans to go to New York for the Democratic National Convention.

It was still a different group of Democrats who gathered in New York on June 12 for Jimmy Carter's convention. For that's what it was. No longer was there the slightest hint that political leaders or blocs of delegates could hijack the nomination or destroy a candidacy with vicious platform battles. This was a party, and New York had so many of them that it hardly noticed the Democrats in 1976. The Tall Ships of the 1976 Bicentennial had just left the harbor. Leisure suits had replaced khaki. The National Education Association had more delegates than the AFL-CIO. There were a lot of Baptists, and "born again" was bandied about more than "Happy Days Are Here Again." Barbara Jordan of Texas, a black woman with a massive voice and the elocution of Henry Higgins, gave the keynote speech. Carter narrowed his list of vice presidential hopefuls to six (including Adlai Stevenson) and then picked Walter Mondale of Minnesota, who had grown up at Hubert Humphrey's political knee. Daley had a good time, but nothing was the same. "They all came to pay their respects," Bill Daley said. "The Kennedys—Jackie and Ted—and everyone else."

Richard Daley enjoyed the display of respect, but he knew he was something of an artifact, a rare relic to be observed one more time. He remarked, "Where were they when they kicked me out of Miami four years ago?"

He stayed at the Waldorf and threw his customary delegation party on the Sunday before the convention. Bob Strauss, the party chairman, told Bill Daley that the mayor could have anything he wanted except a pass to drive into Madison Square Garden. The Secret Service would allow only Carter and his eventual running mate to bring vehicles into the convention hall, Strauss said. "But the head of the Secret Service detail was from Chicago," Bill Daley said, "and we got a car and drove my dad to within ten feet of his seat at the delegation."

New York was the way Daley had feared Miami Beach would be. There was nothing to do, no role to play. The convention era in which he rose to the pinnacle of Democratic power was gone. Somewhere in the arena was a man named Gerald Rafshoon. He had created the commercials that were shown first in Iowa, then New Hampshire, then all across America. They depicted a pleasant peanut farmer in blue jeans whose sole qualification for the presidency was that he would tell the truth. It was a perfect antidote for the years of Watergate and Vietnam. "It's all television now," Daley told his son. It was not even a last hurrah, although Daley made a brief, unnoticed speech. With few exceptions, he didn't know anyone outside the Illinois delegation. There were no Rayburns, McCormacks, Lawrences—even the Kennedys were scarce and inconsequential.

Daley may have felt that for whatever reason this might be his last convention, perhaps the last one he would want to attend even if he were able and invited. He wanted to be there to erase the embarrassment of 1972, to see if one more time he could know that ultimate rush of power when the most important people in America are waiting, beseeching, wondering what decision is being masked by the vague and abrupt statements that come in sentences that can't be parsed but have great clarity. "It was a great convention," he told everyone as he was leaving. "And we have a great candidate."

On November 2, 1976, Richard Daley was in the offices of the Cook County Democratic Party, doing what he always did on election nights, scanning the vote totals and determining what he could do to bring in a winner. Almost from the moment the polls closed it was clear his candidate for governor, Mike Howlett, was doomed. The fratricidal spring primary with Dan Walker had split the Democratic vote so badly that Republican James Thompson would win in a landslide. The Chicago Democrats couldn't even keep Howlett close. He won the city by a scant 150,000 votes. He lost the state by an unbelievable 2,949,850 to 1,574,343, the most lopsided gubernatorial triumph ever.

The Carter camp had been skeptical of Illinois because of polls showing Thompson running so far ahead of Howlett. But the ever-gracious Carter telephoned Daley on election night to thank him for all his efforts—and to see if there was still a chance he could carry Illinois. There was. Daley told him he was holding back a thousand Chicago precincts to see what was happening downstate. Despite the rancor in the governor's race, Daley had done his job for Carter. The Democratic nominee carried the city by 425,000 votes. That was only 50,000 votes less than the miracle vote for Kennedy in 1960, and Carter, with his inoffensive but alien religious utterances, did not have the natural sympathies that Irish-

Catholic Kennedy enjoyed in the city. It was 100,000 votes better than the vaunted Democratic machine had done for Harry Truman in 1948.

But it didn't help. In the end, Illinois went with President Ford by 100,000 votes. It was the first time since 1912 that Illinois hadn't voted with the winner in the presidential contest. Daley was terribly disappointed. A Democratic president had been elected—but not only had Dick Daley not been a decisive factor, he turned out to be no factor at all.

Daley was widely criticized for creating the divisive primary that cost the party the governor's chair and Carter's loss. But that wasn't what happened. The political world of Richard J. Daley was simply changing too much for him to control it. Not because his style of politics didn't work anymore; it did. And not because he had decided to destroy the man who was threatening not only Daley's personal dominance but the whole structure of the Cook County Democratic organization, even if it cost the governor's office or the presidency.

The kind of power that Daley understood demanded that he take whatever steps were necessary to eliminate Dan Walker. The essence of power, above all, is to keep it. And whether he was right or wrong, he believed, his son Bill said, that "Dan Walker was a bad governor, bad for politics . . . . he really wanted him taken out." Daley could not carry Illinois for Jimmy Carter because it was not the same Illinois that he had carried for Kennedy and Johnson, that his predecessors had carried for Truman and Roosevelt.

In 1960, when Daley gave Kennedy a 450,000 margin in Chicago, it held up against the suburban turnout of 500,000 votes. It held up against a total vote in the collar counties of 470,000 votes. In 1976, the Cook County suburbs turned out 1,000,000 votes. The total for DuPage, Lake, Will, Kane, and McHenry was 660,000 votes. Between 1960 and 1976,

700,000 new votes were added to the Republican suburban circle around the city of Chicago, while the city itself declined in presidential turnout from 1.6 million to 1.16 million, a loss of 440,000 votes.

By 1976, party loyalties were vanishing. Voters were far more likely to be ticket splitters, so Howlett's dismal performance didn't really affect Carter's defeat. In Will County, Thompson rolled up 81,000 votes to 32,000 for Howlett. But Ford beat Carter by only 10,000 votes—61,000 to 51,000. It was the same elsewhere in the collar counties and the suburbs. Evanston, for example, went for Thompson by 28,000 to 8,000. Carter carried it by 18,000 to 17,000. Niles Township was a draw between Ford and Carter, but Thompson beat Howlett by 20,000 votes.

Even downstate, where Walker's antimachine posture sold best, voters clearly separated the gubernatorial race from the presidential contest. In St. Clair County, a Democratic stronghold, Thompson beat Howlett 50,000 to 46,000. Yet Carter spanked Ford by 59,000 to 40,000. Democrats in Madison County supported Carter 56,000 to 44,000. They turned their backs on Howlett by a 59,000 to 40,000 margin. Carter ran better than most of his Democratic predecessors in some Republican bastions. In Winnebago County, he lost to Ford by only 10,000 votes, while Thompson beat Howlett by 53,000. It was the same everywhere in the state.

Daley said he had told Carter he would take care of Chicago if Carter took care of downstate. The problem was that neither man could take care of the suburbs. The edge city that John Kennedy had worried about in 1960 had become too big, too Republican to be offset by Chicago's vote.

It might be argued that Daley had cranked out every possible Democratic vote available in 1960 for Kennedy but couldn't repeat the performance in later years. But that reflects the city's population decline. The argument could be made a great many ghost voters had turned out in 1960 and they couldn't be found in 1976. But the reality is that the city was shrinking. The 24th Ward, which once pumped out 20,000 or 23,000 Democratic votes, could find only 13,000 votes in 1976, whether they were alive or not. The 50th Ward on the far North Side, which in 1964 produced 47,000 votes and gave Lyndon Johnson a three to one margin, dwindled to 32,000 votes.

The bulk of the decline was in the black community, which now made up 40 percent of the city's 3.1 million population. The civil rights movement, the urban rioting, the rise and fall of expectations, and the Vietnam War had created an increasingly uninterested black electorate. The 2nd, 3rd, and 4th Wards—the foundation of Bill Dawson's fiefdom— had routinely produced 25,000 votes for the Democratic party. By 1976, the numbers were 16,000, 14,000, and 16,000—all huge majorities, but far fewer total votes. Even had the five black wards that once produced Democratic votes in the 20,000s delivered that number for Carter, it wouldn't have been enough. Daley's twenty-year rule could not be characterized in the black community as "enlightened," but beginning in the 1970s the black vote nationally followed Chicago's patterns of decline.

It wasn't until Harold Washington's mayoral candidacy in 1983 that black voters returned to their 1950 numbers. In the April general election, the 2nd, 3rd, and 4th wards each gave Washington 22,000 to 24,000 votes while the 6th poured out 34,000 votes, reminiscent of Daley's early wins. But they quickly began to drift. In the 1984 presidential race, with Washington enthusiastically supporting Walter Mondale, only the 6th Ward, with 27,000 Democratic votes, was noteworthy.

By 1988, with Washington dead of a heart attack and his interim successor, Eugene Sawyer, in the mayor's chair, the black wards reverted to their 1976 lack of enthusiasm. Michael Dukakis got approximately the same vote from the 2nd, 3rd, and 4th Wards as Carter had polled a dozen years earlier (in the low teens), while some West Side wards turned out as few as 5,000 Democratic votes. The machine that had once been all white, then turned to Daley's advantage with an influx of black votes, had now been split on racial lines. It was still another Democratic Party that Dick Daley was trying to control in the final days of his life.

On December 20, 1976, Daley and his wife attended the annual Christmas party for city department heads in the Bismarck Hotel. Then he traveled to the 10th Ward on the Southeast Side, where he joined Alderman Edward Vrdolyak and Park District chief Ed Kelly, the committeeman of the 47th Ward. They were two of the men who lately had been pictured as his possible successors, the latest in a long list that had appeared and vanished during his unchallenged regime. He was there to dedicate a new park gymnasium. He accepted in silence all the homage that he had been accustomed to over the years and then was presented with a basketball, which he flipped into the hoop, causing him to giggle.

That afternoon he kept his 2 P.M. appointment in Dr. Coogan's office at 900 North Michigan Avenue. Coogan gave him an electrocardiogram and didn't like what he saw. He prepared to have Daley admitted to the hospital. Daley called his son Michael, talked briefly, and hung up the telephone. He collapsed on the floor. He was dead.

They buried Richard J. Daley at Nativity of Our Lord. It was the biggest funeral Chicago had seen since Joe McDonough was laid to rest there forty-two years earlier. Thousands stood all night in the frigid cold outside the Bridgeport church. The powerful and the friendly were admitted through the basement to go upstairs and pay their respects to the family, who maintained the vigil through the night to greet all those who had come to say good-bye to their husband and father. "You could tell," Bill Daley said, "who had been waiting outside. When you went to shake hands, their hands were frozen even if they had gloves."

They all came to the funeral. They listened as the Shannon Rovers, an Irish bagpipe band that appeared almost mystically at Daley's shoulder during every public celebration of his administration, solemnly played "Garry Owen," the Irish battle hymn adopted by George Custer, the 82nd Airborne, and Richard Daley as a theme song of triumph. The Kennedys, the Rockefellers, the Carters, the Mondales, the old governor and the new governor, every Democrat of rank, and many thousands who had no rank and were not even Democrats came. They came because for many of them he was the only mayor they had ever known. For others, he was the minstrel for the city they loved, the voice that led them in worship to the buildings, the lake, the streets, the ballparks, the ball teams, the theaters, the restaurants, the pageants, the parks, and the parades. His admirers and critics were there.

They all knew that whatever else he was or wished he could be, Daley singularly personified an era when a single political leader could solve problems, exert power from LaSalle Street to Pennsylvania Avenue, and get things done. Whether anyone who mourned him in Chicago or noted his death from afar realized it, that time in American politics was gone. And now, too, was Richard J. Daley.

Epilogue

RICHARD DALEY WAS FASCINATED BY GOVERNMENT AND THE process of government. It taught him all he needed to know about power. He became captivated by power. He understood it and used his vast knowledge of the processes of government and politics to expand it and preserve it. He superimposed his own morality on the process and wielded his power in a way that would bring society the benefits he deemed necessary and ignore the excesses he disdained. He understood that winning elections results in power, but power cannot be measured like wealth. He won elections and he lost them, but in either case he was able to convince the public and his peers that the outcome had depended solely on him.

He was not unlike others of his time who achieved lasting political success: John Kennedy, Richard Nixon, Lyndon Johnson. He shared with them the love of the system and the unique ability to make it work for their public and personal ambitions. He was in many ways like his close friend Lyndon Johnson. They were secretive, suspicious, and at times tyrannical. They believed that authority should be upheld and respected and immune to the whims of the dissident or rebellious. They believed in the purest spirit of representative democracy, that officials elected by the people were empowered to do what they thought best for the general good—even when the people who elected them disagreed.

The remedy was at the ballot box, and when the people repeatedly approved, as they did of Daley, he became convinced of his absolute rectitude and comfortable in his absolute power. If he was insensitive to the demands of change, it was because he believed that change can emanate only from power. That was the sum total of his experience in politics and government. He had seen it flourish as Roosevelt, then Truman, then Kennedy and Johnson moved America from a country ruled by the elite to a country where a poor Irish immigrant or the most impoverished Texas hill-country farmer could live in an affluence that much of the world would never know. It was politics and power that brought those changes, and it was the men who used them who made it happen. Dick Daley believed that and he tried to emulate it. He was the last of the breed.

Endnotes

CHAPTER 1

1. Theodore H. White, *The Making of the President 1960* (New York: Atheneum Publishers, 1962).
2. Eugene Kennedy, *Himself* (New York: Viking Press, 1978).
3. Kennedy, *Himself*.
4. Author, "Jane Byrne Wins," *Chicago Tribune*, February 28, 1979, mayoral election.
5. Kennedy, *Himself* (New York: Viking Press, 1978).
6. Kenneth P. O'Donnell and David Powers, *Johnny, We Hardly Knew Ye* (Boston: Little, Brown & Co., 1970).
7. Benjamin C. Bradlee, *Conversations with Kennedy* (New York: W. W. Norton & Co., 1975).

CHAPTER 2

1. O'Donnell and Powers, *Johnny, We Hardly Knew Ye.*
2. White, *The Making of the President 1960.*
3. John Bartlow Martin, *Adlai Stevenson and the World* (Garden City, NY: Doubleday, 1977).
4. White, *The Making of the President 1960.*
5. Larry O'Brien, *Oral History No. 23*, Lyndon Baines Johnson Library.
6. Martin, *Adlai Stevenson and the World.*
7. Author interview with Newton Minow, February 15, 1996.
8. Milton Rakove, *We Don't Want Nobody Nobody Sent* (Indiana University Press, 1979).
9. White, *The Making of the President 1960.*
10. "Convention Briefs," *Chicago Tribune*, July 23, 1960.

CHAPTER 3

1. Ed Kelly, Martin Kennelly, Richard J. Daley, Michael Bilandic, and Richard M. Daley.
2. Rakove, *We Don't Want Nobody Nobody Sent.*
3. Len O'Connor, *Clout* (Chicago: Henry Regnery Co., 1975).
4. Rakove, *We Don't Want Nobody Nobody Sent.*
5. John Bartlow Martin, *Adlai Stevenson of Illinois* (Garden City, NY: Doubleday, 1976).
6. O'Connor, *Clout.*

CHAPTER 4

1. Jack Beatty, *The Rascal King* (New York: Addison-Wesley Publishing, 1992).
2. James MacGregor Burns, *Roosevelt: Soldier of Freedom* (New York: Harcourt Brace Jovanovich, Inc., 1970).
3. Herbert Eaton, *Presidential Timber* (Glencoe, IL: Free Press of Glencoe, 1964).
4. Rakove, *We Don't Want Nobody Nobody Sent.*
5. Harry S Truman, *Memoirs* (New York: Doubleday, 1955).
6. Eaton, *Presidential Timber.*
7. Martin, *Adlai Stevenson of Illinois.*
8. Truman, *Memoirs.*
9. O'Donnell and Powers, *Johnny, We Hardly Knew Ye.*
10. D. B. Hardeman and Don C. Bacon, *Rayburn* (Austin: Texas Monthly Press, 1987).
11. John Bartlow Martin, *Adlai Stevenson and the World* (Garden City, NY: Doubleday, 1977).
12. Hardeman and Bacon, *Rayburn.*

CHAPTER 5

1. William J. Grimshaw, *Bitter Fruit* (University of Chicago Press, 1992).

CHAPTER 6

1. David Halberstam, *The Fifties* (New York: Random House, 1993).
2. Larry O'Brien, *Oral History No. 1*, LBJ Library. (New York: Viking Press, 1978).
3. O'Connor, *Clout.*
4. Daley interview with John Madigan in *Chicago's American*, January 22, 1961.
5. Theodore Sorenson, *Kennedy* (New York: Harper & Row, 1965).
6. O'Donnell and Powers, *Johnny, We Hardly Knew Ye.*
7. Author interview with Dan Rostenkowski, March 1, 1996.
8. Rostenkowski interview.

CHAPTER 7

1. White House Central Files (WHCF), *Daily Diaries* (1963–1968), LBJ Library.
2. Larry O'Brien, *Oral History No. 5*, LBJ Library.
3. Joseph A. Califano, Jr., *The Triumph and Tragedy of Lyndon Johnson* (New York: Simon & Shuster, 1991).
4. Rostenkowski interview.
5. Rostenkowski interview.
6. WHCF, *Daily Diaries*, LBJ Library.
7. Rostenkowski interview.
8. Larry O'Brien, *Oral History No. 8*, LBJ Library.
9. WHCF, *Names File* (Daley), 1957, LBJ Library.
10. Califano, *The Triumph and Tragedy of Lyndon Johnson*.
11. Irving Bernstein, *Guns and Butter* (New York: Oxford University Press, 1996).
12. Califano, *The Triumph and Tragedy of Lyndon Johnson*.
13. Bernstein, *Guns and Butter*.
14. Califano, *The Triumph and Tragedy of Lyndon Johnson*.
15. WHCF, *Legislative Chicago*, LBJ Library.
16. WHCF, *Names File* (Daley), 1966, LBJ Library.
17. Larry O'Brien, *Oral History No. 5*, LBJ Library.
18. WHCF, *Names File* (Daley), 1965, LBJ Library.
19. WHCF, *Daily Diaries*, LBJ Library.

CHAPTER 8

1. *The World in 1966* (Associated Press, 1966).
2. Califano, *The Triumph and Tragedy of Lyndon Johnson*.
3. Lady Bird Johnson, *White House Diary* (New York: Holt, Rinehart and Winston, 1970).
4. The Supreme Court later overturned the death sentence and Speck died in prison in 1991.
5. Rostenkowski interview.
6. Minow interview.
7. WHCF, *Names File* (Daley), May 4, 1967, LBJ Library.
8. William Manchester, *The Glory and the Dream*, Volume II (Boston: Little, Brown & Co., 1973).
9. WHCF, *General Political Affairs File*, LBJ Library.
10. Larry O'Brien, *Oral History No. 23*, LBJ Library.
11. WHCF, *General Political Affairs File*, LBJ Library.

CHAPTER 9

1. Larry O'Brien, *Oral History No. 23*, LBJ Library.
2. Author interview with William Daley, March 12, 1968.
3. Theodore H. White, *The Making of the President 1968* (New York: Atheneum Publishers, 1969).
4. White, *The Making of the President 1968*.
5. William Daley interview.
6. WHCF, *Daily Diaries*, March 13, 1968, LBJ Library.
7. WHCF, *Names File* (Daley), LBJ Library.
8. Uss *Pueblo* was captured by North Korea on January 23, 1968. Its crew of eighty-two men was held until December 23, 1968.
9. WHCF, *Names File* (Daley), LBJ Library.
10. Lyndon B. Johnson, *The Vantage Point* (New York: Holt, Rinehart & Winston, 1971).
11. WHCF, *Daily Diaries*, March 31, 1968, LBJ Library.
12. WHCF, *Daily Diaries*, April 5, 1968, LBJ Library.
13. Califano, *The Triumph and Tragedy of Lyndon Johnson*.
14. WHCF, *Daily Diaries*, April 5, 1968, LBJ Library.

CHAPTER 10

1. WHCF, *Names File* (Daley), May 20, 1968, LBJ Library.
2. WHCF, *Names File* (Daley), June 18, 1968, LBJ Library.
3. WHCF, *Names File* (Daley), July 27, 1968, LBJ Library.
4. Burton Hersh, *The Education of Edward Kennedy* (New York: William Morrow and Co., 1972).
5. Lady Bird Johnson, *White House Diary*.
6. White, *The Making of the President 1968* (New York: Atheneum Publishers, 1969).
7. WHCF, *Names File* (Daley), August 24, 1968, LBJ Library.
8. Minow interview.
9. William Daley interview.
10. Hubert H. Humphrey, *The Education of a Public Man* (New York: Doubleday and Co., 1976).
11. Larry O'Brien, *Oral History No. 23*, LBJ Library.
12. *Congressional Quarterly*, Democratic Convention, 1968.

CHAPTER 11

1. Theodore White, *The Making of the President 1972* (New York: Atheneum Press, 1973).
2. Massachusetts was the only state to carry McGovern in the 1972 election.
3. White, *The Making of the President 1972*.
4. Larry O'Brien, *Oral History No. 29*, LBJ Library.
5. WHCF, *Names File* (Daley) December 1968, LBJ Library.
6. Rakove, *We Don't Want Nobody Nobody Sent*.
7. Jules Witcover, *Marathon* (New York: Viking Press, 1977).

Index